"I'm so thankful that someone fin and criticisms of the multisite churcn moael. Dustin Slaton's insightful *Multisite Churches: Biblical Foundations and Practical Answers* is the definitive book making the biblical case for the legitimacy of the multisite church model historically, theologically, and ecclesiastically."

—Jim Tomberlin,
Pastor and Church Consultant,
Author of *Better Together: Making Church Mergers Work*

"Dustin has written a masterclass on the history, theology, governance, and practices of the modern-day multisite church movement. Filled with research-based conclusions and interesting case studies, *Multisite Churches* is an incredibly rich resource for anyone wanting to better understand the benefits—and even the critiques—of a healthy multisite church strategy. How I wish we had this book twenty years ago!"

—Kadi Cole,
Multisite Consultant and Leadership Coach,
Author of *Developing Female Leaders*

"A comprehensive and well-researched study. Whether you are pro, con, indifferent, or uninformed, you should definitely consult this excellent work by Dustin Slaton to better understand the multisite church movement."

—Daniel L. Akin,
President,
Southeastern Baptist Theological Seminary, Wake Forest, NC

"In *Multisite Churches: Biblical Foundations and Practical Answers*, Dustin Slaton provides the latest research on multisite congregations. Although I remain an ardent supporter of single-site, single-service churches, I can tell you that Slaton's arguments theologically and biblically engage multisite critics' arguments in a very healthy way."

—Matt Queen,
Professor and L. R. Scarborough Chair of Evangelism ("Chair of Fire"),
Southwestern Baptist Theological Seminary, Fort Worth, TX

"Biblically astute and theologically rich, Dustin Slaton answers what I've wondered for years: 'What are the differences in leading a multisite church compared to leading an established church?' With incredibly helpful insights and next steps, Slaton unfolds the unique aspects of leading a multisite church chapter by chapter and page by page. If you are a disciple of ministry, this book is for you."

—Jonathan Smith,
Director of Church Health Strategy,
Texas Baptists, Dallas, TX

"If you are considering a multisite approach to church or generally thinking through the ongoing discussion, I cannot commend Dustin Slaton's book *Multisite Churches* highly enough. You'll find his work biblically faithful, theologically rich, and practically helpful. Slaton writes with a scholar's mind and a pastor's heart, making his work one of the leading voices in understanding multisite churches. Read this book, study it, put it to use in your church; you'll be blessed by doing so."

—Travis S. Kerns,
Associational Mission Strategist,
Three Rivers Baptist Association, Taylors, SC

"*Multisite Churches* is an essential tool for churches and pastors seeking direction and planning for multisite ministries. Dustin Slaton does an excellent job sharing both the rich biblical and historical foundation to the theology and philosophy of the multisite concept. Further, *Multisite Churches* offers a clearly defined approach and guidebook for starting a multisite ministry. If your team is considering what a multisite ministry may look like in your church, this is a valuable resource that you cannot do without."

—Kirk Wooldridge,
Certified Church Consultant,
Executive Director of Williamson Baptist Association, Georgetown, TX

"Dustin Slaton's well-written and fair approach meets a real need for a good theological basis for multisite churches. It's a good read!"

—Keith Evans,
Pastor to Pastors, Resonate Church, Pullman, WA

MULTISITE CHURCHES

BIBLICAL FOUNDATIONS AND PRACTICAL ANSWERS

DUSTIN SLATON

Multisite Churches: Biblical Foundations and Practical Answers

© 2023 by Dustin Slaton

Published by Kregel Ministry, an imprint of Kregel Publications, 2450 Oak Industrial Dr. NE, Grand Rapids, MI 49505-6020.

ISBN 978-0-8254-4829-4

Printed in the United States of America

23 24 25 26 27 / 5 4 3 2 1

For Melody
who, for twenty years, has been
telling me to write a book

CONTENTS

FOREWORD

"The multisite congregation is the single most profound change in American congregations in the past century."
—Thom Rainer,
Former CEO and President of Lifeway Christian Resources

WHEN I STARTED DOWN THE MULTISITE PATH as a senior pastor in Colorado in the 1990s, multisite was a *radical idea.*

What began as a *Band-Aid* strategy for megachurches that were out of room or limited by zoning restrictions progressed through several identifiable stages. It quickly evolved into a *growth* strategy for healthy churches of all sizes. Stable but stuck churches found multisite to be a *revitalization* strategy that reenergized their base and leveraged their influence beyond the walls of their congregation. It has become a *rebirth* strategy for struggling churches that merge with a multisite church. (Nearly half of all multisite campuses have come about through a church merger.) And for some multisite churches it has become a *movement-making* strategy of reproducing and multiplying campuses.

What began as a radical idea has spawned a movement of more than five million people attending thousands of multisite churches in urban, suburban, and rural communities across North America. The multisite model has proven to be an effective vehicle for outreach, church growth, volunteer mobilization, leadership development, revitalization, and regional impact . . . *but is it biblical?*

That is the question that Dustin Slaton skillfully tackles in his book, *Multisite Churches: Biblical Foundations and Practical Answers*. Slaton has performed a long overdue and needed service for the multisite movement by thoroughly addressing the legitimate concerns, valid criticisms, and frivolous attacks of the multisite church model from a biblical perspective. As he says:

> I have written this book in the hope that multisite churches would be challenged to think biblically about their churches, encouraged that a biblical multisite model exists, and equipped with biblical concepts to help them find a biblical structure.

This growing movement of an estimated ten thousand multisite churches is comprised of Protestant churches across the theological and denominational spectrum. Baptist churches are one of the largest groups represented in this movement, yet Baptists (especially of the Reformed tribe) have also generated most of its criticism *(full disclosure—I am an ordained Southern Baptist pastor)*. I mention this because Slaton's book is written by a Southern Baptist largely for Southern Baptists whose congregational ecclesiology struggles more than most other theological streams with the multisite model of "one church with multiple congregations under one centralized governance."

No armchair theologian, Slaton served as a campus pastor in a Southern Baptist church before becoming the lead pastor of a Southern Baptist church. His book wrestles with the tension of *regulative* (practices like multisite are not allowed because it is not mentioned in Scripture) versus *normative* (practices like multisite are allowed because it is not prohibited in Scripture) that has divided church leaders about church practices since the first century. Though this book is written with Baptists in mind, it well serves all multisite practitioners by addressing all the theological and ecclesiastical issues through a biblical lens.

I'm so thankful that someone finally wrote a book to address the concerns and criticisms of the multisite church model. Dustin Slaton's *Multisite Churches* is the definitive book making the biblical case for the legitimacy of the multisite church model historically, theologically, and ecclesiastically.

If the following report of Scripture will ever be said of today, then I dare to predict that God's work through the practice of multisite churches will be one of the essential contributors to seeing this happen:

> "*So the church* throughout all Judea and Galilee and Samaria had peace and was being *built up*. And walking in the fear of the Lord and in the comfort of the Holy Spirit, it *multiplied*" (Acts 9:31, emphasis added)

—Jim Tomberlin

LIST OF ABBREVIATIONS

BFM	Baptist Faith and Message 2000
CGM	Church Growth Movement
FBCD	First Baptist Church of Dallas, TX
FPCS	First Presbyterian Church of Seattle, WA
HPBC	Highland Park Baptist Church of Chattanooga, TN
IMB	International Mission Board of the Southern Baptist Convention
MCM	Multisite Church Movement
MCR	*The Multi-Site Church Revolution*
MRT	*Multi-Site Church Road Trip*
NAMB	North American Mission Board of the Southern Baptist Convention
SBC	Southern Baptist Convention

LIST OF TABLES

ACKNOWLEDGMENTS

I HAVE WRITTEN THIS BOOK in the hope that multisite churches would be challenged to think biblically about their churches, encouraged that a biblical multisite model exists, and equipped with biblical concepts to help them find a biblical structure. I began this journey unaware of many of the ecclesiological issues with multisite models, and I was challenged in my own views on the topic. Nevertheless, I felt confident, and still do, that multisite churches could function in a biblical way. My hope is that this will be a valuable resource that will bless current and future multisite church leaders.

This book, and whatever benefit it may provide, has been a labor of love that would not have been possible without the support of numerous people along the way.

To Melody: You are, and always will be, the love of my life. This would not have been possible without your constant love, encouragement, and support. Your graciousness during this process has given me the freedom to read and write while you picked up my slack around the house and with our kids. This project is a testimony to your love for me and your confidence in me. For almost twenty years you have told me, "One day you need to write a book." Thanks to you, that day has finally come. "He who finds a wife finds a good thing and obtains favor from the LORD" (Prov. 18:22).

To Preston, Addison, Blake, and Jackson: You kids are God's precious gift to your Mommy and me, and I love you so much. Thank you for your sweet encouragement as I've sat in my office chair, typing away at my computer, night after night. Thank you for bringing me candies and drink refills, cards and notes, goodnight kisses and hugs. Thank you for letting Daddy miss out on some family time, and thank you for being a great help to your Mommy. Daddy is finally done with his book. Now, it's time to catch up on some family time! "Behold, children are a heritage from the Lord, the fruit of the womb a reward" (Ps. 127:3).

To Mom and Dad: Thank you for forty-three years of encouragement and for always reminding me to give my very best. You have invested in this project, and I hope the return will be in heavenly rewards that are yet to be seen. Most of all, thank you for introducing me to Jesus, and modeling a life of faithfulness before God. "Train up a child in the way he should go; even when he is old he will not depart from it" (Prov. 22:6).

To Larry and Donna: I am blessed to have such great in-laws. You have been a blessing to me and an example of godliness for our whole family. Thank you for your unceasing encouragement in this endeavor, and for your constant prayer. "And pray in the Spirit on all occasions with all kinds of prayers and requests. With this in mind, be alert and always keep on praying for all the Lord's people" (Eph. 6:18, NIV).

To Drs. Allison, Biles, Kerns, Kiker, Morris, and Queen: Thank you for challenging me and encouraging me. My time spent with each one of you has tremendously impacted my journey and the contents of this book. I am indebted to each one of you. "Let the wise hear and increase in learning, and the one who understands obtain guidance" (Prov. 1:5).

To my former church family at Green Acres Baptist Church's Flint (Texas) Campus and my current church family at First Baptist Church Round Rock, Texas, for patiently allowing me to grow in my understanding of what it means to be a pastor. God has used both of these wonderful churches to shape me in so many ways, one of which was to give me a desire to see multisite churches thrive. "I thank my God in all my remembrance of you, always in every prayer of mine for you all making my prayer with joy, because of your partnership in the gospel from the first day until now" (Phil. 1:3–5).

Finally, to my Heavenly Father: Thank you for the unmerited gift of salvation and eternal life in Jesus Christ. Thank you for the call you placed upon my life. My one, true desire is to be the faithful servant you designed me to be, and I pray this project, and whatever fruit may come of it, will bring glory to your name. "Now to him who is able to do far more abundantly than all that we ask or think, according to the power at work within us, to him be glory in the church and in Christ Jesus throughout all generations, forever and ever. Amen" (Eph. 3:20–21).

—Dustin Slaton
Georgetown, Texas

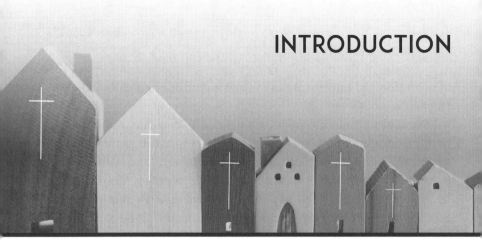

INTRODUCTION

IN THE LATE TWENTIETH CENTURY, a new model of church structure began emerging in North America.[1] This model has been described
in various ways, but it exists today as the multisite church model.[2] People are often introduced to multisite churches in numerous ways. They
find a multisite church when they accidently walk into one of a multisite church's campuses, not realizing it's "only a campus." Or, maybe
a local church opens one of their new campuses down the street from
their neighborhood. Maybe one of their friends starts going to a multisite church. If they are ambitious, maybe they read one of the foundational books, *The Multi-Site Church Revolution* or *A Multi-Site Church
Roadtrip*.[3] Or, maybe they read one of the many blog articles or listen
to a podcast that bemoans the spread of multisite campuses. The landscape of multisite churches' various models and sizes can lead to a lot

---

1   Ferguson, "The Multi-Site Church and Disciplemaking," 18–26; McIntosh, *Make Room
for the Boom*, 138–40.

2   In *The Multi-Site Church Revolution*, the authors list multiple models and labels often used to describe multisite churches and models (Surratt, Ligon, and Bird, *Multi-
Site Church Revolution*, 28–42). Elmer Towns referred to the model as the "extended
geographical parish church" (Towns, *An Inside Look at 10 of Today's Most Innovative
Churches*). The book *One Church, Many Locations* uses the term "key church" in its
descriptions of its model (Ahlen and Thomas, *One Church, Many Congregations*). This
book will use the term "multisite" when referencing the multisite church model. It will
not use common variations, such as "multi site," "multi-site," "multi-campus," or "multichurch," except when quoting from a source.

3   Surratt, Ligon, and Bird, *Multi-Site Church Revolution*; Surratt, Ligon, and Bird, *A
Multi-Site Church Road Trip*.

of confusion and uncertainty as to what a multisite church is and even whether it is biblical.

A multisite church is popularly defined as one church meeting in multiple locations that "shares a common vision, budget, leadership, and board."[4] These churches vary in size, number of locations, format of operation, and numerous other aspects. Their campus locations may be contained inside a single city, or may extend through multiple cities, across state lines, or may even spread around the globe to multiple countries.[5] The multisite church movement (MCM) has no set polity, as multisite churches include churches from many denominations, as well as non-denominational churches.[6] Churches are free to use whatever multisite structure they choose, so long as it fits within their own understanding of a biblical church paradigm.

In the twenty-first century, the number of multisite churches has multiplied significantly. What began with only ten documented multisite churches in 1992 grew to over five thousand by 2018.[7] Many churches within the Southern Baptist Convention (SBC), the largest evangelical denominations in the United States, have joined the movement. Scott McConnell, the Executive Director of the SBC's Lifeway Research, claims there are at least five hundred known multisite churches in the SBC, and

---

4   Surratt, Ligon, and Bird, *Multi-Site Church Revolution*, 18.
5   Surratt, Ligon, and Bird, *Multi-Site Church Revolution*, 18. Green Acres Baptist Church in Tyler, Texas, is an example of a church with multiple campuses in a single city ("New Here?," *Green Acres Baptist Church*). Family Church, a church with ten locations based in West Palm Beach, Florida, is an example of a church with locations in a multi-city region ("Family Church Network," *Family Church*). Life Church, based in Tulsa, Oklahoma, is a single church with thirty-five locations stretched across eleven states ("Locations," *Life Church*). Hillsong Church, based in Sydney, Australia, is a single church with locations in twenty-eight countries around the world, touching every continent except Antarctica ("About Hillsong," *Hillsong Church*). Some, such as Surratt, Ligon, and Bird, also include churches with multiple worship venues on the same campus in the multisite category. This book will not address the multi-venue format, but will only address multisite churches that have two or more separate campus locations. This book will also not address internet churches or online campus formats.
6   Surratt, Ligon, and Bird, *Multi-Site Church Revolution*, 30.
7   Bird, "Big News"; Bird, "Latest Multisite Trends"; Rainer, "Is the Multisite Church Movement Still Growing?" In these documents, Bird notes that multisite churches have grown from around fifty at the end of the twentieth century to more than five thousand as of 2018.

suggests there are many more multisite churches of which the SBC is not aware.[8]

My interest in the multisite church model began when I was serving as a youth pastor at First Baptist Church in Terrell, Texas, from 2008 to 2014. My church began a process of strategic planning, which included a discussion about possibly relocating from a downtown area to an area on the edge of town that was projected to experience significant growth. I began studying multisite church options and became convinced that a multisite model was a strong option for the future of our church. I saw the appeal of either a gradual transition from one location to another or the possibility of maintaining two locations, to reach two distinct groups of people. I was impressed with the apparent success of the multisite model for many churches and was especially enamored with how it apparently helped churches grow.

In 2014, I became the campus pastor at the Flint Campus of Green Acres Baptist Church in Tyler, Texas.[9] This position provided me the opportunity to gain firsthand experience in a multisite church and helped shape my view of how multisite churches should function. I have seen positive and negative aspects of multisite ministry, and I had the opportunity to develop and shape systems that helped improve the way Green Acres's multisite model functions. As I researched and attempted new methods, I became familiar with the practices of multisite churches around the country, and studied the work of multisite advocates such as Leadership Network, The Unstuck Group, Ed Stetzer, Thom Rainer, Jimmy Scroggins, Geoff Surratt, Greg Ligon, Warren Bird, Jim Tomberlin, and others.

The conversation on the multisite church has predominately been carried out online and in sections of books on general church growth. The

---

8   Earls and Pipes, "Multisite Church ID Shift to Help SBC Ties." According to the SBC's Annual Church Profile survey, SBC churches corporately reported 585 campuses in addition to their primary locations (Earls, "Southern Baptists Grow in Attendance").

9   When I originally wrote this book, Green Acres Baptist Church was a multisite, multivenue church. On the original campus, near downtown Tyler, they had four services each Sunday in two separate venues, with concurrent hours of combined small groups. They have since combined those into two worship services meeting in the same venue at different times. The Flint Campus, south of Tyler, now also has two services and two Bible study hours ("Flint Campus," *Green Acres Baptist Church*). I served as the campus pastor of the Flint Campus from October 2014 to January 2021.

available printed literature dedicated specifically to the multisite church model is very limited. As I began studying more about congregational ecclesiology, I began to see many multisite churches were structured in a way that did not fit well within a congregational model. While I was not turned away from the multisite model, this new realization led me on a journey to carefully read and consider the critiques of authors such as Thomas White, John Mark Yeats, and Ed Stetzer, as well as the very strong warnings from 9Marks authors such as Mark Dever, Jonathan Leeman, and Bobby Jamieson. I also discovered a growing number of academic critiques of the model that were strong in their conclusions that multisite churches did not fit congregational polity.

I then turned back to sources in favor of multisite church models to see if I could uncover their theological foundations. What I found was disheartening. There was very little in-depth theological consideration and defense in favor of the multisite model. The primary defender of the model has been Gregg Allison. In 2016, the only resource he had available was an article in the *9Marks Journal* and a brief section in his ecclesiology *Sojourners and Strangers*.[10] This, along with an article by John Hammett in the *Great Commission Research Journal*, were the only theological pieces truly favorable to multisite churches. I also discovered Brian Frye's dissertation, which was the lone PhD dissertation available at the time that had significant theological and historical support for the multisite model.[11]

I then began looking at other church models, such as house churches and cell churches, to see if their undergirding ecclesiology offered support for the multisite model. These sources helped me discover principles applicable to multisite churches, and also to evaluate many of the critiques of those opposed to the model. I consulted sources on church history to evaluate proponents' claims that the multisite model was nothing new, but simply the continuation of a model that has been in place for centuries.

Finally, I have spent much time studying Scripture, seeking to discover the scope of the biblical guidelines and to see what practices the early

---

10   Allison's book, *MultiChurch*, written with Brad House, was not released until 2017.

11   Since 2016, many more dissertations have been written that are favorable to the multisite model. However, these have typically focused on functional aspects of a specific practice within the model, such as preaching or leadership.

church embraced. This has required hours of conducting word-study analysis, consulting theology sources and commentaries, and reading the thoughts of theological voices to gain their ecclesiological insights.

Although I now serve as the senior pastor of a single-site church, I still view the multisite model favorably, and our church's new vision includes a desire to embrace church planting, church revitalization partnerships, and multisite campuses to reach our city and county. I believe that a multisite model, structured rightly, is a valid church structure and can be used effectively to reach more people with the saving knowledge of Jesus Christ. I do also acknowledge that many multisite churches are structured in a way that is not truly congregational and that would not qualify as a single church under congregational polity.

I believe in the complete inerrancy and authority of Scripture, and read Scripture with a normative view of the text. Daniel Block, though specifically writing about corporate worship, expresses my viewpoint on how we should read the biblical text in all areas of ministry when he writes,

> Many prefer the *normative principle*, which allows Christians to incorporate in their worship forms and practices not forbidden by Scripture, provided they promote order in worship and do not contradict scriptural principles. While the [*regulative principle*] is quite restrictive, the latter opens doors to creative and expressive worship. Our challenge, then, is ensuring that even when forms of worship are culturally determined, the principles underlying them are biblically rooted and theologically formed (emphasis original).[12]

I believe where the Scripture speaks with clear direction on a subject, the direction should be followed. Where Scripture does not present clear direction, there is flexibility to utilize appropriate, biblically and theologically sound ministry forms that adhere to the primary mission of the church: to win the lost and create true disciples. For me, this limits using structures that only attract nonbelievers or that create shallow "believers."

12   Block, *For the Glory of God*, 2–3.

A church's structure and practice must create true multiplying disciples who adhere to the inerrant and sufficient Word of God.

MULTISITE CRITICS

On a recent trip to Italy, my wife and I met a wonderful couple from Long Island. As we talked during many visits the conversation turned to church, and my wife, as she loves to do, mentioned I was writing this book. The couple asked what my topic was, and assuming they were not really that interested, I simply said, "It is on multisite churches." Surprisingly, they perked up, turned in their chairs, and said, "Really? What's your take on them? Are they good or bad?" Unfortunately, the answer is not as simple as that.

As the MCM has grown, it has received plenty of criticism from various voices, most of which are within the Southern Baptist Convention. Articles, blog posts, dissertations, and books that question the biblical validity of multisite churches, or which at least raise serious questions about the method, are numerous. These authors specifically claim multisite churches do not, or cannot, meet the definition of a church as defined in the denomination's doctrinal statement, the Baptist Faith and Message (BFM) 2000.[13] They address concerns with the MCM definition of a multisite church, as provided above, and identify examples of how the practical applications of multisite ministry fall outside the BFM's definition of an autonomous, congregationally led, local church.[14]

Thomas White summarizes nine issues he has with multisite churches in the same *9Marks Journal* Allison wrote his article.[15] Jonathan Leeman lists even more issues by identifying "Twenty-Two Problems with Multisite Churches" in a later blog post on the 9Marks website.[16] White expands

---

13   "The Baptist Faith and Message," *Southern Baptist Convention*. If the reader is not familiar with the BFM2000, I would recommend taking a moment to read through it. It provided much of the background theology for the book's conclusions, especially in regard to the ecclesiological arguments found in White's and Leeman's articles.

14   Leeman, "Twenty-Two Problems with Multi-Site Churches"; Sullivan, "Examining the Ecclesiological Soundness of the Southern Baptist Multisite Movement," 140–42; White and Yeats, *Franchising McChurch*, 189–90.

15   White, "Nine Reasons I Don't Like Multi-Site Churches."

16   Leeman, "Twenty-Two Problems with Multi-Site Churches."

his multisite summary into a thorough critique in *Franchising McChurch*, cowritten with John Yeats.[17] This book, which is a critique of consumer driven models of church ministry, includes three chapters critical of the multisite model.

The edition of *9Marks Journal*, already mentioned, is devoted entirely to the discussion of multisite churches. While it gives an opportunity for both multisite critics and advocates to voice support for their views, the journal leans heavily in opposition to the multisite model. This issue includes seven articles arguing against multisite (compared to three in the pro-multisite category), and also has three book reviews, all with a negative slant toward multisite church ministry.[18] These articles question the ecclesiological soundness and historical validity of multisite, present theological and exegetical critiques, and suggest alternatives to multisite. This issue of the *9Marks Journal* reveals the strong bias against multisite models that is consistent throughout the 9Marks ministry organization, especially with the journal's editor, Jonathan Leeman. Leeman is one of the most outspoken critics of the multisite church model. His book, *One Assembly: Rethinking the Multisite and Multiservice Church Models,* is the first book completely devoted to critiquing the multi-models of church ministry. In the book, he explains his belief that multisite and multiservice churches actually do a disservice to the biblical prescription for churches, and he claims that a single-service church is better able to make a gospel impact than a multisite or multiservice church. By including multiservice churches in this book, Leeman successfully eliminates a glaring hole in the arguments of most multisite critics, which is that almost all of their

17 White and Yeats, *Franchising McChurch*.
18 Articles against multisite: Gaines, "Exegetical Critique of Multi-Site," 33–37; Gilbert, "What Is This Thing, Anyway?," 25–27; Hammett, "Have We Ever Seen This Before?," 28–31; Jamieson, "Historical Critique of Multi-Site," 46–48; Leeman, "The Alternative: Why Don't We Plant?," 52–54; Leeman, "Theological Critique of Multi-Site," 38–45; White, "Nine Reasons I Don't Like Multi-Site Churches."
    Articles in favor of multisite: Allison, "Theological Defense of Multi-Site"; Chandler, "Clouds on the Horizon," 32; Greear, "A Pastor Defends His Multi-Site Church," 19–24.
    Book reviews: Jamieson, "Book Review: Multi-Site Churches," 55–57; Jamieson, "Book Review: One Church, Many Congregations," 61–62; Leeman, "Book Review: Franchising McChurch," 61–62.

arguments against multisite churches also apply to multiservice churches, yet multiservice churches are rarely targeted in their critiques.[19]

MULTISITE ADVOCATES

Multisite scholars and practitioners have not addressed many of the concerns presented. The vast majority of pro-multisite literature has primarily focused on the practical side of multisite ministry, not addressing the theological concerns.[20]

Elmer Towns, the prolific church growth author, was the earliest to identify multisite church as a viable, and commendable, model for churches. He included three chapters on multisite churches in his book *10 of Today's Most Innovative Churches*.[21]

Another early proponent who wrote more extensively on the multisite model was Lyle Schaller. He included the model in many of his church growth books from the early 1990s into the 2000s.[22] He also wrote the foreword to the earliest book written specifically on the topic of multisite ministry, *One Church, Many Congregations: The Key Church Strategy*.[23] In this book, the term "key church strategy" is used to describe a specific model of what is now known as the multisite church model. This early

---

19   Leeman, *One Assembly*. Dissertations critical of the multisite model are plentiful. Grant Gaines's dissertation on multisite churches questions the validity of a church that never assembles as a single group (Gaines, "One Church in One Location"). Patrick Willis builds upon this argument in his dissertation, questioning the biblical validity of multisite, but also questioning if multisite ecclesiology is compatible with Baptist church identity (Willis, "Multi-Site Churches and Their Undergirding Ecclesiology"). Heath Kahlbau's dissertation analyzes the ecclesiology of multisite churches and concludes that it is almost impossible for a multisite church to function with true congregational polity (Kahlbau, "Is Anything New Under the Sun?"). Dennis Sullivan's dissertation looks at the issues from the perspective of Southern Baptist history, practice, and ecclesiological definitions (Sullivan, "Examining the Ecclesiological Soundness").

20   Surratt, Ligon, and Bird, *Multi-Site Church Revolution*; Surratt, Ligon, and Bird, *A Multi-Site Church Road Trip*; McConnell, *Multi-Site Churches*.

21   Towns, *Today's Most Innovative Churches*.

22   Schaller, *44 Questions for Church Planters*; Schaller, *Discontinuity and Hope*; Schaller, *Innovations in Ministry*; Schaller, *A Mainline Turnaround*. Ahlen and Thomas do not consider their model to be a multisite model, and neither does Bryan Frye. However, it shares such common characteristics that it will be considered alongside other multisite models. Chapter 2 will make the case that the key church strategy is a form of multisite.

23   Ahlen and Thomas, *One Church, Many Congregations*.

text describes a process by which churches can add satellite campuses to their ministry, and it includes case studies of churches that have used the key church strategy.

The primary source for the multisite church, and what is often considered to be the foundational work on the subject, is *The Multi-Site Church Revolution* (*MCR*).[24] Both the definition of a multisite church and the practical guidance found in this book serve as the starting point for much of the conversation surrounding multisite ministry. Multisite critics often use the principles, claims, and applications from this book as a generalized stereotype in their critiques.[25] This early book functions as a multisite model promotional tool, as does the authors' subsequent book, *A Multi-Site Church Road Trip* (*MRT*).[26] *MCR* is primarily a book of multisite principles with a few included case studies, whereas *MRT* is primarily a survey of multisite church case studies and their strategies. *MCR* does include a chapter with a title that suggests some theological reflection, "Are You Sure This Isn't a Sin?" However, the chapter is simply ten pages focused on quickly rebutting criticisms of the multisite church, with only four passing references to biblical warrant. Both *MCR* and *MRT* are the work of Leadership Network, an influential group in the multisite church arena.

Another Leadership Network book, *Better Together*, focuses on church mergers.[27] The first full chapter in this book gives hope for a biblical argument for church mergers with the title, "God Is Doing Something New: Biblical Basis for Mergers." Yet, the brief biblical warrant for mergers the chapter presents has nothing to do with actual church mergers or multisite churches. It is simply a compilation of passages of Scripture showing God's desire for unity and for all people to be brought together under the banner of the church.[28]

---

24   Surratt, Ligon, and Bird, *Multi-Site Church Revolution*. Dennis Sullivan is one example of many who consider MCR to be the foundational work on the MCM (Sullivan, "Examining the Ecclesiological Soundness," 1).

25   Leeman, "Twenty-Two Problems with Multi-Site Churches"; White, "Nine Reasons I Don't Like Multi-Site Churches," 49–51.

26   Surratt, Ligon, and Bird, *A Multi-Site Church Road Trip*.

27   Tomberlin and Bird, *Better Together*.

28   Tomberlin and Bird, *Better Together*, 8–12.

The lone book from an SBC publisher is *Multi-Site Churches* by Scott McConnell, with contributions from many multisite experts.[29] The book, based on research conducted by Lifeway Research, is full of practical advice but has very little theological reflection on the multisite church. The chapters by McConnell are partnered with practical multisite reflections and advice written by leading multisite practitioners and experts.

When it comes to true theological reflection on the multisite church, Gregg Allison is one of the few scholars who has consistently sought solid biblical warrant for the practice. His first published defense is the article in the Spring 2010 edition of the *9Marks Journal* mentioned previously.[30] In this article, he summarizes a few variations of multisite ministry, summarizes the biblical and theological assessment, and then provides what he believes to be the best model for multisite churches. In his ecclesiology, *Sojourners and Strangers*, Allison includes an eighteen-page section on multisite ministry in his chapter on church governance.[31] This brief analysis is the most thorough pro-multisite theological treatment that is currently available. Allison has written another book, *MultiChurch*, along with Brad House, which includes sections on the ecclesiology of multisite churches.[32] Both Allison and House formerly served as elders at Sojourn Church, a multisite church in Louisville, Kentucky.[33] *MultiChurch*, while containing some theological reflection, has its primary focus on the practical aspects of multisite ministry.

Mark Driscoll, former pastor of Mars Hill Church in Seattle, Washington, a multisite church under his leadership, wrote a modern ecclesiology, *Vintage Church*, along with Gerry Breshears.[34] The book is "about the church of Jesus Christ," and covers topics such as what constitutes a biblical church, church structures, church leadership, and other aspects of ecclesial life. It also includes a chapter on multisite churches. This

29   McConnell, *Multi-Site Churches.*
30   Allison, "Theological Defense of Multi-Site."
31   Allison, *Sojourners and Strangers*, 310–17.
32   House and Allison, *MultiChurch.*
33   "Gregg R. Allison," *The Southern Baptist Theological Seminary*; "Staff," *Sojourn Church.*
34   Driscoll and Breshears, *Vintage Church.*

book is an important resource because it is an ecclesiological work, albeit brief, and it is written by multisite advocates.[35]

Another article written in support of multisite churches comes from John Hammett in the *Great Commission Research Journal*.[36] This article sets two parameters by which a multisite church must function to be considered one church. Hammett should not be considered a staunch multisite advocate, however. In an earlier article, in the same *9Marks Journal* as Allison's article mentioned previously, Hammett voices concern over the multisite model.[37]

The academic world has seen numerous projects published on the multisite church since the beginning of the new millennium. Of those that consider the multisite church model as a whole, as opposed to focusing on only one aspect of a multisite church, only two papers can truly be considered pro-multisite. Brian Frye's dissertation, "The Multi-Site Church Phenomenon in North America: 1950–2010," is focused primarily on multisite's history in the United States. While he does address some ecclesiological issues, his dissertation is not an attempt to make a biblical or theological case for multisite's validity.[38] Scott Revealy's DMin project, "An Ecclesiology for Multi-Site Churches: Thinking Biblically About the Local Church in Multiple Locations," is an early project that presents an overview of multisite churches and much information on how to go about the process of becoming a multisite church. It also includes a basic church

---

35 Subsequent to writing his book, Driscoll resigned from Mars Hill Church and stepped out of leadership and membership in the Acts 29 Network, a church planting association. These moves were made at a time when accusations of alleged heavy-handed and abusive leadership tendencies on the part of Driscoll were made public (Cosper, "The Rise and Fall of Mars Hill"; Welch, "The Rise and Fall of Mars Hill Church"). I am not making any judgment on the truthfulness of these allegations and in no way approve of abusive leadership practices. *Vintage Church* will be referenced frequently, especially in Part 2, because of the importance, and rarity, of having ecclesiological insight from multisite advocates and practitioners. This is in no way an approval, recommendation, or endorsement of Driscoll.

36 Hammett, "What Makes a Multi-Site Church One Church," 95–107.

37 Hammett, "Have We Ever Seen This Before?," 28–31.

38 Frye, "The Multi-Site Church in North America: 1950–2010." Other examples of dissertations that focus on one aspect of multisite ministry are Edwards, "Leadership Structures and Dynamics in Multisite Churches"; Floyd, "A Multi-Plantation Ministry"; Kouba, "Role of the Campus Pastor"; Taylor, "Sermon Preparation Methods."

ecclesiology and attempts to match that ecclesiology to multisite churches. It is a very minimal presentation in favor of multisite churches and cannot be considered a fully developed multisite ecclesiology.[39]

Numerous articles and blog posts in support of multisite church ministry are available, especially from sources such as Thom Rainer, Ed Stetzer, and Leadership Network. These articles trend toward the practical, methodological, and research side of multisite churches, but rarely get into the theological side of the practice.[40] The exception would be Stetzer, who does include some articles questioning certain aspects of the movement.[41]

THE PURPOSE OF THIS BOOK: PROVIDING A FOUNDATION

The authors mentioned above never intended to provide a theological description of multisite church ecclesiology. Their primary purpose was the practical application of the model, and to that end they definitely achieved their purpose. Their directions and applications are thoughtful and provide good analyses of the multisite models available for evaluation. What is needed now is a theological underpinning that provides biblical support. Those who have presented theological defenses have not yet provided a holistic defense of the multisite model, nor have they provided a fully formed ecclesiology for multisite churches.[42] The lack of these two foundational tools for multisite churches is a severe blow for the movement and for church leaders who desire to be biblically faithful while expanding their churches to multiple campuses. For churches and church leaders it is unwise, if not irresponsible, to use an ecclesiological structure without first considering if it is biblically valid. If a church structure falls outside the biblical description of how a church should function, then it should be abandoned in favor of an approach that does adhere to biblical mores. If, however, a multisite model can be shown to

---

39   Reavely, "An Ecclesiology for Multi-Site Churches."
40   Examples include: Bird, "Campus Pastor as Key to Multisite Success"; Rainer, "Is the Multisite Church Movement Still Growing?"; Stetzer, "Multisite Churches Are Here, and Here, and Here to Stay."
41   Stetzer, "Multisite Evolution."
42   Allison, *Sojourners and Strangers*, 310–17; Allison, "Theological Defense of Multi-Site"; House and Allison, *MultiChurch*.

fall within the biblical parameters, then, when appropriate, it should be used wisely by churches for the sake of reaching the lost.

The hope of this book is to be able to provide a simple theological foundation that gives credibility to multisite churches as a legitimate, biblical church model, not simply another fad of a consumeristic church. It will challenge the conclusions that multisite models are incompatible with congregational polity and will make the case that a form of multisite church exists that is compatible with congregationally led churches.[43] It will provide a new definition for multisite churches that is compatible with congregational definitions of churches, and it will provide guidance for how multisite churches can function in a biblical way.[44] The following chapters will support this thesis by evaluating multisite church models and definitions, evaluating the church practices and structure described in the New Testament, considering historical church practices that support multisite models, and engaging current arguments against the multisite church. Along the way, the reader will discover a biblical ecclesiology for multisite churches, and an expression, or model, of multisite church that is fits within congregational polity. The conclusion will suggest a new definition of a multisite church that includes both theological and practical considerations.

Ultimately, the goal is to be thorough enough to provide a pastor and his church leaders, or even a denominational leader, with enough biblical validation to move forward with a multisite model if the Lord is leading them in that direction. It also, hopefully, is accessible enough that the same pastor could confidently put it in the hands of his members

---

43 The content in this book was originally a part of a dissertation written specifically on Southern Baptist multisite churches. Therefore, many of the examples and citations will be from Baptist sources. This should not, however, detract from the application to all congregationally led churches, and even to those with other polity structures. The vast majority of the content is applicable to multisite churches of any tribe.

44 As mentioned in footnote 2, the term "multisite" will be the exclusive term used when discussing various multi-location church ministries. Additionally, only churches that have gatherings in two separate physical campuses will be considered to be multisite. Those who have multiple worship locations on the same physical campus, multi-venue, will not be considered in the argument, although they will be mentioned at times in Part 1 in the section on definitions and models. While Part 1 will provide many various definitions and models of multisite churches from multisite proponents, all of these models will be considered under the one category of "multisite church."

who, like my new friends from New York, have questions about whether multisite will be "good or bad" for the church they love.

IS THIS BOOK JUST FOR BAPTISTS?

As mentioned previously, the original work was done specifically with Southern Baptist polity and the BFM in mind. The theological foundations, and the examples used throughout the book, are almost all from historic and current Baptist authors and pastors. This, however, does not negate the value of the book for non-Baptist churches. All of the principles are based upon an assumption of congregational polity, so a congregationally led church, whether democratically managed or led by elders, can universally apply these principles. Even non-congregational churches will find most of the principles in the book fully applicable to their own contexts.

The BFM describes a church as follows:

> A New Testament church of the Lord Jesus Christ is an auton-
> omous local congregation of baptized believers, associated by
> covenant in the faith and fellowship of the gospel; observing
> the two ordinances of Christ, governed by His laws, exercising
> the gifts, rights, and privileges invested in them by His Word,
> and seeking to extend the gospel to the ends of the earth. Each
> congregation operates under the Lordship of Christ through
> democratic processes. In such a congregation each member
> is responsible and accountable to Christ as Lord. Its scriptural
> officers are that of pastor/elder/overseer and deacons. While
> both men and women are gifted for service in the church, the
> office of pastor/elder/overseer is limited to men as qualified
> by Scripture.[45]

The BFM article on the church reveals the basic underpinnings of local church autonomy, covenant membership, congregational leadership, and the offices of pastor and deacon. These assumptions will be present

---

45   "Baptist Faith and Message 2000," *Southern Baptist Convention.*

throughout the book whenever the BFM is referenced, but even if the readers do not have these same theological assumptions, the content can still be invaluable for a discussion on multisite churches.

The eleven marks of a healthy church that are used as an outline for the book's Part 2 are also universally applicable to all churches. Even if a church is not congregational, it should seek health in all eleven areas; and the guidelines discussed in the book should, at the very least, encourage all churches in the general direction of healthy churches and healthy multisite strategies.

PART 1

THE MULTISITE CHURCH MOVEMENT

FOR MANY, INCLUDING PASTORS and church leaders, discussing a multisite church is a foreign subject. They have probably heard of it, and they might know someone who attends a multisite church. But they really don't know anything about it. What would help is a crash course to help learn the basic history, terminology, and tenets of the multisite church model. Part 1 is that crash course.

This section will provide an overview of the modern multisite church movement (MCM).[1] The time period evaluated, however, will extend beyond what is considered to be the "movement," and will include examples from late 1800s to the present.[2] The breadth of practices within the movement are too varied to provide an analysis of every unique practice of every multisite churches. Therefore, Part 1 will describe the most common practices and definitions within the multisite movement.

---

1   Brian Frye's dissertation, "The Multi-Site Church Phenomenon: 1950–2010," has been a tremendous resource in this section. This section makes great use of Frye's historical analysis of multisite churches, and his bibliography was a great source of information.

2   Frye, "The Multi-Site Church Phenomenon," 3–4, 33–34. Frye says the movement began in 2001, and that no true multisite churches existed until near the end of the twenty-first century.

Chapter 1 will initially discuss popular definitions of a multisite church, as well as various models of multisite churches from leading researchers and practitioners. Chapter 2 will then explain some of the foundational assumptions of the multisite church movement, both in philosophy and practice. Chapter 3 will give an overview of the history of the multisite movement, noting various developments along the way, including a re-evaluation Bryan Frye's analysis of historical examples of multisite-like ministries.[3]

---

3   Frye, "The Multi-Site Church Phenomenon," 33–62.

A SURVEY OF MULTISITE CHURCH SCHOLARSHIP

WHEN I WAS STILL A YOUTH PASTOR, I was beginning to learn about multisite churches from conversations and observations. Some of my wife's extended family attended a local multisite megachurch in Dallas, and I picked up bits and pieces of how their multisite model worked. Each campus had some local leadership but was basically a copy of the central campus and received its direction from the central campus. I saw similar models in other multisite churches across the country. So, when I began interviewing at Green Acres to become their next campus pastor, I assumed it would work the same way. I would provide local leadership, along with the campus leaders, but we would receive our directions from the central campus. I was wrong. The internal workings were not wrong. They were simply different than what I assumed. My assumptions were based in observing how a few multisite church examples worked, but I was completely unaware that there were innumerable ways for multisite churches to function. In reality, the history of multisite shows there have been many definitions and many models.

DEFINITIONS AND MODELS OF MULTISITE CHURCHES

As the multisite church began to gain popularity from the 1980s to the 2000s, more church growth experts began to take notice. Many of these scholars began writing on the subject, providing definitions of multisite churches and describing various multisite models. This chapter will describe the definitions and models put forth by leaders in the movement's development.

Randy Pope

Randy Pope is considered one of the pioneers of the multisite movement.[1] A pastor in the Presbyterian Church, he planted Perimeter Church in Atlanta, Georgia, in 1977 with the intention of having one church with one hundred campuses around and throughout Atlanta.[2] That plan was never realized and, as a result, Perimeter Church modified its model. Along the way, the church has used two models of multisite ministry. The initial model was one church meeting in multiple locations around the city. Under this model, the senior pastor was the primary elder for the whole church. Each campus had a lead campus pastor as well as elders, and each campus was subject to a central campus board composed of three elders from each campus. The church as a whole functioned under one vision and budget.[3]

As the church progressed, Pope modified his vision from one church with multiple locations and a centralized leadership to multiple autonomous churches, unified under a central ministry that facilitated church planting and cooperative ministry efforts.[4] This new model left

---

1   Frye, "The Multi-Site Church Phenomenon," 97–98, 100–101.
2   Pope, "3 Reasons We Stopped Doing Multisite Church."
3   Towns, *An Inside Look at 10 of Today's Most Innovative Churches*, 90.
4   Pope, "3 Reasons We Stopped Doing Multisite"; Towns, *Today's Most Innovative Churches*, 96–97. Pope says the model was adjusted because he realized the vision of beginning one hundred churches across Atlanta could not be realized within the single church organizational structure, but it could be realized through a network of individual churches. Since modifying the model, Perimeter Church has grown from four campuses under the single church model to "40 daughter, granddaughter, and great-granddaughter churches planted around Atlanta" as of 2015 (Pope, "3 Reasons We Stopped Doing Multisite"). Towns uses the same number of four campuses that Pope uses (Towns, *Today's Most Innovative Churches*, 95). However, Russell Chandler suggests there were eight campuses when the transition to autonomous churches linked by a network. He does not, however, include a source for his number (Chandler, *Racing Toward 2001*, 242).

the autonomous churches to contextualize their ministries, choose their own leadership, and manage their own budgets, just as a single-site, autonomous church would do. However, the connection through the network allowed these multiple locations to collectively carry out ministry initiatives they may not otherwise have been able to do on their own.[5]

RANDY POPE'S TWO MULTISITE MODELS[6]	
Church Model	**Model Description**
One Church in Multiple Locations	This model is one church that has multiple locations governed by a central leadership, vision, and budget.
Autonomous Churches Organized Together for Ministry	This model is autonomous churches that are organized together for church planting and specific ministries, and that contribute a set portion of money to facilitate those efforts.

Elmer Towns

Elmer Towns was the first church growth writer to identify the multisite model early within the multisite church movement. In *An Inside Look at 10 of Today's Most Innovative Churches*, he uses three of the ten churches to discuss multisite models.[7] Towns labels multisite "The Extended Geographic Parish Church." His model creates a very general category, large enough to hold most of the more specifically defined multisite categories that would come later. He defines the model, "An extended geographic parish church is spread out over a larger area so that it: (1) meets in several locations, (2) operates different ministries in different locations, and (3) has expanded its location geographically in

---

5   Pope, "3 Reasons We Stopped Doing Multisite."

6   Towns, *Today's Most Innovative Churches*, 90; Pope, "3 Reasons We Stopped Doing Multisite."

7   Towns, *Today's Most Innovative Churches*, 59–72, 89–103, 163–73. The three churches include two Atlanta-based churches, Perimeter Church and Mount Paran Church of God, and Church on the Way in Van Nuys, California. Towns somewhat also includes churches that use cell group home group models in the Extended Geographic Parish Model. He says that "by another definition" these churches can be included, but he does not clarify what that definition is (238).

order to reach a larger 'Jerusalem.'"[8] He further clarifies that the model has multiple ministries, places of ministry, and ministers, but "one central organization and one senior pastor."[9] This early definition is foundational to many of the definitions and models that came after it.

ELMER TOWNS'S EXTENDED GEOGRAPHIC PARISH CHURCH[10]	
Church Model	**Model Description**
Extended Geographic Parish Church	An extended geographic parish church has multiple ministries, places of ministry, and ministers, but one central organization and one senior pastor.

Lyle Schaller

Lyle Schaller was the first church growth writer to categorize multisite churches into various models. Schaller was a prolific contributor to the church growth and church health conversation for over a half century and wrote or edited ninety-four books in his lifetime.[11] While he does not provide a clear definition of a multisite church early on in his discussion of multisite, he does provide one later in his writing. Schaller writes, "They continue as one congregation with one staff, treasury, one membership roster, one governing board, and one name, but with [multiple] worship services every weekend and an open-ended commitment to continue to function as a two- (or three-) site congregation."[12]

---

8   Towns, *Today's Most Innovative Churches*, 238.
9   Towns, *Today's Most Innovative Churches*, 238–41.
10   Towns, *Today's Most Innovative Churches*, 238.
11   Bird, "Lyle E. Schaller."
12   Schaller, *Discontinuity and Hope*, 176.

LYLE SCHALLER'S EIGHT MULTISITE MODELS[13]

Multisite Model	Model Description
Downtown Church	The downtown multisite church uses satellite campuses primarily as a place for teaching, and not a fully developed ministry station.
Urban Church	The urban church has multiple off-campus meeting locations.
Relocation	A church that is using multisite as a part of a relocation process.
Heterogeneous Campuses	A church with campuses that mirror the demographic contexts of the neighborhoods in which they are located.
Key Church Strategy	Mission focused satellites to reach specific target groups of people.
Wounded Bird Merger	A church that is dying joins with a strong church, which then provides new vision, leadership, resources, and people to begin establishing a healthy satellite location.
Small Church Merger	Small churches join together with one another, or with a larger church, to form a single church with a single administrative body, shared leadership, and shared ministries.
Church Planting	Multisite is used as a church planting strategy.

Schaller describes eight models of multisite churches.[14] The first is the downtown church that has a satellite location primarily for preaching rather than a full-fledged ministry. The second model is an urban church that has multiple off-campus meeting places. The third is the church that is using multisite as a part of a relocation process.

---

13   Schaller, *Innovations in Ministry*, 71–72, 121.
14   Schaller, *Innovations in Ministry*, 121. The first seven, Schaller refers to as the "seven most highly visible expressions of the multisite option." The eighth model, "mergers," Schaller refers to as "What probably will turn out to be the most widely followed use of the concept" (121). Frye concludes Schaller's prediction that the merger model would become predominant did not prove accurate (Frye, "The Multi-Site Church Phenomenon," 123).

The fourth is a diverse church whose campuses are contextualized, fitting the demographic context of the neighborhoods in which they are located. The fifth is a church that has adopted the "Key Church Strategy," which is a mission-focused satellite campus methodology.[15] The sixth model is when a larger church adopts struggling churches as a means of rehabilitating and strengthening them. The seventh model is using multisite campuses as a means of church planting. The eighth, and final, model Schaller describes is church merging, whereby two churches come together to form one church while retaining their separate locations.[16]

Earl Ferguson

Earl Ferguson wrote the first scholarly work on the multisite church, a Doctor of Ministry project focused on discipleship processes in multisite churches.[17] Ferguson served as pastor at Living Creek Christian Church in Monroe, Illinois, for thirty-seven years before becoming the campus pastor for Community Christian Church's Carillon Campus.[18] The Carillon Campus is one of the church's seven locations and is based in the community center of a senior adult community.[19]

---

15   The Key Church Strategy will be discussed later in this section.
16   Over a decade earlier, Schaller described a "multi-church" parish, in which two or more small churches combine their financial resources to hire a single, full-time pastor who preaches at each location on an established cycle. He concluded then that there were at least sixty thousand Protestant churches in the United States and Canada that used this method. Specifically, he said 40 percent of United Methodist churches at the time were in such a partnership including two or more churches. This model harkens back to the days of the circuit-riding preachers (Schaller, *The Small Church Is Different!*, 145–46).
17   Ferguson, "The Multi-Site Church and Disciplemaking."
18   Ferguson, "Earl Ferguson," *Facebook*; Ferguson, "Earl Ferguson," *LinkedIn*; "Our History," *Living Creek Christian Church*; "Carillon," *Community Christian Church*.
19   "Community Locations," *Community Christian Church*; Ferguson, "Earl Ferguson," *LinkedIn*. Ferguson's legacy as a multisite pastor includes Community Christian Church, as the two founding pastors are his sons, Dave and Jon Ferguson. Community Christian Church is also a part of the case study in Ferguson's DMin project (Ferguson, "The Multi-Site Church," 26–27; "Leadership Team," *Community Christian Church*). CCC lists seven campuses on their website, in addition to three prison ministries that they identify as campuses. They also have microchurches, which are small groups with more church-like function than a typical small group. There will be more said about microchurches in Part 3.

Ferguson's contribution to the multisite conversation is minimal, but important. His definition of multisite churches is not unique and is actually a quotation of Charles Olsen's definition of satellite base churches from *The Base Church*.[20] Ferguson's primary contribution to the conversation is his two categories of multisite churches, each with additional sub-categories. Like Schaller, Ferguson bases his multisite categories on the purpose behind the church's multisite strategy, rather than the structure of the church.[21]

Ferguson's first category of multisite churches is "reactive multisite churches," which Ferguson claims makes up the majority of multisite churches. A reactive church is a church that pursues the multisite model out of compulsion. Reactive churches find they must expand to multisite either because of a growth explosion in the church, or because the church wants to relocate, and uses multisite as the relocation tool.[22]

Ferguson's second category is "proactive multisite churches." These churches intentionally implement a multisite model for the purpose of reaching more people with the gospel. Some of these churches use the multisite model intentionally to remain in their original location while making room for future growth. Others use satellite locations as bases for ministry in new areas, typically centered around a certain affinity group or a need-based ministry. A third group of churches use multisite ministry as a tool for evangelism and widening their base for reaching more people.[23]

---

20 Ferguson, "The Multi-Site Church," 18. Ferguson quotes Olsen's definition of multisite churches. However, Olsen's intent was not to describe or define a multisite church. Rather, *The Base Church* was written to provide a method for "reshaping the church by building a base church of small-group communities both within and outside the congregation . . ." (19). The language and defined structures Olsen uses are similar to multisite language and models, especially the satellite base church and cluster base church. However, since Olsen's purpose was developing small group communities and not multisite churches, his definition and models will not be included in the current discussion. The communities Olsen described did not show all the marks of a local church, which is a disqualifying characteristic (Olsen, *The Base Church*, 72–87).

21 Ferguson, "The Multi-Site Church," 19.

22 Ferguson, "The Multi-Site Church," 19–22.

23 Ferguson, "The Multi-Site Church," 22–27.

EARL FERGUSON'S TWO CATEGORIES OF MULTISITE CHURCHES[24]	
Church Model	**Model Description**
Reactive Multisite	
Relocating	A church begins a second location in an area of town to which it plans to eventually relocate the ministry leadership and activity.
Growth Explosion	A church experiences a sudden explosion in attendance growth and must begin a second location in order to facilitate continued growth.
Proactive Multisite	
Expanding Reach	This church seeks to use multisite to continue growing and to expand its reach into new areas, with no intention of relocating the original campus. (This differs from the Reactive Growth Explosion model because it is done in preparation for growth, rather than in response to growth.)
Ministry-Based	These churches use multisite as a means of ministering to a community with specific needs.
Intentional Outreach Strategy	These churches are begun with the intention of expanding into multiple locations as a part of their outreach and growth strategy.

Timothy Ahlen and J. V. Thomas

Timothy Ahlen and J. V. Thomas's book *One Church, Many Congregations* is an expansion of Thomas's original satellite church strategy described in *Investing in Eternity*.[25] The authors label the model "the Key Church Strategy."[26] In the foreword, Lyle Schaller says the Key Church Strategy "boils down to the discovery that one congregation can meet

---

24   Ferguson, "The Multi-Site Church," 19–27.
25   Thomas, *Investing in Eternity.*
26   Ahlen and Thomas, *One Church, Many Congregations*, 17–20.

in two different locations."[27] The strategy is a model based largely on the concepts in Donald McGavran's "Homogenous Unit Principle," which states, "People like to become Christians without crossing racial, linguistic, or class barriers."[28] About putting this principle into practice, McGavran says, "One goal of missions is to plant churches in every homogeneous unit, culturally in harmony with that unit, jealously guarding its cultural diversities, and considering the tribe or caste, the clan or other unit one of God's orders of preservation, to be respected till He replaces it."[29]

This is the same viewpoint and purpose of the Key Church Strategy. The strategy is built upon the belief that churches will be healthier and more sustainable when "*started and developed in the context of the socio-economic conditions and culture of the people who are to be evangelized or congregationalized*" (emphasis original).[30] This missionary language defines the heart and purpose of the Key Church Strategy. To summarize a definition of the strategy based on its principles, one could conclude that the Key Church Strategy is a method by which a local church can begin additional congregations that are culturally determined by their location. The original congregation provides the vision for the church, as well as minimal leadership, financial support, and oversight.[31] Those who

---

27   Schaller, Foreword to *One Church, Many Congregations*, 13–14. Schaller credits Ahlen and Thomas with "the discovery that one congregation can meet in two different locations." This is an overstatement. It will become apparent later in the book that many churches have experimented with these principles prior to the Key Church Strategy.

28   McGavran, *Understanding Church Growth*, 163.

29   McGavran, *The Bridges of God*, 162.

30   Ahlen and Thomas, *One Church, Many Congregations*, 32; Thomas, *Investing in Eternity*, 14–19.

31   Ahlen and Thomas, *One Church, Many Congregations*, 34–36. The thirteen principles that guide the Key Church Strategy are: (1) Take the gospel to people of different cultures. (2) Allow the resulting church to develop within the indigenous culture. (3) Recognize that socioeconomic and lifestyle factors affect culture as much as language and the country of birth. (4) Expect the new congregation to express itself differently than yours. (5) Send out leaders from the sponsoring church into the culturally different community. However, keep the total number of such leaders to a minimum. (6) Employ missionary methods. (7) Let the people's perceived needs determine the strategy, programs, and ministries. (8) Discover, and then plug into, the community's existing assets and resources. (9) Serve for the Kingdom's sake—not your own and not your church's! (10) Expect problems. (11) Expect great blessings from God because you are obedient to the Great Commission. (12) Expect to experience accelerated church growth. (13) Keep financial support to a minimum.

become members of the satellite congregations are incorporated into the
sponsoring church's membership and are under the oversight of both the
campus leadership and central leadership.[32]

Within the Key Church Strategy, Ahlen and Thomas identify three different models from which a church may choose one or multiple models for
their strategy. The first model is "church-type congregations." These congregations are planted with a specific unreached target group in view and
have an ultimate goal of becoming a self-sustaining, autonomous church.
The target group will share some unifying trait, typically a nationality
or language. The second model is "indigenous satellite congregations."
These are similar to the first model in that they target a specific group of
people. However, they begin with the understanding that they will likely
require a strong ongoing connection to the original congregation for the
purpose of leadership and financial support. The third model within the
KeyChurch Strategy is the "multihousing congregation." These are similar
to the second model in that they will maintain a strong ongoing connection to the original location. However, they are different because they are
located within a multihousing community and have the goal of reaching
all of the residents within that community rather than a certain affinity
group.[33] These three models within the Key Church Strategy sound very
similar to Ferguson's three proactive category examples.[34] Like Ferguson's
models, the Key Church Strategy is more of a purpose-based model than
a structural model.

The Key Church Strategy is unique in the multisite movement because
it has more of a missionary focus. It was developed when urban churches
in the middle of transitioning neighborhoods decided to reach their new
neighbors by beginning congregations that were culturally relevant to
those neighbors.[35] It is likely that not all of these congregations would
qualify as true multisite campuses, since they do not include the full

---

32   Thomas, *Investing in Eternity*, 42–47.
33   Ahlen and Thomas, *One Church, Many Congregations*, 22.
34   Ferguson, "The Multi-Site Church," 22–27.
35   Most multisite churches, on the other hand, have campuses that are an extension of the
     DNA of the original campus, rather than intentionally different than the original cam-
     pus.

marks of a New Testament church. However, the ultimate goal is to begin and/or develop groups that demonstrate the marks of a church.[36] Thomas describes the model as a "church-type mission that remains a permanent part of the sponsoring church."[37] He adds, "This method presents an alternative to starting new churches. The [Key Church Strategy] makes it possible for a single church to reach thousands of people for Christ."[38]

TIMOTHY AHLEN AND J. V. THOMAS'S THREE KEY CHURCH MODELS[39]	
Key Church Model	**Model Description**
Church-Type Congregations	These congregations [are] traditional churches started to reach specific unchurched groups of people . . . . In each case, the goal [is] to plant new churches that [will] one day be completely self-supporting, self-governing, and self-propagating.
Indigenous Satellite Congregations	These congregations, mostly house churches, [minister] to the needs of the blue-collar residents of the surrounding neighborhoods. While each [is] encouraged to become as autonomous as possible, all parties involved [recognize] the value of a strong ongoing relationship to the sponsor church.
Multihousing Congregations	Multihousing congregations are special examples of indigenous satellite congregations . . . . They also minister to blue-collar people. In addition to depending on the sponsor church for support, multihousing congregations rely on the apartment management for permission to minister on the property.

---

36 Ahlen and Thomas, *One Church, Many Congregations*, 130–33; Thomas, *Investing in Eternity*, 21–33, 42–47.

37 Thomas, *Investing in Eternity*, 1.

38 Thomas, *Investing in Eternity*, 2. In this quote, Thomas refers to the "ISC" instead of the Key Church Strategy. ISC stands for Indigenous Satellite Congregations, a title that was later changed to Key Church Strategy.

39 Ahlen and Thomas, *One Church, Many Congregations*, 22–23.

Bill Easum and Dave Travis

Bill Easum and Dave Travis offer their own definition of multisite churches in *Beyond the Box*. They write, "[A multisite church] meets in many locations but has the same core values, mission, administration, budget, treasury, and staff as a single site church."[40] Their definition is the only one to mention single site churches, suggesting the only true difference between single site and multisite churches is the aspect of multiple locations.

After defining multisite, Easum and Travis give seven models of multisite churches. The first model is "The Apostle Approach." In this model, the senior pastor functions much like the New Testament apostles, with teaching oversight and authority over all locations. The goal in this approach is widespread expansion under the primary leadership of one lead pastor.[41] The second model is the "Video Venue Approach," which utilizes video-based teaching at each location. The third model is "The Rent Approach." With this model, the church rents the facility that houses its satellite campus rather than purchasing or building a permanent location. Easum and Travis say this makes the church more adaptable and frees up resources for ministry that would otherwise be spent on facilities.[42] The fourth model is "The Apartment Approach," which uses a house church or cell church form of multisite by having multiple congregations meeting in multiple apartments or apartment complexes. This allows churches to have "specialized congregations to meet the needs of many micro-niches based on culture and social need."[43] The fifth model is "The Strong Church, Weak Church Approach." This model is a merger between a church that is

---

40   Easum and Travis, *Beyond the Box*, 86. This definition differs from Easum's definition written ten years earlier, which stated, "These [multisite campus] experiments are called satellites, or geographically expanded (or perimeter) parish churches. They operate on the hub and spoke concept with one central congregation and many branch congregations" (Easum, *Dancing with Dinosaurs*, 92).

41   Easum and Travis, *Beyond the Box*, 86–89. This model/description is unique to Easum and Travis, although it is assumed in some of the models by other writers. The description that the apostles held authority over the New Testament churches is Easum and Travis's view, not the view of this author.

42   Easum and Travis, *Beyond the Box*, 89–93.

43   Easum and Travis, *Beyond the Box*, 93. This model is similar to the Key Church Strategy's multihousing model.

struggling and a strong church, whereby the strong church takes ownership and leadership of the struggling church, incorporating it into the church, and revitalizing it as a campus.[44]

BILL EASUM AND DAVE TRAVIS'S SEVEN APPROACHES OF MULTISITE CHURCHES[45]	
Multisite Approach	**Approach Description**
The Apostle Approach	In this model, the senior pastor functions much like a New Testament apostles, with teaching oversight and authority over all locations.
The Video Venue Approach	This approach utilizes video-based teaching at each location.
The Rent Approach	With this approach, the church rents the facility that houses its satellite campus rather than purchasing or building a permanent location.
The Apartment Approach	An approach that uses a house church or cell church form of multisite by having multiple congregations meeting in multiple apartments or apartment complexes.
The Strong Church/ Weak Church Approach	This model is a merger between a church that is struggling and a strong church, whereby the strong church takes ownership and leadership of the struggling church, incorporating it into the church, and revitalizing it as a campus.
The Mainline Approach	Churches in mainline denominations are using multisite church models.
The Small Church Approach	Small churches are using multisite church models

Easum and Travis provide two other models of multisite churches, "The Mainline Approach" and "The Small Church Approach." However, these are not really distinct multisite models, but simply categories of two

---

44   Easum and Travis, *Beyond the Box*, 95–96.
45   Easum and Travis, *Beyond the Box*, 86–96.

types churches that are using multisite models. The Mainline Approach refers to mainline denominations that have begun using multisite, and the Small Church Approach simply shows that small churches are using the multisite model as well.[46]

Easum and Travis's models signify a shift in the focus of multisite model definitions. Previous writers defined their models primarily by the purpose for which they are being used by a church, and secondarily by the church's multisite organizational structure. Easum and Travis's models are defined primarily by organizational structure, and secondarily by purpose. The shift to focusing on structure over purpose will continue in the following definitions and models, and throughout the development of the multisite movement.

Rodney Harrison, Tom Cheyney, and Don Overstreet

Rodney Harrison, Tom Cheyney, and Don Overstreet are well-respected authors and practitioners in the church planting community.[47] Their book *Spin-Off Churches* is focused on church planting, and as a part of their recommended church planting options, they include multisite.[48] The book does not provide a definition for multisite churches, apparently assuming the reader is well aware of what a multisite church is. However, it does provide ten "approaches" to multisite churches.[49] The "Franchise Approach" uses locations that are clones of the original location, seeking to create the same experience across multiple campuses. The authors also include "The Déjà Vu" model, which ironically, sounds very similar to the franchise model. The only apparent difference is that the Déjà Vu model only mentions copying the worship service, whereas the Franchise model is concerned with the overall brand and image of the church, including similarly styled facilities.[50]

---

46   Easum and Travis, *Beyond the Box*, 93–95.
47   "Rodney A. Harrison," *Midwestern Baptist Theological Seminary*; "Dr. Tom Cheyney, Executive Director of Missions"; "Don Overstreet," *Touch Publishing*. Don Overstreet passed away in 2017.
48   Harrison, Cheyney, and Overstreet, *Spin-Off Churches*, 4, 75–80.
49   Harrison, Cheyney, and Overstreet, *Spin-Off Churches*, 77–78. These approaches, or models, are much more specific than some other writers' categories, which accounts for the high number of models.
50   Harrison, Cheyney, and Overstreet, *Spin-Off Churches*, 77–78.

RODNEY HARRISON, TOM CHEYNEY, AND DON OVERSTREET'S TEN MULTISITE MODELS[51]	
Multisite Model	**Model Description**
The Franchise	The Franchise Approach uses locations that are clones of the original location, seeking to create the same experience across multiple campuses.
The Déjà Vu	The Déjà Vu model duplicates the worship experience of the primary location across all locations.
The Licensee	The Licensee Approach uses similar elements across all campuses, but the ministries are contextualized based on their location.
The New Venture	The New Venture model is an approach with the intentional purpose of using multisite to eventually launch a separate, autonomous church.
The Encore	The Encore model uses the same worship presentation and personnel at different times and different locations.
The Satellite	The Satellite model looks similar to a cell church, meeting in numerous homes and other small locations. However, unlike a cell, there is no expectation that the groups will ever join together for worship.
The Third Place	The Third Place model seeks to locate campuses in places people are already accustomed to going, such as theatres, cafes, coffee shops, and other community locations.
The Video Venue	The Video Venue model uses a pre-recorded or live-feed video of the preaching from one campus to be shown at the satellite campuses.
The Resurrection	The Resurrection model is a merger between a dying church and a healthy church, where the healthy church takes the dying church on as a campus and revitalizes the church and its ministries.
The Multicultural	The Multicultural model uses the same worship and ministry experience but translates it into different languages and cultures.

---

51   Harrison, Cheyney, and Overstreet, *Spin-Off Churches*, 77–78.

The "Licensee Approach" uses similar elements across all campuses, but the ministries are contextualized based on their location. The "New Venture" model is an approach with the intentional purpose of using multisite to eventually launch a separate, autonomous church. The "Encore" model uses the same worship presentation and personnel at different times and different locations. The "Satellite" model looks similar to a cell church, meeting in numerous homes and other small locations. However, unlike a cell, there is no expectation that the groups will ever join together for worship. The "Third Place" model seeks to locate campuses in places people are already accustomed to going, such as theaters, cafes, coffee shops, and other community locations. The "Video Venue" model uses a pre-recorded or live-feed video of the preaching from one campus to be shown at the satellite campuses. The "Resurrection" model is a merger between a dying church and a healthy church, where the healthy church takes the dying church on as a campus and then revitalizes the church and its ministries. Finally, the "Multicultural" model uses the same worship and ministry experience but translates it into different languages and cultures.[52]

Geoff Surratt, Greg Ligon, and Warren Bird

When critics of multisite churches address a definition of multisite churches, they most often refer to the one provided by Geoff Surratt, Greg Ligon, and Warren Bird in *The Multi-Site Church Revolution* (*MCR*).[53] This was the first book written exclusively on modern multisite churches and it has become the foundational document for churches considering multisite ministry.[54] *MCR*, and its sequel, *A Multi-Site Church Road Trip*, are the two most thorough books on multisite church philosophy and practice.[55]

MCR defines a multisite church as "one church meeting in multiple locations—different rooms on the same campus, different locations in the

---

52   Harrison, Cheyney, and Overstreet, *Spin-Off Churches*, 77–78.
53   Sullivan, "Examining the Ecclesiological Soundness," 1.
54   *Investing in Eternity* and *One Church, Many Congregations* are solely focused on multisite-type models and were written before *MCR*. However, they are about particular models of multisite churches, and not the movement in general (Ahlen and Thomas, *One Church, Many Congregations*, 78–79; Thomas, *Investing in Eternity*, 1–2.)
55   Surratt, Ligon, and Bird, *Multi-Site Church Revolution*; Surratt, Ligon, and Bird, *A Multi-Site Church Road Trip*.

same region, or in some instances, different cities, states, or nations. A multisite church shares a common vision, budget, leadership, and board."[56] From this definition, one can see the authors provide a wide lane in which churches can legitimately function as a multisite church. In fact, they state, "The variety of ways in which churches today can adapt the multi-site approach is unlimited."[57] Out of this vast array of possible options, *MCR* describes five primary models of multisite churches, each of which fit within the parameters of *MCR*'s definition.[58]

The first model is the "Video-Venue" model. This model uses a video feed, either live or pre-recorded, to broadcast the preacher's message to another location. *MCR* equates this model with a church that has multiple venues at a single location, but the concept feeds into the second model, which is the "Regional-Campus" model. This model seeks to replicate the original campus's worship experience to satellite campuses, using a videoed message, live worship, community groups, and facility experiences that are similar to the original campus. In some cases, a teaching pastor rotates to each location to preach live at each campus. The primary purpose of this model is to make the worship experience at the original location accessible to people who are far away from that location. The regional campuses bring the experience closer to home. In order to begin a new location, the church will identify an area where a large area of church members live, or a place with a need for a new church, and begin a new campus nearby.[59]

The third model in *MCR* is the "Teaching-Team" model. This model uses live preaching at each campus location. Some churches have a primary preacher at each campus, while others rotate their teachers among the campuses. This approach allows the teacher to have a more incarnational

---

56   Surratt, Ligon, and Bird, *Multi-Site Church Revolution*, 18. *MCR* provides a shorter definition later in the book when it says, "A church is considered multi-site if it has more than one worship venue, more than one campus, or a combination of both" (28). This book will not evaluate or discuss churches that have services meeting at multiple venues on the same campus but do not have campuses at a separate location. The book will also not discuss internet campuses.

57   Surratt, Ligon, and Bird, *Multi-Site Church Revolution*, 29.

58   Surratt, Ligon, and Bird, *Multi-Site Church Revolution*, 29–41.

59   Surratt, Ligon, and Bird, *Multi-Site Church Revolution*, 30–36.

connection with the congregation because he is there in person.[60] The fourth model is the "Partnership" model. This model is distinct from the regional campus model because the satellite campus meets in a rented or borrowed facility, rather than in a facility owned by the church. The church works out a partnership with the building owners based on a financial commitment or some other form of mutual benefit. This location will not seek to replicate all aspects of the original campus but will still attempt to offer a full slate of ministry opportunities.[61] The final model in *MCR* is somewhat nebulous. It is called the "Low-Risk" model, and it also uses borrowed facilities. However, unlike the partnership model, it provides a very simplified approach to ministry, offering only the basics of what might be available at the original campus.[62] It is a very entrepreneurial model that is very similar to the T4T model of rapid church planting.[63] In the low-risk model, a church advertises the pending arrival of a new church in the area and asks for people to come alongside and invest in leading the new church. These lay leaders are trained and equipped to lead a church, and very quickly, a new campus is born.[64]

Surratt, Ligon, and Bird introduce a sixth model in *MRT*, although they do not identify it as such. This model is the "Internet Campus." With the internet campus, a church presents a live or pre-recorded worship opportunity online, where people can log on using their digital device. Once connected, they can worship, interact with others, ask questions, get answers, and make decisions for Christ. These internet campuses provide one more connection point for members to "attend church" and to stay connected to their fellowship.[65]

---

60   Surratt, Ligon, and Bird, *Multi-Site Church Revolution*, 36–37.
61   Surratt, Ligon, and Bird, *Multi-Site Church Revolution*, 37–39.
62   Surratt, Ligon, and Bird, *Multi-Site Church Revolution*, 39–40.
63   Smith and Kai, *T4T*, 35–36. The book describes its discipleship and church planting strategy as a rapid training process. The book says, "T4T trains believers to witness to the lost and then disciple them in a reproducible pattern that cascades out for generations. Trainers and disciples together hold one another to witness to the lost and train new believers to form reproducing discipleship communities led by rapidly maturing leaders generation by generation. . . . T4T is an all-inclusive process of training believers over the course of twelve to eighteen months to witness to the lost and train new believers to form reproducing discipleship communities generation by generation" (36–37).
64   Surratt, Ligon, and Bird, *A Multi-Site Church Revolution*, 39–40.
65   Surratt, Ligon, and Bird, *A Multi-Site Church Road Trip*, 85–100. The authors do not define internet campuses as a true multisite model, but in their description, it is obvious that internet campuses form a distinctly different model that can be used as a part of an overall

GEOFF SURRATT, GREG LIGON, AND WARREN BIRD'S SIX MULTISITE MODELS[66]	
Multisite Model	**Model Description**
Video Venue	Creating one or more on-campus environments that use videocast sermons (live or recorded), often varying the worship style
Regional-Campus Model	Replicating the experience of the original campus at additional campuses in order to make church more accessible to other geographic communities
Teaching-Team Model	Leveraging a strong teaching team across multiple locations at the original camps or an off-site campus
Partnership Model	Partnering with a local business or nonprofit organization to use its facility beyond a mere "renter" arrangement
Low-Risk Model	Experimenting with new locations that have a low level of risk because of the simplicity of programming and low financials investment involved but that have the potential for high returns in terms of evangelism and growth
Internet Campus	A virtual online worship presence that includes authentic teaching and intentional opportunities to make a personal connection to the church

multisite strategy with multiple campuses, or as a unique "campus" within a church that has only one physical site.

In *MRT*, published in 2009, the authors identified seventeen churches that had online campuses. Contrast this to research published in 2019, which surveyed 176 churches that have online campuses. This number is merely a sample of the churches that were using the model in 2019 (Rainer, "New Research and Insights on the Online Church"). The COVID-19 pandemic of 2020 has pushed even more churches to use an online presence for connecting with members and guests. According to Lifeway Research, only 22 percent of churches in America live streamed their worship before the pandemic. That number grew to 66 percent of churches by the end of March 2020. By that same time, 99 percent of churches had begun having, at minimum, sermons available on some digital platform, up from 41 percent in fall 2019 (Wax, "New Research").

66   Surratt, Ligon, and Bird, *Multi-Site Church Revolution*, 30; Surratt, Ligon, and Bird, *A Multi-Site Church Road Trip*, 88. The authors list their original five models in *MCR*. They do not specifically label the internet campus as a model, but this book considers it a sixth model because of its distinct difference from the other five models.

All of these models fall within the parameters of *MCR*'s multisite church definition. However, each of these models themselves have so much flexibility within them that churches practicing the same models can look radically different. *MRT* demonstrates this reality by identifying and describing how fifteen churches are using multisite church models.[67] Each of these churches is unique, yet all of them fit within *MCR*'s definition.

Brad House and Gregg Allison

The most recent contribution on behalf of the multisite model is from Brad House and Gregg Allison. Both House and Allison previously served as elders at Sojourn Church, which describes itself as a "family of churches" whose "mission is to reach people with the gospel, build them up as the church, and send them into the world."[68] These interdependent churches meet in five locations in the Louisville, Kentucky, metro area, which includes one location in New Albany, Indiana.[69]

In his *9Marks Journal* article, published in 2010, Allison bases his concept of multisite churches on *MCR*'s definition, which he refers to as the "operative definition."[70] In the article, he defends "one church [which] exists in various locations or campuses," using language that shows he considers the organization to be a single church and a single congregation.[71] Allison's understanding of a single church and single congregation meeting in multiple locations carries over into his ecclesiology study, *Sojourners and Strangers*, written in 2012.[72] Allison confirms the core elements of *MCR*'s multisite definition, including a "shared vision, budget, leadership, and

---

67   Surratt, Ligon, and Bird, *A Multi-Site Church Road Trip*, 20–21, 33–34, 41–42, 56–57, 73–74, 85–86, 101–2, 114–15, 129–30, 146–47, 158–59, 173–74, 186–87, 198–99.

68   "Staff," *Sojourn Collective*; "Gregg R. Allison," *The Southern Baptist Theological Seminary*; "Mission, Values, and Beliefs," *Sojourn Church*; "Sojourn Midtown," *Sojourn Church*. Sojourn Church began in 2000 as Sojourn Community Church and later took the name Sojourn Collective for a time. At the time House and Allison wrote *MultiChurch* in 2017, the church still functioned under its original name (House and Allison, *MultiChurch*, 14).

69   "I'm New," *Sojourn Church*.

70   Allison, "Theological Defense of Multi-Site," 7.

71   Allison, "Theological Defense of Multi-Site," 13, 16. Allison uses the singular "church" when describing his model, and he considers it a single congregation since he writes, "The congregation—which exists at multiple sites . . .".

72   Allison, *Sojourners and Strangers*, 310–11, 314, 316.

board."[73] However, Allison differs from *MCR*'s belief that multisite churches can have unlimited reach, stating that multisite churches should be relegated to a single city and its outlying areas.[74] Allison writes in his article,

> The church exists for city reaching. Accordingly, there is a geographical limitation placed on the multi-site church, which is the city the church is attempting to reach with the gospel and its ministries. Its strong sense of missional identity translates into the church as a whole reaching out to the city's residents, including adding other sites to expand the church's reach into heretofore outlying areas of the city.[75]

MultiChurch, written in 2017, reveals Allison's evolved, or perhaps fully developed, definition of a multisite church, which he and House label a "multichurch." They define a multichurch as follows:

> As we define it, multichurch is a local community of Christians that matures and multiplies its influence through launching, developing, and resourcing *multiple congregations to reach its city*, with the gospel of Jesus Christ. This is one church with multiple congregations or "churches" in a set geographic area (bounded by an identifiable population that shares proximity and accessibility).[76]

According to the authors, a multichurch is distinguished from a multisite church because "the *multichurch model* features one church that expresses itself in *multiple churches* that have a form of polity that provides the responsibility and authority to make decisions about budget,

---

73   Surratt, Ligon, and Bird, *Multi-Site Church Revolution*, 18; see also Allison, "Theological Defense of Multi-Site," 16; Allison, *Sojourners and Strangers*, 316–17.

74   Allison, "Theological Defense of Multi-Site," 16; Surratt, Ligon, and Bird, *Multi-Site Church Revolution*, 18.

75   Allison, "Theological Defense of Multi-Site," 16, emphasis original.

76   House and Allison, *MultiChurch*, 16–17. House and Allison consider "multichurch" to be the logical evolution of the multisite church phenomenon (11–12).

contextualization of ministries, and more."[77] These distinguishing characteristics reveal a level of autonomy in the multichurch model that is not as evident in the common multisite church models, which are more centrally governed and moderated.[78]

House and Allison provide a spectrum of seven church models, two of which they label "multichurch."[79] The determining factor for a church's place on the spectrum is the "locus of power," by which the authors mean "the authority and responsibility to establish vision, make decisions, and spend money" at each location of the church. The spectrum proceeds from a completely centralized power model to a strongly decentralized power model. The first model, labeled "The Pillar Church," is a standalone, single congregation church that meets in only one service. All of the authority within the church is vested in a single group that meets together each week.[80]

House and Allison describe the second through fourth models as multisite churches. The second model, "The Gallery Church," is one church in a single location with multiple services or venues. The locus of power in this model remains at one location, but those who hold the authority, the congregation, gather in multiple services or venues.[81] This category shows a distinction between *MultiChurch*'s concept of multisite and *MCR*'s concept of multisite. *MCR* does not consider a church to be multisite until they have at least begun holding services in two different locations on the same campus. By *MCR*'s definition, a church with multiple services in the same room remains a single site church.[82] However, *MultiChurch* categorizes a church that has two or more services in the same room in the multisite category.[83]

House and Allison's third model, the second of their three multisite categories, is "The Franchise Church." This model clones the original

77   House and Allison, *MultiChurch*, 65, emphasis original.
78   Surratt, Ligon, and Bird, *Multi-Site Church Revolution*, 18.
79   House and Allison, *MultiChurch*, 47–75. These models include examples that are not multisite churches.
80   House and Allison, *MultiChurch*, 47, 51–55.
81   House and Allison, *MultiChurch*, 55–58.
82   Surratt, Ligon, and Bird, *Multi-Site Church Revolution*, 27, 30.
83   House and Allison, *MultiChurch*, 50.

location at one or more additional locations, where the original location's style of ministry and presentation is mirrored to the fullest extent possible. The power in this model remains highly centralized, and the church is especially concerned with maintaining the original location's identity, or brand, across all campuses. Campus leaders' flexibility to contextualize their ministry is limited by the church's overall brand and messaging. These churches often use some form of video preaching during the worship services.[84]

The fourth model, the final in the authors' multisite category, is "The Federation Church." This model has a centralized leadership that allows the campuses the flexibility to contextualize their ministry to fit their location. This frees the campuses to venture away from the original location's image in order to create an image that fits within their own locale, while maintaining the overall mission and vision of the whole church. These churches typically use live preaching at each location to enhance the contextualization.[85]

Models five and six on House and Allison's spectrum comprise the multichurch category of churches. The fifth model is called "The Cooperative Church." This model is "one church composed of multiple interdependent churches."[86] In this model, the power structure tips in favor of the individual locations. However, there is still a centralized governing body made up of equal numbers of members from the individual locations which oversees leadership, vision, and budgeting. Each location is responsible for contextualizing the vision of the church and for carrying out the mission in its own way. It is also solely responsible for allocating its budget and selecting its own leadership.[87]

---

84 House and Allison, *MultiChurch*, 58–61.
85 House and Allison, *MultiChurch*, 61–65.
86 House and Allison, *MultiChurch*, 65–66.
87 House and Allison, *MultiChurch*, 65–68. House and Allison describe Sojourn Church as a Cooperative Church (67). However, in an email, Brad House confirmed that Sojourn has transitioned to a collective model. He noted that in the spectrum, some aspects overlap as a church settles in on a certain model. House functioned as the Director of the Collective, which means he served in many ways as an executive pastor (Brad House, "Email between Brad House and Dustin Slaton," August 5, 2020).

BRAD HOUSE AND GREGG ALLISON'S SEVEN-CHURCH SPECTRUM[88]	
Church Model	**Model Description**
Non-Multisite	
Pillar Church	It is a stand-alone church with a single congregation meeting in a single space.
Multisite	
Gallery Church	This model is one church in one location with multiple services and/or venues.
Franchise Church	The franchise church is one church cloned to multiple sites, each of which is granted the responsibility and authority to express the church's "brand," that is, its vision, worship, preaching, discipleship, care, and mission.
Federation Church	The federation model focuses on being one church that is contextualized in multiple locations.
Multichurch	
Cooperative Church	A cooperative model is multichurch because it is one church composed of multiple interdependent churches
Collective Church	A collective model church is a multichurch because it is a collection of individual churches which collaborate as one church.
Network	
Network Churches	A network implies the concerted participation of individual churches that band together for a limited purpose.

The sixth model, second in the multichurch category, is "The Collective Church." This model is a collection of individual churches, which are

---

88   House and Allison, *MultiChurch*, 51, 55, 58, 61, 65–66, 69, 73.

"largely independent," but which "collaborate as one church."[89] The locus of power for these churches is highly decentralized, and the churches only share a limited number of ministries and resources. A central operations team functions primarily to oversee administrative responsibilities, and leaves most, if not all, ministry decision to the individual churches.[90]

The seventh model on *MultiChurch*'s spectrum steps out of the multichurch category and is called "Network Churches." In this model, independent churches are loosely connected for the purpose of partnerships in specific ministry areas. The centralized leadership holds no governing authority over the individual churches, except in defining what is required to be a part of the network. There is no structure which obligates the individual churches to the network.[91]

MultiChurch expands the multisite conversation to consider additional church structures. *MCR*'s five models, plus *MRT*'s addition of the internet campus, all fit within the three multisite models on *MultiChurch*'s seven model spectrum.[92] The Cooperative model still carries multisite characteristics, while the Collective and Network models step outside of the true multisite category because of the lack of strong centralized leadership.

CONCLUSION

As can be seen in this chapter, many of the models set forward by multisite advocates are similar, and some of the models themselves are blends of multisite variations. As *MCR*'s authors state, "The approaches are not easy to categorize because most multi-site churches, especially larger congregations, are a blend of several models. Although we have chosen to confine our discussion to five broad models, these models are being tailored to fit local contexts in numerous ways."[93]

Having surveyed the various definitions of multisite churches, a summary definition needs to be established for the sake of the rest of

---

89   House and Allison, *MultiChurch*, 69.
90   House and Allison, *MultiChurch*, 69–72.
91   House and Allison, *MultiChurch*, 72–75. These churches are not multisite, but autonomous churches loosely connected.
92   House and Allison, *MultiChurch*, 50–51; Surratt, Ligon, and Bird, *Multi-Site Church Revolution*, 29–41; Surratt, Ligon, and Bird, *A Multi-Site Church Road Trip*, 87–98.
93   Surratt, Ligon, and Bird, *Multi-Site Church Revolution*, 41.

the book. For this purpose, a modified version of *MCR*'s definition will be used.[94] The definition of a multisite church the remainder of the book will work from is, "A multisite church is one church meeting in multiple separate physical campuses. These locations may be in the same city or region, or they may be in different cities, states, or nations. A multisite church shares a common vision, budget, and leadership." This definition will serve as the multisite church definition of the multisite church movement. A new definition of multisite churches that is more consistent with congregational ecclesiology will be recommended in the final chapter.

---

94   Surratt, Ligon, and Bird, *Multi-Site Church Revolution*, 18.

CHAPTER 2

A SURVEY OF MULTISITE CHURCH HISTORY

WHILE THIS BOOK WILL ARGUE that the multisite church model has historical precedent that dates as far back as the early church, the modern multisite movement in the United States is very young. Bryan Frye, whose dissertation is the foremost treatment of the history of the multisite movement in the United States, concludes the multisite church, as currently defined, is a development of the second half of the twentieth century. He dates the official beginning of the MCM as September 11, 2001.[1] On that infamous day in American history, Leadership Network hosted a meeting of multisite church leaders with the purpose of discussing the growing trend of multisite churches and beginning to study how they function.[2] The conclusion of this report was that the multisite church model would continue to grow in popularity and effectiveness, a prediction that has been proven true since its publication.[3] This chapter will provide a brief history of the MCM,

---

1   Frye, "The Multi-Site Church Phenomenon," 1, 33–34.
2   Travis, "Multi-Site/Multiple-Campus Churches," 1.
3   Rainer, "Is the Multisite Church Movement Still Growing?"; Travis, "Multi-Site/Multiple-Campus Churches," 11.

including possible multisite examples that reach even back into the eighteenth century.

MULTISITE CHURCHES OR NOT?

In Frye's dissertation, he describes five different types of churches and ministries, dating as far back as the eighteenth century, which had similar characteristics as multisite churches. Frye concludes these five models, for one reason or another, do not meet the criteria of a multisite church.[4] He notes that some of the satellite locations within the

---

4   Frye, "The Multi-Site Church Phenomenon," 33. The models that Frye concludes are not multisite models are Methodist circuit riders, unaffiliated mission Sunday schools, church-affiliated missions and chapels (Frye specifically considers First Baptist Church of Dallas, Texas, First Presbyterian Church of Seattle, Washington, and Highland Park Baptist Church of Chattanooga, Tennessee), and the Key Church Strategy. These models will be reevaluated in this section. Frye also includes the fifth example of J. Frank Norris pastoring both First Baptist Church of Fort Worth, Texas, and Temple Baptist Church of Detroit, Michigan, which he also concludes was not a multisite church situation. Frye points out that the arrangement to have Norris pastor both churches was indeed innovative for its time, but, "While his work is intriguing, the primary commonality that Norris' dual pastorate ministry has with multi-site churches of today is that one individual was doing ministry in two distant locations over an extended period. Though they may have shared much in common in terms of their principles and practice (cf. Sunday school methods of Louis Entzminger), First Baptist Church, Fort Worth, Texas, and Temple Baptist Church, Detroit, MI *were two autonomous churches* operating in *two different locations*" (Frye, "The Multi-Site Church Phenomenon," 51). Norris's own description shows he was serving two different churches (Norris, "How Dual Pastorate Was Brought About," 270–71). This is further proven by the fact that Norris was fired from Temple Baptist Church while remaining the pastor at First Baptist until his death (Pigott, "A Comparison of the Leadership of George W. Truett and J. Frank," 34–54)

   O. S. Hawkins writes, "Norris originated the use of multisite campuses in the practice of church evangelism and growth." He points to Norris using multiple tabernacles around the city of Fort Worth and to him pastoring two churches simultaneously. He writes, "The modern craze of establishing multisite locations of one church is high on the popularity scale in the SBC today. Multitudes of local congregations now meet in myriad locations across metropolitan areas and beyond. Eight full decades earlier J. Frank Norris originated the idea" (Hawkins, "Two Kinds of Baptists," 196–97). Hawkins is correct in considering Norris an early proponent of multisite for his use of multiple tabernacles around Fort Worth. However, Norris's work will not be considered in the reevaluation of Frye's work because the reevaluation of First Presbyterian Church of Seattle, Washington, and First Baptist Church of Dallas, Texas, will suffice.

models are disqualified from being "campuses" because "the various outlying [locations] are not always churches."[5] This is an important point. For a church to be considered a multisite church, its campuses must not only demonstrate the foundational characteristics of a multisite church (multiple locations, shared vision, shared leadership, and shared budget), but must also demonstrate the marks of a true church. For Baptist churches, the minimum standard for the marks of the church have historically been the right preaching of the Bible and the correct practice of the ordinances of baptism and the Lord's Supper.[6] Therefore, for any of these models to be considered a multisite model, they must not simply demonstrate the elements of a multisite church, but also these two marks of a church. This section will reevaluate four of Frye's examples to see if the multisite attributes and church marks are present.[7]

Circuit Riding Preachers

The first of the forms Frye evaluates is the circuit riding preaching method used by the developing Methodist church during the late eighteenth century. During the First Great Awakening in Britain, John Wesley began organizing groups of Christians in various cities around the country.[8] Initially, these societies met in the homes of members,

---

This example will not be considered in this book, because it clearly falls outside the realm of multisite churches. The two churches were two autonomous churches sharing a pastor and nothing else.

5   Frye, "The Multi-Site Church Phenomenon," 33.

6   This will be discussed in chapter 7.

7   The examples included will be reevaluated because Frye included them in his analysis, and because they provide a period of time that spans across the entire twentieth century, and even back into the nineteenth (Frye, "The Multi-Site Church Phenomenon," 33–62). Other examples of potential early multisite churches do exist but will not be evaluated. John Vaughn lists First Baptist Church of Fort Worth, Texas, Akron (Ohio) Baptist Church, Florence (South Carolina) Baptist Temple, Landmark Baptist Temple of Cincinnati, Ohio, and the Crystal Cathedral of Orange County, California (Vaughn, *The Large Church*, 56–59).

8   Cairns, *An Endless Line of Splendor*, 79. These groups, intentionally still within the Church of England, were known as societies, and were designed to facilitate Bible study and growth in holiness. Wesley's goal was not to break away from the Church of England, but to reform it.

but as they grew, they constructed buildings, which Wesley called "chapels." Even with these chapels, his original intention was to remain within the English church.[9] As the societies grew, Wesley continued to organize them, first holding a conference of leaders in 1744 consisting of six Church of England clergymen and four laymen. The numbers of societies and leaders continued to grow, to the point that Wesley organized the societies into circuits. He established a superintendent and preachers for each circuit. In addition, Wesley required each society member to give a penny a week, which remained with the local society for the provision of the chapel.[10] When Wesley began separating his movement from the Church of England in 1784, he registered the chapels under the ownership of one hundred lay preachers rather than under a single organization.[11]

As these societies developed and eventually became the Methodist church, they demonstrated similar characteristics as the multisite church movement. The societies/churches were spread around various locations, and they shared common mission, evangelism, and discipleship strategies. However, each society was focused on its own area and ministry goals. Some of them shared common leadership, but they maintained their own finances and owned their own properties. The only true connection between the churches was the leadership structure, which eventually developed into an episcopal structure connecting all of the churches in a hierarchical organization.[12] In his analysis of the Methodist circuit riding model, Frye is correct in stating they were not multisite churches, because they did not have a shared vision or budget.

---

9   Terry, *Evangelism*, 104–5.
10 Cairns, *An Endless Line of Splendor*, 79; Terry, *Evangelism*, 104–5.
11 Cairns, *An Endless Line of Splendor*, 79. This same process was followed in the United States following the First Great Awakening, and even into the Second Great Awakening. Francis Asbury was the leader of the Methodist movement in America, and his team of circuit riding preachers established churches all over the middle states and the American frontier. Asbury guided the preachers and societies with a firm hand. Asbury's work in America paralleled Wesley's in England, as the Methodist movement continued to grow (Cairns, *Endless Line of Splendor*, 79; Orr, *An The Eager Feet*, 64; Terry, *Evangelism*, 105).
12 Orr, *The Eager Feet*, 64; Terry, *Evangelism*, 128–29.

METHODIST SOCIETIES UNDER CIRCUIT RIDERS				
Multiple Locations	Shared Vision	Shared Budget	Shared Leadership	Church Marks
Yes	No	No	Yes	Yes

Unaffiliated Mission Sunday Schools

Frye next turns his attention to the mission Sunday school model.[13] Robert Raikes is credited with originating this model of ministry in England in the late 1700s that still exists around the world, in various forms, to this day.[14] Raikes intended for Sunday school to provide "instruction in reading and in the elementary truths of religion."[15] Raikes details how the Sunday schools functioned in a letter written in 1784. He writes,

> The children were to come soon after ten in the morning, and stay till twelve; they were then to go home and stay till one; and after reading a lesson they were to be conducted to church. After church they were to be employed in repeating the catechism till half-past five, and then to be dismissed, with an injunction to go home without making a noise and by no means to play in the street.[16]

Although the children were "conducted to church," Raikes's original Sunday schools were not affiliated with or overseen by a local church. They were individual efforts that spread through various cities in England and, eventually, into other parts of the world. It was not until later that the model eventually made its way into churches' ministries and was widely adopted.[17]

The fact that this model began as a ministry outside the purview of a local church disqualifies the unaffiliated mission Sunday school as

---

13   Frye, "The Multi-Site Church Phenomenon," 38–40.

14   Trumbull, *The Sunday-School*, 109–10. Many scholars consider the Sunday school model to be something that has continued in various forms since the early church. For a full discussion on this topic the first chapter of Trumbull's book.

15   Trumbull, *The Sunday-School*, 109–10.

16   Raikes, "Letter from Robert," 110.

17   Trumbull, *The Sunday-School*, 113–14.

a multisite church model. The Sunday schools at times used church-owned facilities, but the church did not provide a budget, leadership, or vision for the schools.[18] Thus, it is not a multisite ministry by current definitions.

UNAFFILIATED MISSION SUNDAY SCHOOLS				
Multiple Locations	Shared Vision	Shared Budget	Shared Leadership	Church Marks
Yes	No	No	No	No

Church-Affiliated Mission Sunday Schools

The third multisite-type ministry Frye evaluates is the church-affiliated mission Sunday school model.[19] Frye examines three churches that had multiple Sunday schools meeting in various locations around their cities. One of these churches is the First Presbyterian Church of Seattle, Washington (FPCS), who welcomed a new pastor, Mark Matthews, in February 1902.[20] Under Matthews's leadership the church grew to become the largest Presbyterian church in the world with over eight thousand members by the end of his pastorate in 1940.[21] A part of the significant growth can be attributed to its branch system of Sunday schools which met in multiple locations around the city.[22]

---

18   Trumbull, *The Sunday-School,* 113–14.
19   Frye, "The Multi-Site Church Phenomenon," 42–48, 52–53. In the category of church-affiliated mission Sunday schools, many terms are used interchangeably by Frye and other authors. These outreach models are referred to as mission Sunday schools, branch Sunday schools, chapels, mission chapels, satellite chapels, satellite locations, and satellite outposts. Some of these labels will be used interchangeably in this section as well.
20   Frye, "The Multi-Site Church Phenomenon," 45–48; Giboney and Potter, *The Life of Mark A. Matthews,* 24.
21   First Presbyterian Church of Seattle, "A Brief History of the First Presbyterian Church of Seattle."
22   Soden, *Reverend Mark Matthews,* 41, 55. These groups were often started by a group of Christians who recognized a need for a church in a new area and began coming together. They would then contact FPCS and begin the process of becoming a part of the church. As a part of the process, the church would help the new group build a building to meet in, provide pastoral leadership, and provide financial support.

Over time, FPCS began twenty-eight branch Sunday schools each of which had its own teachers.[23] All the teachers were trained by Matthews and would meet with him on a regular basis to prepare for their teaching assignments. Each one was required to sign a statement of faith, acknowledging they agreed with the church's beliefs.[24] The leaders were also required to be accountable to the mother church, specifically to Matthews himself.[25] Members of the schools, from children to adults, were encouraged by Matthews to engage in evangelism, meeting needs, and in ministry. Each Sunday school even had its own music ministry. As people joined the schools, their membership was in the First Presbyterian Church. Many of these locations grew quite large, with one having over three hundred members. Each year, the church would have an annual Sunday school picnic, where all the locations were encouraged to come together for a day of celebration.[26]

The First Presbyterian Church of Seattle, Washington, under the leadership of Mark Matthews was, by the current definition, a multisite church.[27] The church members gathered in multiple locations and had a shared ministry vision, a shared budget, and shared leadership. In addition to these foundational multisite characteristics, worship was taking place at these locations, which involved music and teaching. Ministry was taking place to serve the community, and the members of the schools were identified as members of FPCS. The only uncertainty about the schools is whether or not the ordinances were administered at these branch locations.[28] If it can be

---

23 First Presbyterian Church, "A Brief History of the First Presbyterian Church"; Soden, *Reverend Mark Matthews*, 55. FPCS made a distinction between three different types of outlying posts: branch Sunday schools, mission churches, and Bible classes (Welsh, *The Presbytery of Seattle*, 589–90).

24 Soden, *Reverend Mark Matthews*, 55–56.

25 Giboney and Potter, *The Life of Mark A. Matthews*, 75.

26 Soden, *Reverend Mark Matthews*, 55–56.

27 Following the end of Matthews's tenure at FPCS, the local presbytery consolidated the branches of FPCS under the leadership of a committee in order to facilitate developing those locations into autonomous churches. Many became independent churches, while others were closed (Welsh, *The Presbytery of Seattle*, 161).

28 As the intention of these branch Sunday schools was to provide a "church" to a group of people who were removed by distance from the primary FPCS location, it makes sense that the ordinances would have also been provided. It would not make sense to provide evangelism, teaching, and worship, yet withhold baptism and the Lord's Supper. Still, this assumption cannot be proven by the available literature.

assumed they were administered at the locations, then these characteristics would point to FPCS as being a multisite church.[29]

FIRST PRESBYTERIAN CHURCH OF SEATTLE, WASHINGTON				
Multiple Locations	Shared Vision	Shared Budget	Shared Leadership	Church Marks
Yes	Yes	Yes	Yes	Teaching: Yes Ordinances: Unknown

Frye also evaluates the mission Sunday schools of the First Baptist Church of Dallas (FBCD).[30] As far back as the late 1800s, FBCD had a system of branch Sunday schools meeting in multiple locations in and

---

29   Frye disagrees, writing, "One aspect of the [FPCS], however, which makes the church look so much like a multi-site is also the single attribute that removes if from multi-site classification. That attribute is its use of the branch system. . . . While it is clear that the relationship of the branch churches and the mother church was close (and in some ways integrally woven together), the branch churches remained semi-autonomous, preserving their right to become autonomous . . . . This distinction may seem small, but it stands at the core of multi-site identification. A multi-site church necessitates bilocation or multilocation, or more specifically the presence of a single entity existing simultaneously in two or more locations" (Frye, "The Multi-Site Church Phenomenon," 48). His conclusion is that the branch's opportunity to split off as an autonomous church removes it from the category of multisite church, and that the branches actually existed as a separate "church."
     Soden, however, makes a distinction between two strategies at FPCS when he writes of the church's "ability to spawn new churches and to build a branch system." There was apparently a church planting effort and a branch system. The branch system could have, and likely did, feed the beginning of new churches, but Soden does not equate the two as synonymous of one process. This branch system, Soden writes, allowed FPCS to "surpass ever other congregation," noting a single congregation was in view. Additionally, since the members were recorded as members of FPCS, it seems the branch churches must be considered a part of FPCS (Soden, *Reverend Mark Matthews*, 55). Otherwise, members of a branch church, with their membership tied to FPCS, would not actually hold membership in their home church.
     The right to become an autonomous church also does not automatically remove FPCS and its branches from the multisite category. Church spin-offs are a viable option for multisite churches, and are even encouraged. *MCR* states, "Could multi-site also be a church-planting model? Absolutely. Many churches are doing just that" (Surratt, Ligon, and Bird, *Multi-Site Church Revolution*, 51).
30   Frye, "The Multi-Site Church Phenomenon," 42–45.

around Dallas, with at least twenty-two different locations between 1873 and 1967.[31] These mission outposts varied in purpose and structure. Some began as outreaches to children, while others began with the purpose of beginning a new church. Some borrowed property, while others purchased or built facilities. FBCD provided paid staff, volunteer leadership, and financial resources to support the works, which led to the success of many, although not all, of the missions. FBCD purchased property for some of the missions and chapels.[32] Leon McBeth says in the early years of the twentieth century FBCD fully supported mission schools, until such a time as they became a strong enough mission that they were able to become a separate church. He notes that under W. A. Criswell, in the 1950s, each mission had its own budget and carried the majority of the responsibility for finances, but FBCD was ready to supplement their expenses when needed.[33] The supplemental funds were usually "not from the regular budget of First Baptist Church, but from special offerings."[34] While the missions carried much of the financial load of their ministries, FBCD's central leadership did maintain oversight and leadership.[35] The staff met regularly with the pastor for leadership and direction.[36] One reason for

---

31   McBeth, *First Baptist Church of Dallas*, 354. McBeth's list of chapels and missions in Appendix B is likely incomplete. In the narrative, he mentions that the first (at least) four chapels had been begun by 1885, and that all of these became independent churches. However, the list in Appendix B only shows two missions, the "Rock College SS" and "Oak Cliff Mission." These two are listed as having become independent churches. Eight more are listed to have begun in the 1890s, and of these, McBeth only identifies the two churches that came from the missions and a third that "may have become" an independent church. These hints indicate that McBeth's information is likely not complete, and there were possibly many more branch Sunday schools, missions, and chapels begun by FBC Dallas (84, 354).

32   McBeth, *First Baptist Church of Dallas*, 104, 127, 278–81.

33   Slaton and Gray, "Interview with Rick Gray." Rick Gray, a former pastor in East Texas, grew up attending FBCD from 1955 to 1974, and his parents were highly involved in FBCD leadership. He spent much time being mentored by W. A. Criswell and maintained close friendship with current FBCD pastor, Robert Jeffress. Gray passed away in 2023.

34   McBeth, *First Baptist Church of Dallas*, 280.

35   As an example of the commitment to central leadership while the mission schools were under the purview of FBCD, one mission in the Cedar Springs area was closed, rather than released, when those being reached out to wanted to manage their own church (McBeth, *First Baptist Church of Dallas*, 279).

36   Slaton and Gray, "Interview with Rick Gray."

FBCD's desire to maintain responsibility was the understanding that the members of the missions were members of FBCD.[37] Most of the mission schools included time in class teaching as well as corporate worship.[38] A full worship service and observing the ordinances of baptism and the Lord's Supper were common at most of the chapels.[39] These characteristics would validly place First Baptist Dallas and some of its mission Sunday schools in the multisite category.[40]

---

37   Vaughn, *The Large Church*, 74–75.
38   McBeth, *First Baptist Church of Dallas*, 278–79.
39   Slaton and Gray, "Interview with Rick Gray."
40   Frye concludes FBCD was not a multisite church for three different reasons. First, he says, "FBCD wanted to multiply churches and multi-sites . . . churches want to multiply new sites. . . . Most multi-site churches, while perhaps open to the possibility of their sites becoming autonomous, would not initiate new sites with the intention of those sites becoming a new autonomous church" (Frye, "The Multi-Site Church Phenomenon," 43n29). This conclusion may be true, but just as with FPCS, the intended end of a campus does not define whether a church is multisite or not. *MCR* poses and answers the question, "Could multi-site also be a church planting model? Absolutely. Many churches are doing just that." The authors also quote Jim Tomberlin, "In the future, multi-site will be a primary church-planting tool" (Surratt, Ligon, and Bird, *Multi-Site Church Revolution*, 55, 177). Lyle Schaller included church-planting as one of his multisite models, as did Harrison, Cheyney, and Overstreet, with their "New Venture" model. These examples show that a church planting purpose, whether intentional or not, does not by default disqualify a church from the multisite categroy (Harrison, Cheyney, and Overstreet, *Spin-Off Churches*, 78; Schaller, *Innovations in Ministry*, 127). It is also clear that not all mission Sunday schools were intended to start new churches in the first place. John Vaughn writes, "Mother churches often view the satellites as branch Sunday schools merely located away from the main site of the church. They all seem to encourage some of the units to become autonomous churches. Many churches would never consider releasing a satellite chapel any more than the average American church would consider having an adult Sunday-school department, inside the church, meeting independently of the main church" (Vaughn, *The Large Church*, 74).
     Second, Frye focuses on the function of the on-location pastors. Frye notes FBCD's on-site pastors, "though paid by and responsible to a mother church, functioned as a typical pastor fulfilling all the pastoral duties of an autonomous church. Conversely, in more multi-site churches the site leader is a campus pastor responsible for all pastoral duties except preaching and teaching during the main weekly worship gathering" (Frye, "The Multi-Site Church Phenomenon," 43n29). Again, Frye mislabels a common practice within multisite churches as a definitive mark of multisite churches, even when *MCR* and others do not support his conclusion. *MCR* includes the "Teaching-Team Model" of multisite churches, which intentionally uses live preaching at the various locations (Surratt, Ligon, and Bird, *Multi-Site Church Revolution*, 30, 36–37). Scott McConnell lists live teaching as one of three preaching options at the campus, with the campus pastor being the primary

FIRST BAPTIST CHURCH OF DALLAS, TEXAS				
Multiple Locations	Shared Vision	Shared Budget	Shared Leadership	Church Marks
Yes	Yes	Yes	Yes	Yes

Frye's third example of mission Sunday schools is Highland Park Baptist Church of Chattanooga, Tennessee (HPBC).[41] Lee Roberson became the pastor of HPBC in 1942. The first Sunday he preached there, before accepting the call, there was only a "small crowd" in attendance. A couple of years before his 1983 retirement, the church had grown to an average weekly Sunday school attendance of 8,969. Of that average,

---

teacher as one of the live-teaching options (McConnell, *Multi-Site Churches*, 82–83). Tomberlin includes ability to effectively teach as a part of the teaching team as a quality of a good campus pastor (Tomberlin, "What Makes a Great Campus Pastor").

Third, Frye points out that FBCD's mission chapels were largely supported by FBCD and created a financial loss each year. He notes, correctly, "it is doubtful that most current multi-site churches would purposefully launch a new site of their church if they perceived that the site would not be able to pay for itself immediately or after a few years" (Frye, "The Multi-Site Church Phenomenon," 43–44n29). Frye is correct to conclude that most multisite churches would not start a campus that would not be able to support itself financially. However, again, this is a common practice of multisite churches that Frye has elevated to an essential attribute. The fact that a church has a site or sites that cannot, or will not, fully support itself financially does not remove a church from the multisite category. *MCR* notes the example of National Community Church in Washington, DC, which has a coffee-shop campus, located just blocks from the United States Capitol, which they launched with no expectation that it would be self-supporting. It was more important to have the location, and opportunity to impact that community, than it was for the location to be self-supporting (Surratt, Ligon, and Bird, *Multi-Site Church Revolution*, 71–73, 104; "Ebenezer's Coffee House," *National Community Church*).

Frye used characteristics that are common to multisite churches but not essential characteristics, to make his determination about FBCD's mission Sunday schools and chapels. His conclusion is not supported by the provided criteria. The verdict must be decided based on stated definitions of multisite churches, not by practices that are the most common. Given the wide variety of models and practices, flexibility must allow some expressions to look different, even if they are wildly different than most the "typical" multisite church. So long as they show the identified core elements of multisite churches and the marks of the church, they can fit in the multisite category.

41   Frye, "The Multi-Site Church Phenomenon," 52–53.

46 percent attended at least one of the seventy chapels that were a part of the church covering a seventy-mile radius of the church.[42] The chapel ministry was in part a way of training pastoral students who attended Tennessee Temple College, providing them a place to learn in preaching and pastoral ministry. The chapels were under the full authority and oversight of HPBC. Their property was purchased and owned by HPBC, and their administrative decisions were guided by the central church leadership, most notably by Roberson himself.[43] As such, these satellites very rarely became autonomous churches.[44]

HPBC, under the leadership of Lee Roberson, functioned similarly to FPCS and FBCD. The sponsoring campus and the chapels had shared leadership, budgets, and vision. Evangelism, teaching, and worship were taking place in the satellite chapels, and the ordinances were being practiced at the chapels. The membership of those who attended the chapels was in HPBC, not only the chapel itself.[45] With these elements in place, HPBC would fit the criteria of a multisite church. In fact, David Bouler, pastor of HPBC from 1991 to 2008, considers the church a multisite church, saying in a 2005 interview, "We started in 1942 developing the multisite ministries and from about 1942 until about 1970 we went up to seventy off-campus sites. We had seventy chapel sites that we operated as a part of the ministries of Highland Park Baptist Church."[46] When discussing the reason for spinning off some of their campuses, Bouler identifies key multisite characteristics that show the chapels fit the multisite mold. He says,

> We were so large that the people would go to the chapel ser-
> vice but there was no sense of responsibility for their local

42   Wigton, *Lee Roberson*, 62, 158. In 1971, the total membership of Highland Park Baptist Church was listed at 57,325.

43   Slaton and Groves, "Interview with J. C. Groves"; Towns, *The Ten Largest Sunday*, 27; Wigton, *Lee Roberson*, 204–5.

44   Vaughn, *The World's Twenty Largest*, 111; Wigton, *Lee Roberson*, 204–5.

45   Groves, Edwards, and Cravatt, "The Power of a Story: JC's Story"; Slaton and Groves, "Interview with J. C. Groves." Evidence of the ordinances and location of the membership comes from J. C. Groves. Groves attended a HPBC chapel from 1992 to 1997 and from 2000 to 2005. His father pastored one of the chapels, Old Stone Chapel, for three years.

46   Ludden, "Big Churches Use Technology."

church or their local community because they were related to the overall plan of Highland Park Baptist Church and our vision scheme of things. And, as we evaluated it we noticed if we gave them responsibility along with owning the church and the property and accountability for it, there was a greater vigor and interest in evangelizing that local community in which that chapel was located.[47]

This comment from Bouler confirms HPBC chapels had a shared ministry vision, a shared budget, and shared leadership[48] with the mother campus. All of these characteristics align with the definition of a multisite church.[49]

---

47 Ludden, "Big Churches Use Technology."

48 Ludden, "Big Churches Use Technology." "They were related to the overall plan of Highland Park Baptist Church and our vision scheme of things," indicates shared vision. "And, as we evaluated it we noticed . . ." indicates shared leadership and board. "Owning the church and the property . . ." indicates a change in the ownership of the property, from one shared by the whole church, to one where only the satellite (new church) owns the property. This indicates a transition from a shared budget to one that is not shared.

Incidentally, this is a similar conclusion that was reached in 2010 by the leadership at Green Acres Baptist Church before I became the campus pastor in 2014. The church realized the satellite campus members had little ownership and responsibility for the ministries and maintenance taking place at the Flint Campus, and therefore ministry to the local community was suffering. However, rather than releasing the satellite as an autonomous church, the church modified the leadership and financial responsibilities to a model in which the satellite campus took on responsibility for ministry development and implementation, staff hiring and oversight, and budgetary responsibility. The model is similar to a Cooperative model on the *MultiChurch* spectrum. This caused more personal buy-in on the part of the Flint Campus membership and created an atmosphere of more effective ministry at the Flint Campus. In 2022, about a year after I departed, the model shifted back toward something closer to the Franchise Model on Allison and House's spectrum, with the Flint Campus modeling more of their ministry practice after the Tyler Campus, and the central leadership calling more of the shots on what is happening at the satellite campus.

49 Frye does not consider HPBC to be a multisite church. His reason is that the chapels tend to either drift toward autonomy or being fully dependent on the mother church. He says, "No category exists in the mission or branch system for churches to be somewhere in the middle of these positions." His point is that the branch system does not generally create a situation where an outpost location supplies enough resources to support itself, yet chooses to remain with the original church as "a part of a single church expressing itself in two locations" (Frye, "The Multi-Site Church Phenomenon," 53). Again, Frye is elevating common characteristics to the level of foundational principles. So long as a church shares common leadership, vision, and budget, and also demonstrates the marks of a church, it fits the model of a multisite church. As mentioned previously, the flexibility of multisite

HIGHLAND PARK BAPTIST CHURCH OF CHATTANOOGA, TENNESSEE				
Multiple Locations	Shared Vision	Shared Budget	Shared Leadership	Church Marks
Yes	Yes	Yes	Yes	Yes

These examples show the church-affiliated mission Sunday school model parallels the multisite movement in many ways. Towns adds additional support when he lists the characteristics of mission Sunday schools, in comparison to an autonomous local church. A mission Sunday school first, "Depends on sponsoring church. Property owned by sponsoring church. Offerings go to central treasurer."[50] This is a shared budget. Second, in a mission Sunday school, "Ministry is led by Christians from sponsoring church. Mission people help in ministry."[51] This is shared leadership.[52] Third, with a mission Sunday school, "Decisions for ministry and organization made by sponsoring church."[53] This is shared vision and leadership. The only thing missing from Towns's description is the marks of a church. While the mission Sunday schools presented above may not look like the modern idea of a multisite church, they still share the foundational principles identified by multisite advocates and should be considered as an early example of multisite church.

---

models allows for churches to use it as a church-planting strategy, a perpetual mutually-beneficial relationship, or even an ongoing dependent relationship.

50   Towns, *Getting a Church Started*, 59–60. Towns mixes the titles of mission Sunday schools and satellite chapels. Of Landmark Baptist Temple in Cincinnati, Ohio, he says, "The satellite churches are actually mission Sunday Schools, except they include a preaching service where one of the staff members form the sponsoring church preaches." He adds another example from his own experience, "The author pastored a mission Sunday School from the Scofield Memorial Church, Dallas, Texas as he was attending seminary. The work was called Denison Street Chapel when the people called him as a pastor in 1955."

51   Towns, *Getting a Church Started*, 59–60.

52   Compare to the "Low-Risk Model" in *MCR*, which uses a combination of leaders sent by the mother church and leaders developed from the new area (Surratt, Ligon, and Bird, *Multi-Site Church Revolution*, 39–40).

53   Towns, *Getting a Church Started*, 59–60.

The Key Church Strategy

Frye's next example of a multisite-type model is the Key Church Strategy.[54] This model has already been defined as a multisite model. This model uses satellite locations of different types for the purpose of reaching certain segments of the population and is very similar to the mission Sunday school models described previously. These locations have shared leadership, budget, and vision, and when demonstrating the marks of a true church, meet the characteristics of a multisite church.[55]

KEY CHURCH STRATEGY				
Multiple Locations	**Shared Vision**	**Shared Budget**	**Shared Leadership**	**Church Marks**
Yes	Yes	Yes	Yes	Sometimes

The reevaluation of Frye's examples shows the church-affiliated mission Sunday schools and Key Church Strategy do show the basic characteristics of multisite churches. They meet in multiple locations, have a shared vision, shared leadership, and shared budget, and in situations where they demonstrate the marks of the church, they should be considered examples of multisite churches. Therefore, the history of multisite churches in the United States, even if it functioned under a different name, dates far earlier than scholars typically assume.

---

54 Frye, "The Multi-Site Church Phenomenon," 54–61.

55 Frye does not consider the Key Church Strategy to be a valid multisite model for two reasons. First, he again disqualifies a model based on the satellite location's opportunity to become an autonomous church (Frye, "The Multi-Site Church Phenomenon," 61). As noted previously, this does not disqualify a church from being multisite, as some multisite churches use the model as a church planting strategy.

His second reason is valid, in that many of the satellite locations in the Key Church Strategy do not display the full marks of a true church. Thus, their ecclesiological structure falls short of being a true campus because it does not show the marks of a true church. However, if a location can be shown to include the right teaching of the Word and the ordinances, then it could be considered a legitimate satellite campus.

MULTISITE FROM THE 1950S TO 1980

In his dissertation on multisite churches in America, Frye limits the primary focus of his research to the years 1950 to 2011, with the latter being the year of the dissertation's publication.[56] This limit is partly based on Lyle Schaller's conclusion that early multisite models began emerging in the 1950s, with church mergers in rural North America.[57] As noted previously, it is the conclusion of this book that valid multisite churches existed as early as the nineteenth century, and, in the case of HPBC, continued as multisite even into the twenty-first century.[58] Few churches have been clearly identified as multisite in the period between the 1950s and 1980s, but some authors have tried to name some. Earl Ferguson claimed multisite churches existed in the 1960s and 1970s. Yet, when he lists multisite churches, he does not indicate whether or not these churches have functioned as multisite since the 1960s or 1970s, or became multisite at a later time.[59] In addition to FBCD and HPBC

---

56   Frye, "The Multi-Site Church Phenomenon," 28–29.

57   Schaller, *Innovations in Ministry*, 121. Frye also bases the limit on a developing trend in the business sector around the same time, one which Schaller identifies in *Innovations in Ministry* and in *Discontinuity and Hope*. This change is the development of "multisite practices" in businesses, with multiple locations of department stores, restaurants, banks, universities, and more. These businesses capitalized on the expansion of communities and began making their services more accessible to a widening population. *MCR* also points to this change in business strategy as an influencer in multisite development (Frye, "The Multi-Site Church Phenomenon," 29; Schaller, *Discontinuity and Hope*, 7, 74–83, 174–79; Surratt, Ligon, and Bird, *Multi-Site Church Revolution*, 9–10).

58   Frye, "The Multi-Site Church Phenomenon," 53–54; Ludden, "Big Churches Use Technology." In the 2005 interview with Ludden, HPBC pastor David Bouler indicated, "in the past 14 years, Highland Park Baptist has let go of 37 satellite churches." The interviewer said the process of letting go of churches was a current process, indicating that as of 2005, HPBC still had satellite chapels (Ludden, "Big Churches Use Technology"). As of Frye's dissertation in 2011, he said there was no indication that HPBC had any remaining campuses (Frye, "The Multi-Site Church Phenomenon," 54). In an article written in 2012, the church's high mark membership of 57,000 had dwindled to a weekly attendance of 370 gathering at one location. The property was being sold so the church could relocate (Cooper, "Chattanooga's Iconic Highland Park Baptist Church Will Move").

59   Ferguson, "The Multi-Site Church," 18–26. One issue with Ferguson's claim is that he bases it on Charles Olsen's research. Olsen's models were not multisite models, but small group models, as has been shown in the previous section on Ferguson's models. The multisite churches Ferguson lists, without dates, are Willow Creek Community Church in South Barrington, Illinois, Druid Hills Presbyterian Church in Atlanta, Georgia, Skyline Wesley-

discussed previously, Vaughn identifies Akron Baptist Temple in Akron, Ohio, and First Baptist Church of Fort Worth, Texas, as having "satellite ministries" as far back as 1969, bringing the total to potentially four identified multisite churches in the 1960s.[60] Gary McIntosh identifies Scott Memorial Church in San Diego, California, as a multisite church during the 1970s.[61] There are likely more examples available, but these scant references show that the multisite models were not widely used in the US through the 1970s. In fact, Surratt, Ligon, and Bird say "interest had expanded" to approximately twenty-five multisite churches in the 1980s.[62] If interest in multisite had "expanded" to twenty-five, then it obviously had very few churches practicing it.

MULTISITE IN THE 1980s AND 1990s

Frye identifies Perimeter Church in Atlanta, Georgia, as "the primo-genitor of the multi-site church movement."[63] The brief history of Perimeter Church has already been discussed. This church set the stage for what would become a multisite formula in the 1990s and 2000s. At the heart of Perimeter Church was a multisite strategy specifically focused on adding locations with similar ministries at various locations to reach different areas of the city, for the purpose of reaching the whole city.[64] While this strategy did not come to fruition for Perimeter Church, their intentional multisite model was highly influential.[65]

---

an Church in Lemon Grove, California, First Baptist Church of Atlanta, Georgia, Mount Paran Church of God in Atlanta, Georgia, The Church on the Way in Van Nuys, California, First Community Church in Columbus, Ohio, Northlands Community Church in Longwood, Florida, The Church of the Saviour in Washington, DC, First Baptist Church of Arlington, Texas, Perimeter Church in Atlanta, Georgia, and Community Christian Church in Naperville, Illinois.

60   Vaughn, *The Large Church*, 57. Vaughn also mentions Florence Baptist Temple in Florence, South Carolina, Landmark Baptist Temple in Cincinnati, Ohio, and Calvary Chapel in Santa Ana, California, but does not include a date. Therefore, it is not possible to pinpoint when these churches went multisite except that it was before 1985, the date of the book's publication.

61   McIntosh, *Make Room for the Boom*, 138–40.

62   Surratt, Ligon, and Bird, *A Multi-Site Church Road Trip*, 17.

63   Frye, "The Multi-Site Church Phenomenon," 97–98.

64   Chandler, *Racing Toward 2001*, 242.

65   Schaller, *Innovations in Ministry*, 122–23.

By the end of the 1980s, Towns included three multisite churches in his "ten most innovative churches." Perimeter Church was listed alongside Church on the Way in Van Nuys, California, and Mount Paran Church of God, in Atlanta, Georgia.[66] Frye identifies North Heights Lutheran Church, Minneapolis, Minnesota, and Mosaic Church in Los Angeles, California, as two other multisite churches that were birthed in the 1980s.[67] Still, the movement was in its infancy. Conservative estimates hold the movement at only ten actual practicing multisite churches by 1990.[68]

The 1990s saw more expansion in multisite. A survey of 228 multisite churches in 2007 found that forty-one (18 percent) of them had become multisite before 2000.[69] By the end of the decade, the number of multisite churches had climbed to at least one hundred, although some believe it could be as high as two hundred.[70] Researchers also began focusing more on the multisite subject. Towns published *An Inside Look at 10 of Today's Most Innovative Churches*, the first book to include a section on multisite churches.[71] Soon, authors published more books with information on the subject, including many that have been discussed previously in this chapter.[72] Leadership Network also emerged as a leading researcher of multisite church ministry. They would be responsible for much of the conversation that would take place in the coming decades.[73]

MULTISITE IN THE TWENTY-FIRST CENTURY

The greatest explosion of multisite churches took place in the twenty-first century, yet because of varying definitions, it is sometimes hard

---

66   Towns, *Today's Most Innovative Churches*, 59–72, 89–103, 163–73.
67   Frye, "The Multi-Site Church Phenomenon," 96–97.
68   Rainer, "Is the Multisite Church Movement Still Growing?"
69   Shields, "Survey of 1,000 Multi-Site Churches," 2. This report is no longer available. The information is quoted in Frye, "The Multi-Site Church Phenomenon," 104.
70   Rainer, "Is the Multisite Church Movement Still Growing?" Surratt, Ligon, and Bird say the number of multisite churches was as high as two hundred at the end of the 1990s. However, they are including multi-venue churches in this tally. After claiming two hundred, they add "in addition to the above, a small number of churches began experimenting with having multiple campuses" (Surratt, Ligon, and Bird, *A Multi-Site Church Road Trip*, 217).
71   Towns, *Today's Most Innovative Churches*, 59–72, 89–103, 163–73.
72   Ahlen and Thomas, *One Church, Many Congregations*; Schaller, *Discontinuity and Hope*, 174–79; Schaller, *Innovations in Ministry*, 112–20.
73   Frye, "The Multi-Site Church Phenomenon," 94–95.

to track specific numbers. Surratt, Ligon, and Bird claim the number of multisite churches grew from two hundred in 1999 to three thousand by 2009.[74] This coincides with Frye's conclusion that "for every one multi-site church begun before 2000, ten more emerged between 2000 and 2007."[75] A 2012 study sponsored by Duke University used a broad multisite definition and found eight thousand multisite churches in 2012, 3 percent of all Protestant churches.[76] In a 2019 blog post, Thom Rainer cites research conducted by Leadership Network in 2012 that says there were "more than five thousand" multisite churches. In the post Rainer says he believes the current number of multisite churches could actually be closer to "ten thousand in North America."[77] Yet Leadership Network published an article in 2019 that says the "more than five thousand" mark was still "big news."[78] How is seven-year-old data "big news," and why do Leadership Network and Rainer's articles, dated within six months of each other, suggest a potential difference of five thousand multisite churches? The rapid expansion of multisite churches in the last two decades, combined with inadequate tracking and data collection, shows the MCM has been a movement that is difficult to categorize and calculate.[79]

These large numbers, however, do suggest the multisite model is not going away. In a 2014 blog post, Ed Stetzer writes, "Multisite churches are on the rise. This is not a fad, this is not some sort of temporary

---

74 Surratt, Ligon, and Bird, *A Multi-Site Church Road Trip*, 217. It seems the authors include multi-venue churches in these numbers, but that is not clear.

75 Frye, "The Multi-Site Church Phenomenon," 105.

76 "National Congregations Study," *Association of Religious Data Archives.* This study included multi-venue churches, with two or more separate venues on the same campus, but no satellite campus, in its multisite calculations. The report findings were summarized in Bird and Walters, "Multi-Site Church Scorecard," 3.

77 Rainer, "Is the Multisite Church Movement Still Growing?" The Leadership Network report cited by Rainer is no longer available.

78 Bird, "Big News."

79 This is one of the reasons the SBC is beginning to assign unique tracking IDs to campuses. The hope is that better tracking will give a clearer picture of the multisite church situation and will help local associations and church planters know where multisite church campuses are located. In the 2023 Annual Church Profile reporting, SBC churches identified 585 campuses in addition to their original location. Thus, the SBC is becoming more aware of the actual locations of their churches (Earls, "Southern Baptists Grow in Attendance"; Earls and Pipes, "Multisite Church ID").

trend—multisite churches are here to stay. It's like the megachurch now—just a part of our church landscape—the new normal."[80] Rainer concludes the movement is moving out of the early adopter stage and into the mid-adopter stage, meaning multisite is officially entering into the mainstream of church life. He concludes this will lead to an even greater breakout of more multisite churches.[81] Leadership Network research released in 2018 notes many interesting statistics about the continuing development of the model. It finds that the larger a church is, the more likely it is to be multisite, showing eighteen of the twenty largest churches and sixteen of the twenty fastest growing churches are multisite.[82] While this may not be surprising, the research also finds that 47 percent of multisite campuses are in small towns and rural areas.[83] In the twenty-first century, roughly four decades after Perimeter Church began experimenting with the intentional multisite model, the movement has grown to the point that multisite churches are found throughout North America, and are present in every imaginable context.

---

80   Stetzer, "Multisite Churches Are Here."
81   Rainer, "Is the Multisite Church Movement Still Growing?"
82   Bird, "Latest Multisite Trends," 13. In a podcast interview with Tony Morgan, Geoff Surratt said fifty of the one hundred largest churches in the United States are multisite churches (Morgan and Surratt, "Is Multisite on the Downslope?").
83   Bird, "Latest Multisite Trends," 14.

THE SOUTHERN BAPTIST CONVENTION AND MULTISITE CHURCHES

MULTISITE'S ENTRANCE INTO THE SBC has been a slow process. As SBC churches began adopting the model, leading to greater numbers of multisite churches in the denomination, the convention began incorporating multisite into its reporting and strategies. There has never been an official statement from the SBC specifically addressing or approving multisite churches and, due to the SBC's convictions on local church autonomy, there likely never will be.

The earliest adoption of multisite strategy by the SBC is unclear, but it appears to be through using the Key Church Strategy. J. V. Thomas, identified previously as the designer of the Key Church Strategy, was the Director of Project Development for the Baptist General Convention of Texas in the late 1970s. Gambrell Street Baptist Church, an SBC church that sits directly across the street from Southwestern Baptist Theological Seminary in Fort Worth, Texas, was looking for a way to reach its community in an area where minority groups were rapidly multiplying. Working with Thomas, Gambrell Street pioneered the Key Church model as a project of the Church Extension Department of the Texas convention. That initial project eventually developed into

85

a nationwide initiative to use the model to begin two thousand new congregations, and by 1997, three hundred Southern Baptist Churches in twenty-seven states had adopted the strategy.[1] In 1995 and 1996, Thomas served as a consultant for the Home Mission Board of the SBC (now North American Mission Board [NAMB]), and he is listed in the SBC Annual for those years as "National Consultant, Key Church Strategy."[2] This shows the Key Church Strategy was a part of the SBC's strategies, but the model is nowhere mentioned in the entity reports. Lyle Schaller notes, ironically, in 1999 in the foreword to *One Church, Many Congregations*, "We invited two Southern Baptists from Texas to write a book to be published by The United Methodist Publishing House."[3] It seems Southern Baptists were using the model but were not ready to identify this emerging form of ministry in an official capacity. Within ten years, however, they would have no choice but to begin addressing the multisite movement.

In 2007, seeing growth of the multisite model both inside and outside the SBC, Lifeway Research conducted a survey of over one thousand churches.[4] Plans for this study were announced at the SBC annual meeting in Lifeway's report, which was the first time an SBC entity had included multisite in a report to the annual meeting.[5] This research was the first study conducted by the SBC on the multisite topic. The study showed many pastors were considering a move toward multisite ministry, and many of them were looking for guidance in how to move forward. Following this study, Lifeway Research interviewed leaders from forty multisite churches seeking to put together strategies for churches moving toward multisite.[6] This information was presented in Scott McConnell's

---

1   Ahlen and Thomas, *One Church, Many Congregations*, 19, 21–22, 151.

2   Atchison, *Annual of the Southern Baptist Convention: Nineteen Hundred and Nine-ty-Five*, 568; Atchison, *Annual of the Southern Baptist Convention: Nineteen Hundred and Ninety-Six*, 561.

3   Schaller, "Foreword," *One Church, Many Locations*, 13.

4   McConnell, *Multi-Site Churches*, 2–3.

5   Yeats, *Annual of the 2007 Southern Baptist Convention*, 165.

6   McConnell, *Multi-Site Churches*, 2. The forty church leaders who were interviewed were not all from Southern Baptist churches. It is not clear if the first study of over one thousand church pastors was conducted among Southern Baptist pastors or if it reached beyond the SBC. It is only clear that it was a survey of "Protestant pastors."

book *Multi-Site Churches: Guidance for the Movement's Next Generation*.[7] This book, published by Broadman & Holman, a publishing arm of the SBC, promotes the multisite model and provides, as the title suggests, information for how churches can implement the multisite model.[8] In the year of the book's publication, at the 2009 SBC Annual Meeting, Lifeway included in its ministry report that *Multi-Site Churches* would be forthcoming.[9] The publication and mention of *Multi-Site Churches* was the another step by the SBC toward embracing multisite ministry.

At the 2011 SBC Annual Meeting, NAMB included multisite campuses in its report of new SBC congregations begun in 2010.[10] This is the first record of multisite churches being tracked and shows that NAMB began recording multisite campuses within its church planting strategies as far back as 2010. In 2013, Lifeway announced leadership training resources that were specifically tailored toward church planters and multisite churches "to include products and services that are unique to doing church in shared venues and rented facilities." These resources were a part of Lifeway's Ministry Grid training platform, which was launched in 2012.[11] This was a step by the SBC to develop ongoing strategies and resources specifically for multisite churches. The initiative spawned a new resource website in 2015, NewChurches.com, dedicated to supporting church planters and multisite churches.[12]

In 2019, the SBC announced a plan to begin issuing SBC ID numbers to help local associations and denominational leaders track the locations

---

7   Walker, "Email Message to Dustin Slaton." Kevin Walker is a research assistant at Lifeway Research. He confirmed the research was not published separately, but was the basis for *Multi-Site Churches*.

8   McConnell, *Multi-Site Churches*, 2–3.

9   Yeats, *Annual of the 2009 Southern Baptist Convention*, 172. The book is also mentioned in the same context in Lifeway's report at the 2010 SBC Annual Meeting in the section regarding what was published in 2010 (Yeats, *Annual of the 2010 Southern Baptist Convention*, 195).

10   Yeats, *Annual of the 2011 Southern Baptist Convention*, 192. The multisite campuses were included in a total number of new congregations, along with newly affiliated churches and new church plants.

11   Yeats, *Annual of the 2013 Southern Baptist Convention*, 161.

12   Yeats, *Annual of the 2016 Southern Baptist Convention*, 162, 165. "Start New Churches. We'll Help," *NewChurches*. The *New Churches* website is now solely focused on church planting.

of multisite churches. Up to that point, a church with multiple locations had only one ID number, which made pinpointing the locations difficult for the local leaders, and made identifying areas for potential church planting difficult.[13] This new way of tracking also allowed NAMB to begin better tracking for multisite campuses in their totals of new congregations across the denomination, and it provided them a clearer picture of how and where churches are growing. This tracking began with the 2019 Annual Church Profiles and was included in the 2020 SBC Book of Reports, as well as every subsequent Book of Reports since then, and 2020 SBC Annual Executive Committee report. It was the first time multisite churches were counted as a specific category, separated from church plants, in the SBC's reporting.[14]

In February 2020, the new President of the SBC Executive Committee, Ronnie Floyd, presented the SBC Executive Committee's "Vision 2025," which is "A call to reach every person in every town, every city, every state, and every nation."[15] As a part of this vision, comprised of five strategic actions, Floyd calls for six thousand new churches in the SBC, including "fifty new campuses identified or added by our multisite churches annually."[16] With this statement, the President of the Executive Committee of the Southern Baptist Convention publicly espoused the multisite church model as an official part of the SBC's evangelism vision. These decisions by key leaders and entities in the SBC show that multisite is gaining traction within SBC ranks. While an official recognition of multisite ministry may never come from the SBC, it is clear the model has become widely accepted within the convention.

---

13   Earls and Pipes, "Multisite Church ID."
14   Yeats, *Book of Reports Prepared for 2020 SBC Advance*, 11, 89, 95, 100; Yeats and Young, *Annual of the Southern Baptist Convention Prepared for the Year 2020*, 65, 151, 157, 162; Yeats, *Book of Reports for the 2021 Southern Baptist Convention*; Yeats, *Book of Reports for the 2022 Southern Baptist Convention*; Finn, *Book of Reports for the 2023 Southern Baptist Convention*. The report clarifies, "Under ACP definitions, a new campus is not considered its own church."
15   "About Vision 2025," *Vision 2025*.
16   Floyd, "Vision 2025 Presentation by Ronnie Floyd."

CHAPTER 3

FOUNDATIONAL ASSUMPTIONS OF THE MULTISITE CHURCH MOVEMENT

IN THE FIRST OF FOUR ARTICLES WRITTEN about The Summit Church's multisite strategy, pastor J. D. Greear writes, "The Summit Church has chosen to pursue a multi-site approach because our elders believed it was the most efficient way to reach the maximum number of people in our city while faithfully pursuing the other biblical beauties God prescribes for his local church."[1] That opening statement reveals a truth that is at the heart of most of the MCM: a desire to be both biblical and practical for the sake of the gospel.[2]

While the MCM literature has focused primarily on the practical aspects of multisite models, that does not mean the reasons for the model are purely pragmatic or consumeristic. The leaders of this movement, whether practitioners, leaders, or writers, have gospel-based purposes behind their methodology. There are some foundational assumptions

---

1   Greear, "Multisite or 'One-Service-Only?'"
2   This analysis of assumptions of the multisite church movement are based on multisite advocates. These assumptions are not necessarily arguments being made by this book. In Part 3, I will evaluate some of these assumptions and the criticisms levied against multisite ministry.

they hold to that can provide clarity as to why they believe multisite is a good model.

MULTISITE FULFILLS A GREAT COMMISSION PURPOSE

In *Multi-Site Churches*, Scott McConnell asks, "When does multi-site make sense?" His first answer to that question sums up the primary focus of most multisite advocates: "When the focus is on the Great Commission."[3] In *MRT*, Surratt, Ligon, and Bird state,

> For many churches, the biblical motivation for embracing the multi-site model isn't very controversial. Churches want to fulfill the Great Commission . . . by giving more opportunities for the gospel to be shared. They want to obey the Great Commandment . . . by taking the love of Christ to the people, meeting them where they are. These churches believe that new campuses are places where . . . lost sheep and lost coins are sought out, and where lost children are welcomed home.[4]

These words reveal the authors' purpose in writing the book, and ultimately what they believe is the purpose behind multisite churches. Similar purpose statements resound throughout the multisite community. Ahlen and Thomas write that the purpose of the Key Church Strategy is to present "new ways of influencing the community and advancing the Kingdom of God."[5] In the foreword to *One Church, Many Congregations*, Schaller says the Key Church Strategy is one of the most effective outreach strategies he has encountered in almost four decades of working

---

3   McConnell, *Multi-Site Churches*, 5.

4   Surratt, Ligon, and Bird, *A Multi-Site Church Road Trip*, 201. In *MCR*, the authors make a similar statement: "The primary motive behind the multi-site approach is to obey the church's God-given directives. The Great Commandment . . . is to love God and one another, the Great Commission . . . is to make disciples of all nations, and the Great Charge . . . reminds us to involve all believers in ministry. Drawing from Scripture and over fifty different contemporary examples, The Multi-Site Church Revolution . . . shows you how any church, regardless of its size or location or denomination, can contribute to fulfilling these essential commands by developing an identity as one church in many locations" (Surratt, Ligon, and Bird, *Multi-Site Church Revolution*, 10).

5   Ahlen and Thomas, *One Church, Many Congregations*, 20.

with churches.[6] McConnell writes, "[Multisite churches'] bent is to make decisions based on a desire for the kingdom of God to grow. The decision to add their second site and sometimes other sites since then was drive from this desire to reach people with the good news of Jesus Christ."[7]

Multisite church pastors voice the same purpose behind their multisite strategies. Chuck Carter, pastor of Family Church in Windermere, Florida, says, "Among the churches where [multisite] is successful, it is because the Great Commission is driving it."[8] J. D. Greear, pastor of The Summit Church, a multisite church in Raleigh, North Carolina, writes, "We have embraced multi-site as a strategy for growing our church and reaching our city. . . . The multi-site approach, in our judgment, best allows us to be effective in evangelism, pastorally responsible over our members, and to develop leaders and church planters."[9]

John Piper, pastor of Bethlehem Baptist Church, a multisite church in Minneapolis, Minnesota, says, "And it almost goes without saying that 'multiplying campuses' and 'planting new churches' is shorthand for spreading a passion for the supremacy of God to more and more people who then need a place to worship with God's people and study and strategize—hence new campuses and church planting."[10]

These are just a few of examples of the many that could be shared that show the purpose of the multisite model is for a church to take the gospel to as many people as possible, in obedience to Christ.

Even critics of the multisite church admit that the purpose behind the model is positive. Thomas White says, "I sincerely believe the basic desire of the multi-site movement is to reach more people with the gospel."[11] Grant Gaines goes so far as to say, "Praise God for our brothers and sisters in multi-site churches who are reaching their communities

---

6   Schaller, "Foreword," *One Church, Many Congregations*, 13.

7   McConnell, *Multi-Site Churches*, 6–7.

8   Carter, "There has got to be something driving the thing . . . ," 8. When cited, Family Church still functioned under the name First Baptist Church of Windermere, Florida.

9   "About J. D. Greear," *Southern Baptist Convention*; Greear, "A Pastor Defends His Multi-Site Church," 19, 24.

10   "John Piper, D.Theol," *Bethlehem College and Seminary*; Piper, "Treasuring Christ Together Above All Things."

11   White, "Nine Reasons I Don't Like Multi-Site Churches," 49.

with the gospel of Jesus Christ! Assenters and dissenters to this approach alike should be able to say with Paul, 'What then? Only that . . . Christ is proclaimed; and in this I rejoice.'"[12]

Even Jonathan Leeman, the most outspoken critic of multisite churches, admits that, on the surface, adding sites "makes *Great Commission sense*" (emphasis original), and that many multisite pastors "prize conversion and spiritual growth."[13]

These descriptions of multisite models and churches make it clear that the underlying purpose of most multisite churches and advocates is spreading the gospel of Jesus. The fact that even critics of the movement see this as the case demonstrates that the central heart of multisite ministry is commendable. The questions critics raise are rarely about the purity of multisite churches' missional intentions, but instead about the wisdom of their processes.

MULTISITE IS A BIBLICAL MODEL

Brad House and Gregg Allison emphatically state, "The very first Christian church was a multisite church."[14] They and other proponents point to Acts 2:46 and 5:42, which they say show the early church met in a large gathering at the temple and in smaller gatherings in homes.[15] *MCR* agrees, concluding that the multisite model can be seen in an undeveloped form in the early church gathering in both large groups and small groups.[16] Multisite advocates also claim Paul gives hints that some early churches met both together and separately when he talked about gathering the "whole church." They say there would be no need for Paul to mention a gathering of the whole church unless there were also gatherings when the

---

12   Gaines, "Exegetical Critique of Multi-Site," 33.

13   Leeman, *One Assembly*, introduction, Section 1.

14   House and Allison, *MultiChurch*, 31.

15   Greear, "A Pastor Defends His Multi-Site Church," 19; House and Allison, *MultiChurch*, 32.

16   Surratt, Ligon, and Bird, *Multi-Site Church Revolution*, 17. The authors base this conclusion on Elmer Towns's conclusion that two levels of gathering existed within the church: the whole church gathered in celebration and small groups gathered in cells (Towns, *Today's Most Innovative Churches*, 242–43). They also cite Aubrey Malphurs's conclusion that the early church was formed as a single church in one city that met together as a whole church, and also in smaller groups, not as the whole group. Malphurs refers to this as a "city church" (Malphurs, *Being Leaders*, 22–25).

whole church was not present.[17] Many advocates see this as evidence of a citywide church that met in homes in small units and also came together in large group settings.[18] Some even claim the churches that resulted from the persecution of the church following the stoning of Stephen constituted a regional multisite church. They base this on the Jerusalem Council of Acts 15 and that churches routinely sought guidance from the apostles.[19] Some multisite advocates claim multisite models allow churches to fulfill Paul's statement in 1 Corinthians 9:22 to "be all things to all people so that by all possible ways I might save some."[20]

Some advocates validate the multisite model by claiming the Bible does not give specific enough directives in certain aspects of ecclesiology.[21] To put it another way, they find support for multisite in that the Bible does not expressly forbid it. John Piper says, "We do [multisite] because I don't think the New Testament forbids it, and it seems to me the New Testament is pretty flexible about its ecclesiology on these matters."[22]

MULTISITE IS PRACTICING GOOD STEWARDSHIP

One of the primary reasons Bethlehem Baptist Church in Minneapolis, Minnesota, began using the multisite model was a desire to be good stewards of the resources and mission God had given them.[23] It is financially wiser, they claim, to extend to regional locations than it is to continually create a larger and larger single campus.[24] Multisite models allow a church to continue to grow and reach more people, and with multiple facilities they can extend into multiple services and utilize their space more efficiently.[25] Dave Ferguson, an early multisite proponent

---

17 Allison, "Theological Defense of Multi-Site," 9; House and Allison, *MultiChurch*, 40; Malphurs, *Being Leaders,* 24–26.

18 Malphurs, *Being Leaders*, 22–25. See also an unpublished paper by this author: Slaton, "The Citywide Church."

19 Surratt, Ligon, and Bird, *Multi-Site Church Revolution*, 92.

20 Surratt, Ligon, and Bird, *Multi-Site Church Revolution*, 29; Surratt, Ligon, and Bird, *A Multi-Site Church Road Trip*, 201.

21 Greear, "A Pastor Defends His Multi-Site Church," 19–20.

22 Piper, "What Are the Key Issues?"

23 Piper, "Treasuring Christ Together, Part 1"; Piper, "Where I Am There Will My Servant Be."

24 Greear, "A Pastor Defends His Multi-Site Church," 20–21.

25 Rainer and Howe, "Why Small Churches Are Going Multisite."

and current pastor of a multisite church with ten locations, agrees, stating, "Multisite strategies reach more people faster, with higher quality, greater results, and lower costs."[26] Advocates claim multisite strategies are the most economical way for them to fulfill the Great Commission.[27]

Multisite is also good stewardship, advocates claim, because of the success rate of multisite campuses. Multisite campuses have a higher success rate than church plants. Only 10 percent of multisite churches have experienced a campus closure, while 30–40 percent of church plant attempts ultimately fail.[28] This means the resources that are poured into multisite campuses have a better chance of leading to a successful, functioning gospel presence in a new area.

MULTISITE IS THE MOST EFFECTIVE MODEL FOR MULTIPLICATION AND EVANGELISM

Research on multisite churches points to their effectiveness in achieving their evangelistic purpose. A study conducted in 2014 found that in churches that used both multisite campuses and church plants in their outreach strategy, 42 percent said that their campuses were more evangelistically effective, compared to only 11 percent who said their church plants were more effective.[29] The same study found that 85 percent of multisite churches surveyed are experiencing growth from all sources, at an average rate of 14 percent per year. Fifty percent of multisite churches that also support church plants say their campuses grow faster than the plants, compared to 14 percent that say the plants grow faster.[30] Bird, who authored the study, noted in 2019 that successful

---

26   "Community Locations," *Community Christian Church*, 88.
27   House and Allison disagree with this assumption in *MultiChurch*. They point to the increased complexity of multisite structures, and conclude that these complexities, especially in the necessary personnel needed to manage the complexities, add to the overall expenses of a multisite model. Thus, where savings may be seen in one area, additional expenses arise in others (House and Allison, *MultiChurch*, 175–76).
28   Bird and Walters, "Multisite is Multiplying"; Malphurs, "The Need for Church Planting and Revitalization."
29   Bird, "Multisite Church Scorecard," 22.
30   Bird, "Multisite Church Scorecard," 4, 22. These figures include evangelistic, transfer, and biological growth. This book is not arguing that transfer growth is an equally satisfactory goal as evangelistic growth.

evangelistic trends are continuing in multisite churches, pointing out that multisite churches reach more people and baptize more people than single-site churches.[31]

When compared to single location churches, the data also leans in favor of multisite churches. Roughly 85 percent of multisite churches surveyed are growing. Compare this to the overall church health landscape in which around 80 percent of churches in the United States are plateaued or in decline.[32] This data suggests the Great Commission purpose for which most multisite churches began using the multisite strategy is successfully being fulfilled. Some advocates say these kinds of effective results are enough evidence to show God approves of the multisite model.[33]

MULTISITE IS NOT A REPLACEMENT FOR OTHER MULTIPLICATION METHODS

Although many advocates laud the multisite model's effectiveness, they are quick to also say that multisite does not replace or eliminate other models of church multiplication. McConnell writes, "The multisite strategy does not replace any other method of participating in kingdom growth. It does not replace church planting, personal evangelism, visitation programs, investing and inviting, servant evangelism, or evangelistic training."[34] Some multisite churches use campuses as a church planting strategy, starting some campuses with the intention of eventually launching them out as autonomous churches, while other campuses are intended to remain in the church. Alongside these, many multisite churches still plant and support fully autonomous churches.[35] The variety and mixture of models shows that multisite is not an exclusive method that is incompatible with others.

---

31 Bird, "Big News." Bird does not explain whether that claim is simply based on the fact that the churches are larger than the average single-site church, or if it is because the churches are more evangelistically effective than single-site churches.

32 Bird, "Big News"; Bird, "Multisite Church Scorecard," 4–5.

33 Surratt, Ligon, and Bird, *Multi-Site Church Revolution*, 94.

34 McConnell, *Multi-Site Churches*, 17.

35 Surratt, Ligon, and Bird, *A Multi-Site Church Road Trip*, 33–40; "Family Church Network," *Family Church*; "Our Mission," *Harbor Network*; "About Us," *Summit Collaborative*; Scroggins and Wright, "Autonomous Launch."

Greer believes the multisite model helps facilitate church planting rather than detracting from it, which is why The Summit Church uses multisite models alongside traditional church planting.[36] The campus model becomes a pipeline to help develop leaders for new independent churches.[37] Bethlehem Baptist Church in Minneapolis, Minnesota, began a capital campaign in 2003 to develop a second location for their church, and as a part of the campaign, they included monies specifically designated to facilitate independent church planting and provide funds for global missions projects.[38] Family Church, an SBC church in the West Palm Beach, Florida, area with thirteen campuses also supports The Family Church Network, which includes a two-year church planting residency.[39]

Missiologist Jeff Christopherson says, "Multi-siting can be extremely missionally effective—in many cases, much more effective than what we often consider as classical church planting."[40] These examples, and many others, demonstrate that the multisite model has not hindered the promotion of other ministry efforts or initiatives. Based on current research for this book and other projects, no multisite advocate has been found who argues for a church to use multisite exclusive of church planting.

---

36   Part 3 will provide more clarification about the similarities and differences between church planting and multisite campuses.
37   Greear, "A Pastor Defends His Multi-Site Church," 20–22.
38   Piper, "Treasuring Christ Together, Part 1."
39   "Our Story," *Family Church*; "Church Planting Residency," *Family Church Network*.
40   Christopherson, "Can Multisite Be Missional?"

PART 2

BUILDING HEALTHY MULTISITE CHURCHES

IN THE TWENTIETH CENTURY, church experts focused on church growth. The goals of the books, journals, and articles written in this area was helping churches grow larger in membership, Sunday School, and in worship attendance. In the late 1990s, and early into the twenty-first century, the language shifted from church growth to church health. Writers such as Rick Warren began talking about how to grow a healthy church that had biblical aspects present throughout its ministries. The focus was not on bigger churches and ministries, but on healthier churches and ministries.

In Part 2, we will look at the aspects of healthy churches in general, and then apply these principles to the multisite context. In doing so, the chapters will analyze eleven healthy church aspects by their biblical and historical relevance. They will then dive into how multisite scholarship and practice has specifically addressed these issues, and conclude with methods for multisite churches to effectively put healthy practices in place. Finally, the chapter will end with a multisite ecclesiological guide for multisite churches.

CHAPTER 4

WHAT IS A HEALTHY CHURCH?

IN *FRANCHISING MCCHURCH*, Thomas White and John Yeats write, "This [multisite] movement, while new, has not had many proponents attempt to find a scriptural basis for its existence."[1] Grant Gaines adds, "The lack of any extended biblical, theological, and historical treatment of the subject . . . calls for such an evaluation and response."[2] The evaluation and response Gaines provides in his dissertation is not favorable to the typical multisite model, and it is indicative of many who have critiqued the subject. The lack of a thorough theological treatment is a conspicuous absence in the multisite church movement's (MCM) credibility.[3] Aside from Gregg Allison and his coauthor Brad House, no multisite

---

1   White and Yeats, *Franchising McChurch*, 172.
2   Gaines, "One Church in One Location," 2.
3   It must be acknowledged that providing a theological analysis is not the *purpose* of books such as *The Multi-Site Church Revolution*, *A Multi-Site Church Road Trip*, *Multi-Site Churches*, and *MultiChurch*. They are written as practical guides, not theological treatises or ecclesiologies. In seeking to provide practical content on how to develop a multisite church, they achieve their goal. The critiques levied by those questioning the movement, however, is that there should be more theological consideration to go along with the practical. The chapter in Part 2 will show how current multisite literature and multisite advocates have addressed these characteristics of healthy churches from a biblical perspective, and will then add additional support for multisite in each aspect. In doing so, the chapters may seem very critical of these writers, or may seem to have misunderstood the practical

99

advocate has done significant work in providing a biblical foundation for multisite churches.[4]

In a chapter evaluating the Church Growth Movement (CGM) of the twentieth century, Gailyn Van Rheenen writes of the movement, "Detractors and proponents, however, agree on one thing: Church Growth 'both infuriates and inspires,' but discussion of it 'has never been boring!'"[5] In his analysis of the CGM, he concludes that a great threat to the mission of the church is "pragmatism—separated from biblical theology—which drives the agenda of the church."[6] Van Rheenen provides four critiques of CGM philosophies that are equally applicable to the MCM. He says the CGM has an "anthropocentric focus," meaning its advocates and practitioners focus too much on what people are doing, rather than on what God is doing. The second critique is "segmentation of theology and praxis," meaning "pragmatic thinking 'de-emphasizes' theological problems, takes for granted the existence of adequate content, and consequently majors in method." Van Rheenen's third critique of the CGM is the movement's "theological level of inquiry," whereby he states the movement does "not begin as a theologically integrated discipline." His final critique is a "focus on numerical growth," meaning the goal of CGM methods is an end result of larger churches, rather than on developed disciples.[7] Van Rheenen's evaluation and critique of the CGM is also a fitting critique of the MCM, which grew out of the CGM.[8] His recommended solution is also appropriately applicable to the MCM. He suggests a "missional helix" composed of theological re-

---

purposes behind their books. This is not the intention. The goal of the chapters is simply to show what *has* been written, provide additional content, and then to provide a brief example of how multisite churches can be a biblically healthy church.

4   See Allison, *Sojourners and Strangers*; Allison, "Theological Defense of Multi-Site"; House and Allison, *MultiChurch*.

5   Van Rheenen, "Reformist View," 170. Quotations within Van Rheenen's comment are from: Guder, "Evangelism and the Debate over Church Growth," 147.

6   Van Rheenen, "Reformist View," 174.

7   Van Rheenen, "Reformist View," 175–86.

8   For similar critiques of the multisite movement see: Leeman, "Twenty-Two Problems with Multi-Site." Thom Rainer includes "multicampus" in his book on the Church Growth Movement, linking it with that movement (Rainer, *The Book of Church Growth*, 207, 212).

flection, historical perspective, cultural analysis, and strategy formation, where the four quadrants work together to form an overall methodology for churches.[9] A more robust theological framework such as this needs to be provided for multisite churches.

The chapters in Part 2 will establish an ecclesiology for multisite churches that is biblically faithful and compatible with Baptist ecclesiology. To do so, the chapters will consider eleven aspects of a healthy church. These aspects have been selected to cover as many facets of ecclesiology and church practice as is reasonable, going well beyond the traditional marks of the church, in order to provide a more holistic foundation for multisite churches. But first, this chapter will introduce the subject by providing an initial evaluation of the traditional marks of the church.

THE MARKS OF A HEALTHY CHURCH

Considering the scope of church history, the discussion about the marks of a true church is still relatively new. Mark Dever points out that what comprises a true church did not become a topic of debate until the Reformation.[10] However, a more accurate statement would be to say that the focus of the conversation shifted at the Reformation. Since the fourth century, church fathers were identifying characteristics that defined a true church. The four marks that would be the primary characteristics of the church for the next thousand years are most clearly described in the Niceno-Constantinopolitan Creed of 381, more commonly known as the Nicene Creed. It states, "We believe . . . in one, holy, catholic, and apostolic Church."[11] John Hammett notes these four elements describe the nature of the universal church comprised of all believers throughout history.[12] Norman Geisler agrees, identifying these four marks as characteristics of the universal church, but not of local churches.[13] What Hammett and

---

9   Van Rheenen, "Reformist View," 186–89.
10 Dever, *Nine Marks of a Healthy Church*, 26.
11 Leith, *Creeds of the Churches*, 28–33.
12 Hammett, *Biblical Foundations for Baptist Churches*, 62.
13 Geisler, *Systematic Theology*, 4:51–57. The descriptions Geisler uses are "Indivisible" (one), "Regenerate" (holy), "Universal" (catholic), and "Apostolic."

Geisler identify as characteristics of the universal church, however, the Roman Catholic Church identifies as characteristics of both the universal and visible (local) church.[14] The Catechism of the Catholic Church states that it alone fully satisfies these four marks, and therefore it alone is the true visible church on earth.[15]

This belief by the Roman Catholic Church, and the abuses thereof, is what ultimately led to the Reformation, and to a new conversation around what constitutes a true church. Since Martin Luther broke away from Rome, Dever notes, the "marks of the church have been a necessary focus of discussion."[16] As the Reformation progressed, many reformers identified two fundamental components as a baseline for a true church: the right preaching of the Word and the right administration of the sacraments, or ordinances, of baptism and the Lord's Supper. Dever beautifully captures the importance of the marks of the church, writing,

> A biblical ecclesiology can largely be organized and presented under these two marks since in them both the creation and preservation of the church are accomplished. The first mark is the fountain of God's truth that gives life to his people, and the second is the lovely vessel to contain and display this glorious

---

14 Melton, *Nelson's Guide to Denominations*, 165–66.
15 "Catechism of the Catholic Church, 1.2.3.9.3: The Church is One, Holy, Catholic, and Apostolic," *The Holy See*. In a summary subsection, this article reads: "The Church is one: she acknowledges one Lord, confesses one faith, is born of one Baptism . . . forms only one Body, is given life by the one Spirit, for the sake of one hope (cf. Eph 4:3–5), at whose fulfillment all divisions will be overcome.

"The Church is holy: the Most Holy God is her author; Christ, her bridegroom, gave himself up to make her holy; the Spirit of holiness gives her life. Since she still includes sinners, she is 'the sinless one made up of sinners.' Her holiness shines in the saints; in Mary she is already all-holy.

"The Church is catholic: she proclaims the fullness of the faith. She bears in herself and administers the totality of the means of salvation. She is sent out to all peoples. She speaks to all men. She encompasses all times. She is 'missionary of her very nature.'

"The Church is apostolic: She is built on a lasting foundation: 'the twelve apostles of the Lamb' (Rev. 21:14). She is indestructible (Mt. 16:18). She is upheld infallibly in the truth: Christ governs her through Peter and the other apostles, who are present in their successors, the Pope and the college of bishops."
16 Dever, *Nine Marks of a Healthy Church*, 26.

work. The church is generated by the right preaching of the
Word. The church is distinguished and contained by the right
administration of Baptism . . . and the Lord's Supper.[17]

With something so important to the reformers, and those who would
come after, one would think there would be a clear consensus on what
the marks of the church are. However, that is not the case.

The Augsburg Confession of 1530 is the first Reformation period statement of faith to identify the marks of the correct teaching of the Scriptures
and the correct observance of the sacraments.[18] The confession states, "For
it is sufficient for the true unity of the Christian church that the Gospel . .
. be preached in conformity with a pure understanding of it and that the
sacraments be administered in accordance with the divine Word."[19] These
two marks were also acknowledged by reformers such as Thomas Cranmer
and John Calvin.[20] The Belgic Confession of 1561 added church discipline as
a third mark of the church.[21] The reformer who saw more church marks than
any others was Luther himself, who identified seven marks of the church.
His marks are: "the possession of the holy word of God . . . sacrament of
baptism . . . sacrament of the Altar . . . the office of the keys exercised publicly
. . . consecrate[d] or call[ed] ministers . . . externally recognized by prayer,
public praise, and thanksgiving to God . . . externally recognized by the holy
possession of the sacred cross."[22]

As the Reformation continued, baptistic groups began emerging,
and many of these groups developed confessional statements. An early

---

17   Dever, *The Church*, chap. 3, sec.1.
18   Dever, *The Church*, 26–28. The sacraments included in these reformed marks are bap-
      tism and the Lord's Supper. These sacraments are referred to as ordinances in Baptist
      life, including in the Baptist Faith and Message. Therefore, they will be referred to as
      ordinances from this point forward except in direct quotes ("The 2000 Baptist Faith &
      Message," *Southern Baptist Convention*).
19   Melancthon, *The Augsburg Confession*, in *Creeds of the Churches*, 70.
20   Cranmer, *The Articles of Religion*, in *A History of the Articles of Religion*, 316; Calvin,
      Institutes of Christian Religion, 19.
21   *The Belgic Confession*, in *The Creeds of Christendom*, 419.
22   Luther, "On the Councils and the Church," in *The Annotated Luther*, 212–16. In modern
      vernacular, these seven are (1) the Scriptures, (2) baptism, (3) the Lord's Supper, (4)
      church discipline, (5) local church appointed leadership, (6) public worship, and (7)
      suffering for Christ's sake.

Mennonite group developed a confessional statement, known as The Waterland Confession of 1588, that later became foundational to the movement of English Separatist John Smyth and the first General Baptist Church.[23] Article fifteen of the confession identifies the "Ministries" of the church as "teaching the Word, use of the sacraments, care of the poor and ministers, and church discipline."[24] Smyth echoed these marks in his brief confession, as his group was seeking to partner with the Waterland Mennonites in 1610.[25] In 1611, Thomas Helwys developed a similar confession, "A Declaration of Faith of English People," that included as practices of the church, prayer, preaching, breaking bread, and the holy ordinances.[26] The first confession to make a clear declaration of the "marks" of a true church was the General Baptist's Orthodox Creed of 1679. It states:

> And the marks by which [a church] is known to be the true spouse of Christ are these, viz. Where the word of God is rightly preached, and the sacraments truly administered, according to Christ's institution, and the practice of the primitive church; having discipline and government duly executed, by ministers or pastors of God's appointing, and the church's election, that is a true constituted church.[27]

Benjamin Keach, the late seventeenth-century English Particular Baptist pastor, notes that a church exists when people assemble for worship, "among whom the Word of God and Sacraments . . . are duly administered, according to Christ's Institution."[28]

Early Baptists in the United States were also concerned with identifying the characteristics that defined a valid church, and they were

---

23 Lumpkin, *Baptist Confessions of Faith*, 43.
24 de Rys and Gerrits, *A Brief Confession*, in *Baptist Confessions of Faith*, 59.
25 Smyth, *Short Confession of Faith*, in *Baptist Confessions of Faith*, 101.
26 Helwys, *A Declaration of Faith of English*, in *Baptist Confessions of Faith*, 120. Helwys writes, "To Pray . . . Prophecie . . . breake . . . bread, and administer in all the holy ordinances."
27 Monck, *An Orthodox Creed*, in *Baptist Confessions of Faith*, 319.
28 Keach, *The Glory of a True Church*, in *Polity*, 64–65. Keach was an influential contributor to the Second London Confession (Lumpkin, *Baptist Confessions of Faith*, 239–40).

influenced by the English Baptists.[29] The Philadelphia Confession of 1742 mirrored England's Second London Confession of 1677, stating a church "completely organized according to the mind of Christ" has officers and members, with "officers appointed by Christ to be chosen and set apart by the church" for the "administration of ordinances, and execution of power or duty."[30] Such duty is given "in any way needful for their carrying on that order in worship and discipline."[31] The New Hampshire Confession of 1833, which became the foundational document for developing the Baptist Faith and Message (BFM) of 1925, reads,

> That a visible Church ... of Christ is a congregation of baptized believers, associated by covenant in the faith and fellowship of the Gospel ... observing the ordinances of Christ; governed by his laws; and exercising the gifts, rights, and privileges invested in them by his word; that its only proper officers are Bishops . . . or Pastors ... and Deacons ... whose qualifications, claims and duties are defined in the Epistles to Timothy and Titus.[32]

As the Southern Baptist Convention (SBC) came into being in 1845 and began establishing its theological foundation, it followed a more simplified approach. William B. Johnson, the first president of the newly formed SBC and an important contributor to the theological development of the convention, concludes that the "materials" of a church are teaching of the Word, baptism, and Lord's Supper.[33] John L. Dagg, considered to be the first systematic theologian of the SBC, was less specific in his ecclesiological work, *A Treatise on Church Order*.[34] Of a church, he writes,

---

29 Lumpkin, *Baptist Confessions of Faith*, 240. Elias Keach, the son of Benjamin Keach, was influential in early American Baptist life. He brought the elder Keach's writing to the states, and it became the foundational work for the Philadelphia Confession.

30 Lumpkin, *Baptist Confessions of Faith*, 348–49; *Confession of Faith*, in *Baptist Confessions of Faith*, 286–87; "The Philadelphia Confession of Faith," *Baptist Studies Online*, 29.

31 "Philadelphia Confession," *Baptist Studies Online*, 29.

32 Lumpkin, *Baptist Confessions of Faith*, 365–66.

33 Caner and Caner, *The Sacred Trust*, 1–8; Johnson, *The Gospel Developed*, in *Polity*, 178. Johnson identifies these as baptism, teaching and doctrine, and breaking of bread.

34 Dever, "John L. Dagg," 52, 63.

"A Christian Church . . . is an assembly of believers in Christ, organized into a body, according to the Holy Scriptures, for the worship and service of God."[35] P. H. Mell, a pastor, author, theologian, and professor who contributed greatly to the growing SBC, says a church is made up of baptized believers "who are able to meet together in one place, and who observe the ordinances and maintain the worship of God."[36]

As the SBC formed its official faith statements—the BFM versions of 1925, 1963, and 2000—it did not specifically mention marks of a church. However, Article VI provides a definition, which states,

> A New Testament church of the Lord Jesus Christ is an auton-omous local congregation of baptized believers, associated by covenant in the faith and fellowship of the gospel; observing the two ordinances of Christ, governed by His laws, exercising the gifts, rights, and privileges invested in them by His Word, and seeking to extend the gospel to the ends of the earth.[37]

---

35   Dagg, *A Treatise on Church Order*, 74.

36   Cathcart, *Baptist Encyclopedia*, in *Polity*, 406–7; Mell, *Corrective Church*, in *Polity*, 443.

37   "The Baptist Faith and Message," *Southern Baptist Convention*. The full text of the three versions, when regarding local congregations, are as follows.
    1925: "A church of Christ is a congregation of baptized believers, associated by covenant in the faith and fellowship of the gospel; observing the ordinances of Christ, governed by his laws, and exercising the gifts, rights, and privileges invested in them by his word, and seeking to extend the gospel to the ends of the earth. Its Scriptural officers are bishops, or elders, and deacons."
    1963: "A New Testament church of the Lord Jesus Christ is a local body of baptized believers who are associated by covenant in the faith and fellowship of the gospel, observing the two ordinances of Christ, committed to His teachings, exercising the gifts, rights, and privileges invested in them by His Word, and seeking to extend the gospel to the ends of the earth. This church is an autonomous body, operating through democratic processes under the Lordship of Jesus Christ. In such a congregation, members are equally responsible. Its Scriptural officers are pastors and deacons."
    2000: "A New Testament church of the Lord Jesus Christ is an autonomous local congregation of baptized believers, associated by covenant in the faith and fellowship of the gospel; observing the two ordinances of Christ, governed by His laws, exercising the gifts, rights, and privileges invested in them by His Word, and seeking to extend the gospel to the ends of the earth. Each congregation operates under the Lordship of Christ through democratic processes. In such a congregation each member is responsible and accountable to Christ as Lord. Its scriptur-al officers are that of pastors/elders/overseers and deacons. While both men and

While these ideas seem nebulous, Herschel Hobbs, who chaired the committee tasked with the writing of the BFM 1963, and who was one of the most influential shapers of Southern Baptists in the twentieth century, writes in 1964, "The church 'local' is made up of baptized believers who are banded together to observe the ordinances, exercise spiritual discipline, and carry out the Great Commission."[38] Reworded, this shows the influential Hobbs considered a church to be a group of believers gathered together, possibly with organization, for teaching of the Word, evangelism, practicing church discipline, and observing the ordinances.

This analysis shows that while the discussion of the marks of the church is fluid, it has consistently included a people who are joined together by covenant and the practices of preaching the Word, observing the ordinances, and practicing church discipline. Therefore, it is clear that these three create a core trio of marks that are widely accepted. However, the question is still not settled. About correct preaching and proper observance of the ordinances, Hammett comments, "They are clearly an essential part of the church's life but do not go to the heart of the church's nature." He continues to note that the improper practice of these "will hinder the church's health and weaken its ministry, but it does not necessarily invalidate the church, unless the impropriety compromises the message of the gospel."[39] Hammett notes that these two marks were selected primarily as a reaction of the Reformers to the abuses of the Roman Catholic Church, and that both marks function as two goals for which healthy churches can strive.[40] The point is that the definition of "right preaching" and "proper observance of the ordinances" will be defined differently by churches of different confessional backgrounds, for example, Baptists and Methodists. Yet, a church of either denomination may still be considered a true church, composed of true believers in Jesus Christ.

Therefore, the conversation in this book moving forward will not identify these, and other elements, as essential marks of a church, but as

---

women are gifted for service in the church, the office of pastor/elder/overseer is limited to men as qualified by Scripture" ("Comparison Chart," SBC).

38   Dockery, "Herschel H. Hobbs," 216; Hobbs, What Baptists Believe, 77.

39   Hammett, Biblical Foundations for Baptist Churches, 65.

40   Hammett, Biblical Foundations for Baptist Churches, 65.

important aspects of a healthy church. The essentials of a healthy church has been a focus of conversation since 1998, when Dever published the first edition of *Nine Marks of a Healthy Church*.[41] About the book, and the 9Marks organization that grew out of it, Justin Taylor at The Gospel Coalition writes, "I would be hard-pressed to think of any other ministry that has been more intentional in helping Southern Baptists and evangelicals recover a healthy understanding of polity and ecclesiology, especially at a practical level."[42] By combining the concepts of church marks and indicators of church health, Dever seeks to turn the focus away from pragmatic church growth, which has dominated conversations about the church for decades, to a more biblically based model for church health.[43] His marks, which he makes clear are not *the* marks of a church, are expositional preaching, biblical theology, the gospel, a biblical understanding of conversion, a biblical understanding of evangelism, a biblical understanding of church membership, biblical church discipline, a concern for discipleship and growth, and biblical church leadership. Dever's point is that while a church can exist without some of these, it is not a healthy church.[44]

Dever has not been alone in identifying attributes of a healthy church. In the last two decades, many scholars, pastors, and organizations have provided lists of healthy church attributes.[45] One such organization is the International Mission Board (IMB), the international missions arm of the SBC. The IMB published "12 Characteristics of a Healthy Church," which they use as a gauge for health in their church planting efforts.[46] Not

---

41 Dever, *Nine Marks of a Healthy Church*. This original version was a pamphlet, which has been expanded many times to the full text it is now. Dever is a major contributor in the area of Baptist ecclesiology, which is why he is referenced so often in this section, and the sections that follow.

42 Taylor, "Mark Dever's Original Letter."

43 Dever, *Nine Marks of a Healthy Church*, 20–23, 28–32.

44 Dever, *Nine Marks of a Healthy Church*, 7, 28. The two marks Dever includes are right preaching and right administration of the ordinances. He also adds that correct church discipline inherently grows out of the correct practice of the Lord's Supper.

45 For examples, see: "Ten Leading Indicators of a Healthy Church," *Evangelical Free Church of America*; Rainer and Akin, *Vibrant Church*; Stetzer and Rainer, *Transformational Church*. Thom Rainer even has health indicators he predicts for churches in 2029: Rainer, "The Healthy Church in 2029."

46 Platt, "12 Characteristics of a Healthy Church."

coincidentally, these twelve traits were developed by David Platt, former president of the IMB, who was highly influenced by Dever's *Nine Marks of a Healthy Church.*[47] These twelve traits are biblical evangelism, discipleship, membership, leadership, teaching/preaching, ordinances, worship, prayer, fellowship, accountability/discipline, giving, and mission.[48] This list represents an expansion of healthy church characteristics that goes even further than Dever's nine, and much further than even the most robust historical understanding of the marks of the church.[49]

Using a combined and modified list of Dever's "nine marks" and the IMB's "twelve characteristics," the following eleven chapters will explore eleven characteristics of a healthy church. Each section will provide a summary of biblical foundation for the trait, will show how congregational churches have historically understood each trait, will show how this trait fits within congregational ecclesiology, and will demonstrate how the trait can be applied in a multisite context.[50]

---

47   "About David Platt," *Radical.* Platt wrote the foreword to the third edition of *Nine Marks of a Healthy Church,* in which he notes how influential the book has been in his ministry (Platt, "Foreword," 9–12).

48   "12 Characteristics of a Healthy Church," *IMB.*

49   This is not to imply that this book, Mark Dever, or the IMB would suggest that historical churches that might not have included all twelves aspects of a "healthy" church in their descriptions of the church were unhealthy. These simply reflect what many within in SBC circles consider essential aspects of a healthy church.

50   As these are widely accepted as biblical characteristics of a healthy church, only a brief summary of the biblical warrant will be included for each characteristic. It is not the purpose of this book to formulate a full expression for each characteristic. For a more complete exposition of each aspect see Allison, *Sojourners and Strangers.*

CHAPTER 5

PREACHING

PREACHING THE WORD OF GOD is an essential in a church. Without the centrality of the Word, a church will not be able to fulfill its mission of evangelism and discipleship. In Matthew 16:18, following Peter's confession that Jesus was the Christ, Jesus says, "And I also say to you that you are Peter, and on this rock I will build my church . . . " To most interpreters outside the Roman Catholic Church, the "rock" upon which Jesus would build the church was the confession of Peter that Jesus is the Messiah.[1] Commenting on this passage, Malcolm Yarnell writes, "The foundation of the church is Jesus Christ, and the apostles, including Peter, share in that foundation alongside the prophets as inspired witnesses to the Word that is now our Bible."[2] This reveals a foundational element of a church, as has been shown previously, that has consistently been a mark of the church for centuries is the centrality of preaching the Word of God.

---

1   Yarnell, "Upon This Rock I Will Build My Church," 48–55. It is beyond the scope of this book to address the Roman Catholic view of Peter's confession and papal succession derived from Peter holding the "keys to the church." Martin Luther wrote the earliest major critique of papal succession in *Against the Roman Papacy, An Institution of the Devil* (1545).
2   Yarnell, "Upon This Rock I Will Build My Church," 55.

Paul makes it clear that the foundational element of faith is the Word of God. He says in Romans 10:17, "So faith comes from what is heard, and what is heard comes through the message about Christ"(CSB).[3] When Paul recounts his initial evangelism in Corinth, he reminds the Corinthian believers, "When I came to you, brothers and sisters, announcing the mystery of God to you, I did not come with brilliance of speech or wisdom. I decided to know nothing among you except Jesus Christ and him crucified" (1 Cor. 2:1–2, CSB). Paul recognizes the foundational element of the church is not methodology, but the simple message of the gospel.[4] He adds that the foundation of faith, and of the church, is nothing other than Jesus Christ. He writes, "For no one can lay any foundation other than what has been laid down. That foundation is Jesus Christ" (1 Cor. 3:11, CSB). Peter says in 1 Peter 2:6–8 that Jesus and his word are the cornerstones of faith and the church.[5] These passages show that the Word of God, specifically the message of the gospel that is the central focus of that Word, is the foundation of faith, and ultimately the foundation of the church.[6]

However, the existence of this Word is not that which identifies or establishes a church. As Calvin states, "Wherever we see the Word of God purely *preached and heard*, . . . there, it is not to be doubted, a church of God exists."[7] In order for a healthy church to exist, the gospel must be preached by a preacher, and it must be heard and acted upon by a listener. Luther considered preaching the Word of God to be the central aspect of the church, higher than any other. He writes about the dual requirements of preaching the Word and hearing the Word, noting, "Christian people are recognized by their possession of the holy Word of God. . . . And even if there were no other sign than this alone, it would suffice to prove that a Christian, holy people must exist there, for God's Word cannot be without God's people, and conversely, God's people cannot be without God's Word."[8]

---

3   Dunn, *Romans 9–16*, 623, 630; Murray, *The Epistle to the Romans*, 60–61. Unless otherwise noted, all Scripture references will be from the Christian Standard Bible.
4   Vaughn and Lea, *1 Corinthians*, 32–33; Verbrugge, "1 Corinthians," 2.c.
5   Blum, "1 Peter," 228; Verbrugge, "1 Corinthians," 3.a.
6   Dever, *Nine Marks of a Healthy Church*, 53–54.
7   Calvin, *Institutes*, 1658, emphasis added.
8   Luther, "On the Councils and the Church," 422–24.

As has been noted previously, the Reformers, and those who came after, emphasized the "right" preaching of the Word. Allison similarly concurs on this point when he writes, "Thus, the church must proclaim—clearly, urgently, persuasively... —the Word of God.... the church must preach the Word of God—'without confusion, without change,' without compromise—as its first order of business."[9]

HISTORICAL PERSPECTIVES ON PREACHING[10]

Baptist churches have historically emphasized biblical preaching. Dagg says God is glorified when biblical preaching takes place, writing, "God is honored when his word is so expounded to the people, that they not only hear the sound with the ear, but receive the meaning of it in their understandings, and feel its power in their hearts."[11] In the foreword to his collection of lectures to young pastors, Charles Spurgeon highlights the immeasurable worth of correctly interpreting and preaching the Bible. He writes,

> The College... aims at training preachers rather than scholars. To develop the faculty of ready speech, to help them to understand the word of God, and to foster the spirit of consecration, courage, and confidence in God, are objects so important that we put all other matters into a secondary position. If a student should learn a thousand things, and yet fail to preach the gospel acceptably, his College... course will have missed its true design.[12]

John Broadus emphasizes the necessary skill of preaching in a way that connects with people, writing,

---

9   Allison, *Sojourners and Strangers*, 435. Allison adds that a "persistent critique" of many churches is that they have significant biblical illiteracy in the pew as well as in the pulpit. This illiteracy results in poor homiletics, which in turn results in poor preaching.
10 Let the reader remember, this project was originally a written specifically with Southern Baptist polity, history, and doctrine in mind. The examples in this section, and in similar sections in the next ten chapters, include examples from and references to Baptist authors and history. Even so, the principles remain valid for non-Baptist churches as well.
11 Dagg, *A Treatise on Church Order*, 240.
12 Spurgeon, *Lectures to My Students*, iv.

That which is not interesting and impressive cannot be the full expression of warm devotion, and then the expression, by a general law, reacts upon the feeling. Externals, however they may appeal to aesthetic sentiment, can never create devotion; but animated and earnest expression will strengthen devotion, and this may be achieved while carefully avoiding the danger of formalism.[13]

In his lectures, Spurgeon emphasizes being faithful to the whole counsel of God, adding,

If we speak as ambassadors for God, we need never complain of want of matter, for our message is full to overflowing. The entire gospel must be presented from the pulpit; the whole faith once delivered to the saints must be proclaimed by us. The truth as it is in Jesus must be instructively declared, so that the people may not merely hear, but *know*, the joyful sound.[14]

These words from Spurgeon represent the importance of biblical preaching that is a heartfelt principle of Baptists, and numerous others, throughout history.[15] E. C. Dargan, like Spurgeon, captures the importance of training men in the ability to preach the Word well. He writes,

We cannot be wrong in inferring from these hints that a previous and continued training for the preacher's task would, in Paul's view, include attention to the manner as well as the content of his message. . . . there are clear indications that the ability to present the truth of God effectively in human speech is both exemplified and enjoined by the highest authority.[16]

---

13   Broadus, *The Preparation and Delivery of Sermons*, 511–12.
14   Spurgeon, *Lectures to My Students*, 1.72.
15   Norman, *The Baptist Way*, 11.
16   Dargan, *The Art of Preaching*, 27.

Andrew Fuller, attempting to capture the gravity of the preaching responsibility, writes, "A pulpit seems an awful place! An opportunity for addressing a company of mortals on their eternal interests. Oh how important! We preach for eternity!"[17] Broadus emphasizes preaching the true Word of God is a way of remaining true to Jesus, saying, "To teach our distinctive views is not only a duty to ourselves, to our fellow Christians, and to the unbelieving world, but it is a duty we owe to Christ; it is a matter of simple loyalty to him."[18] He also acknowledges biblical preaching is central to the overall ministry of the church, writing, "The great appointed means of spreading the good tidings of salvation through Christ is preaching—words spoken whether to the individual or to the assembly. And this, nothing can supersede."[19]

There has also been historic unity on the central topic of biblical preaching, the gospel of Jesus Christ, exemplified by Paul when he writes, "I decided to know nothing among you except Jesus Christ and him crucified" (1 Cor. 2:2, CSB). L. R. Scarborough writes,

> He who side-tracks the gospel in his pulpit misses his greatest opportunity, belittles his call and shames his ordination. It is by the "foolishness of preaching," not by foolish preaching, God is to save the world. The gospel is what God ordained us to preach. The heart of the gospel is Jesus Christ. The glory of Christ is his Cross. . . . The Crossless . . . preacher is a Christ-less preacher.[20]

A. T. Robertson says, "Give us men in the pulpit today above all things that fear God and think the gospel good enough for anybody and make no apology for preaching it."[21] B. H. Carroll says, "If I take up anything else to preach I cannot come in power. I cannot come in the Holy Ghost. I cannot come with a well-grounded conviction that it will do you any

17   Fuller, *The Diary of Andrew Fuller, 1780–1801*, 24.
18   Broadus, "The Duty of Baptists," 152.
19   Broadus, *The Preparation and Delivery of Sermons*, 2.
20   Scarborough, *My Conception of the Gospel Ministry*, 59.
21   Robertson, "Preaching and Scholarship," 159.

good. That is why I cannot do it. But put me to preaching this Christ crucified, and I can preach that with much assurance, for I know that it is the power of God unto salvation."[22]

Biblical sermons are sermons based on the content and the authority of the Bible. J. M. Pendleton writes, "A sermon ought to be vital with Scriptural . . . truth—the truth as it is in Jesus."[23] Dargan writes, "Preaching rests for its authority upon the Holy Scriptures . . . as the Word of God."[24] George Truett declares, "The Word of God is to be proclaimed. The Word of God is to be avowed. The Word of God is to be declared. The Word of God is not bound. The Word of God will take care of itself, if only it be faithfully proclaimed."[25] Broadus makes the distinction between biblical preaching and merely giving a philosophical talk, writing, "You will promote the healthier tendencies by preaching the definite doctrines of the Bible, and by abundant exposition of the Bible text. Men grow weary of mere philosophical speculation and vague sentiment, and will listen again to the sweet and solemn voice of the Word of God."[26]

In a statement identifying the essential aspect of biblical authority for Christians, churches, pastors, and the preaching of the Word, Jimmy Draper writes, "The view of the church down through the centuries, almost without exception, until recent times, has been that the Bible is the authoritative, infallible, inerrant Word of God and that it is our sole source of authority in every given area of human understanding. We have seen that this is true of Baptists as well as other Christians."[27]

The authority of the Word of God has been held in the highest respect. Church leaders have based their teaching on that perfect Word, and they have considered the essential message of preaching to be the gospel of Jesus Christ in his life, death, burial, and resurrection. A pastor's ability and faithfulness in preaching such biblical messages is essential to the

---

22   Carroll, *The Supper and Suffering of our Lord*, 130.
23   Pendleton, *Theological*, 36.
24   Dargan, *The Art of Preaching*, 238.
25   Truett, in *A Quest for Souls*, 68.
26   Broadus, *Lectures on the History of Preaching*, 232.
27   Draper, *Authority*, 65.

health of a local church, and a local church must accept nothing less than such faithful preaching.

PREACHING IN MULTISITE CHURCHES

Multisite advocates have not specifically addressed the aspect of rightly preaching the Word of God, but they have emphasized the importance of preaching within the strategy.[28] Larry Osborne, pastor of North Coast Church in Vista, California, emphasizes in a multisite context that preaching carries an additional level of importance, as he considers it to be the primary medium that unites the campuses.[29] In a multisite model that uses video teaching, a preacher with a commitment to biblical preaching can preach to multiple campuses. This is a simpler way of ensuring biblical preaching, because only one primary pastor must faithfully preach the text each week, and it can also serve as a visible representation that the church places a high value on quality, biblical preaching.[30] This does not mean, however, that live teaching cannot provide quality, biblical preaching. Jimmy Scroggins, lead pastor of Family Church in West Palm Beach, Florida, a church with thirteen campuses, places a high value on biblical preaching. He develops preaching schedules and messages along with his campus pastors. A once-a-year planning retreat helps develop the overall direction of the year's messages and ensures the pastors understand the vision and direction of the sermon series. A weekly preparation meeting allows the pastors to collaborate on the upcoming messages. The team develops the message outline and main idea that will be preached consistently across all campuses. Outside of the outline and main idea, each preacher has the freedom to develop the rest of the message in a

---

28   Surratt, Ligon, and Bird, *A Multi-Site Church Road Trip*, 96. The authors include preaching as an aspect of a biblical church. See Taylor, "A Study of Sermon Preparation Methods."

29   McConnell, *Multi-Site*, 204; "About Larry," *Larry Osborne*.

30   House and Allison, *MultiChurch*, 59. Of course, having a single preacher preaching to multiple locations also creates the risk that a pastor who does not preach the Word faithfully will spread that message to multiple campuses. Therefore, it is essential that the pastor be accountable for preaching a biblically faithful message, and that the congregation hold him to that standard. This must be the same expectation for all churches, regardless if they are multisite or not, or have live preaching or video preaching at their campuses.

way that flows out of his unique personality and that matches the unique context of his local congregation.[31] For Gregg Allison, live preaching is a fulfillment of the biblical expectation of a pastor, as not only does his doctrine serve as a guide for the church members, but his life lived out among the body serves as an accessible model for the church members.[32] House and Allison highlight the importance of preaching as a place where the church shows itself as a bearer of the image of God and the united body of Christ.[33]

Preaching, whether in person or via video, must be grounded in the Word of God. This element must remain consistent, even as the delivery method or the preaching style may vary. Ed Stetzer and Mike Dodson write, "Many will say that there is only one biblical form of preaching, but they miss the point. There are many ways to communicate through preaching, but all of them require a biblical foundation and an appropriate form from which to communicate."[34] This simply means that any sermon must be first of all grounded in the biblical text alone, regardless of whether the sermon is verse-by-verse, topical, narrative, thematic, live, video, or any combination of these forms.[35] All of these variations may be biblically based and true to the Word of God.[36]

This evaluation shows historically, and currently, biblical preaching has been considered an essential component of a healthy church. Therefore, a healthy church, whether single-site or multisite, must be committed to providing preaching that is faithful to the biblical text in interpretation and application. While this is an essential task every church must address, multisite churches will have to take particular care to ensure biblical preaching is taking place not just in one location, but across multiple locations. If this is done via video delivery, a single pastor may control

---

31   Scroggins and Wright, "How Family Church Does Multisite."
32   Allison, "Theological Defense of Multi-Site," 9.
33   House and Allison, *MultiChurch*, 99.
34   Stetzer and Dodson, *Comeback Churches*, 93.
35   Stetzer and Dodson, *Comeback Churches*, 93–94.
36   Smith, "The Essential Elements of Text-Driven Preaching"; Vines and Shaddix, *Power in the Pulpit*, 44–47. The common term for a biblically based sermon, where the content of the biblical text determines the content of the sermon, is "expository preaching." A new term that has also become popular is "text-driven preaching."

the biblical content and should faithfully preach the Word.[37] However, with live preaching, the senior pastor of the church must take particular care to ensure the campus preachers under his leadership are providing biblical content in their messages.[38] The specific church must decide which medium fits best in its context and its model. Whichever choice is made, the church and church leaders must ensure the preaching is biblically based.[39] This added burden is one multisite churches must be prepared to deal with but is not an insurmountable obstacle. Multisite churches can, and many do, provide biblical preaching across all of their campuses.

---

37   McConnell, *Multi-Site Churches*, 204.

38   Greear, "How Do You Prepare for Sermons?"; Scroggins and Wright, "How Family Church Does Multisite."

39   While I believe in-person preaching, or at least a hybrid of in-person and video, is the best model of multisite preaching, I will not make a conclusion on whether video preaching is biblical or not. I do recommend live, in-person preaching at each campus as a means of answering some valid multisite critiques. These are addressed in Part 3. For an evaluation of the biblical validity of video-based preaching, see Herrington, "A Theological and Philosophical Evaluation of Simulcast Preaching."

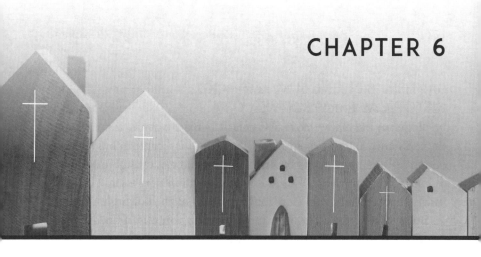

CHAPTER 6

THE ORDINANCES: BAPTISM AND THE LORD'S SUPPER

THE SECOND ASPECT OF A HEALTHY CHURCH, one which the Reformers, and many after, considered an essential mark of the church, is proper observance of the ordinances of baptism and the Lord's Supper. Protestant churches believe these were the two ordinances initiated by Christ and that they are to be perpetuated by churches.[1] They are "a symbolic act commanded by Jesus to signify that which Christ did to effect salvation from sin."[2]

---

1   Hammett, *Biblical Foundations for Baptist Churches*, 63–65.
2   Hobbs, *What Baptists Believe*, 82–83. It is beyond the scope of this book to address the different viewpoints on proper administration of the ordinances or the efficacy of the ordinances. For a good summary on these topics, please see Armstrong, *Understanding Four Views on Baptism*; Armstrong, *Understanding Four Views on the Lord's Supper*; Schreiner and Crawford, *The Lord's Supper*; Schreiner and Wright, *Believer's Baptism*.

　　This chapter works off the assumption that the ordinances are not dispensations of grace, but are significant, symbolic events commanded by Jesus. It assumes both are reserved to be practiced only by those who have made a personal profession of faith in Christ.

BAPTISM: BIBLICAL SUMMARY AND
HISTORICAL PERSPECTIVES

Baptism was a practice in first-century Judaism before Jesus initiated the ordinance at the end of his ministry. Christian baptism has its foundation in John's practice of baptism for repentance. Jesus gave authority to John's baptism when he submitted to it in the wilderness, as described in Matthew 3:13–17. He then commanded that those who became his disciples should also submit to the act of baptism out of obedience to him, as described in Matthew 28:18–20.[3]

In Luke's account of the Acts of the Apostles, it is apparent the disciples considered baptism to be an essential aspect of a believer's life in the early church. Peter commanded the new believers to be baptized following their repentance as they responded to his gospel message on the day of Pentecost (Acts 2:38, 41), as well as those who believed of the household of Cornelius the Centurion (Acts 10:46b–48). Philip's ministry in Samaria also resulted in people believing in Jesus and consequently being baptized (Acts 8:12–13, 36–39). Saul/Paul's process of conversion references his own baptism (Acts 9:18; 22:16), and after he began his missionary ministry, he consistently baptized new believers (Acts 16:15, 33; 18:8; 19:5).[4]

While the Lord's Supper appears to have been conducted in homes and whole church gatherings, the Bible is not specific about the early church's practice of baptism.[5] Acts 2:41 shows a likely mass baptism taking place as thousands were added into the church following Peter's evangelistic preaching.[6] Other examples show people baptized as households (Acts 16:15, 33), small groups (Acts 8:1–7), and individuals (Acts 8:36–39). There are no definitive descriptions of the location of baptisms, although baptismal pools, public baths, private pools, and natural bodies of water are likely places.[7] The baptisms are, however, clearly conducted and validated by a church leader, such as Peter, Philip, or Paul. Thus, it

---

3   Armstrong, "Introduction," in *Understanding Four Views on Baptism*, 13. This assumption is based on the view of believer's baptism, which this author considers to be the correct understanding of Christ's ordinance.
4   Nettles, "Baptist View," 28–38.
5   Akin, "The Meaning of Baptism," 65.
6   Schnabel, *Acts*, 161–68.
7   McGowan, *Ancient Christian Worship*, 144; Schnabel, *Acts*, 167–68.

is apparent that the authority and oversight of the church is an aspect of the early church's baptism.[8]

Baptism is an essential step in the life of a believer, commanded by Christ. It is an act of obedience on the part of a believer, which symbolizes the believer's identity with Christ and with Christ's death, burial, and resurrection. Baptism is also an initiation into a local church and therefore is to be administered under the oversight of a local church body and leadership. Baptism is also a prerequisite to taking the Lord's Supper, and as with the Lord's Supper, Baptist statements throughout the centuries have confirmed these beliefs.[9] Smyth's *Short Confession* of 1609 says, "That the church of Christ is a company of the faithful; baptized after confession of sin and of faith. . . . That baptism is the external sign of the remission of sins, of dying and of being made alive."[10] A 1651 English Baptist confession states, "That the way and manner of baptising . . . both before the death of Christ, and since his resurrection and ascension, was to go into the water, and to be baptised."[11] The New Hampshire Confession captures a full picture of these beliefs, stating, "That Christian Baptism . . . is the immersion of a believer in water, in the name of the Father, Son, and Spirit, to show forth in a solemn and beautiful emblem, our faith in a crucified, buried, and risen Saviour . . . with its purifying power; that it is prerequisite to the privileges of a church relation; and to the Lord's Supper."[12]

Others have written and preached their confirmation of these truths throughout the centuries. John Gill frequently defends the mode of baptism by immersion. He often writes about "proofs for immersion, taken

---

8   White, "What Makes Baptism Valid?," 116.
9   Wright, "Baptism in History, Theology, and the Church," 120–25.
10 Smyth, *Short Confession*, 101.
11 Lumpkin, *Baptist Confessions of Faith*, 182.
12 Lumpkin, *Baptist Confessions of Faith*, 366. The Baptist Faith and Message, in its three iterations, has been a rewording of this confessional definition (Lumpkin, *Baptist Confessions of Faith*, 361). The BFM 2000 reads, "Christian baptism is the immersion of a believer in water in the name of the Father, the Son, and the Holy Spirit. It is an act of obedience symbolizing the believer's faith in a crucified, buried, and risen Saviour . . . the believer's death to sin, the burial of the old life, and the resurrection to walk in newness of life in Christ Jesus. It is a testimony to his faith in the final resurrection of the dead. Being a church ordinance, it is prerequisite to the privileges of church membership and to the Lord's Supper" ("2000 Baptist Faith and Message," *Southern Baptist Convention*).

from the circumstances which attended the Baptism of John, Christ, and his Apostles."[13] He also argues from the meaning of the Greek *baptizo*, writing, "That the proper, primary, common, and natural sense of the Greek word [*baptizo*], is to *dip* or *plunge*, has been acknowledged by the greatest masters of that language."[14] Andrew Fuller writes plainly, "That Christian baptism is properly administered only by immersion, and to those who make a credible profession of faith in Christ, it is no part of our present design to prove. Addressing *you*, we shall take each of these particulars for granted."[15] Robertson writes, "If anything in the New Testament is clear, it is evident that the New Testament baptism is the immersion of the believer."[16] Pendleton adds, "Immersion is so exclusively the baptismal act, that without it there is no baptism."[17]

Baptism is a symbol of Jesus's death, burial, and resurrection, and that there is no salvific grace provided by the act. J. R. Graves, a vehement defender of believer's baptism, writes, "Baptism, then, was appointed to symbolize—1. The death, burial and resurrection of Christ, by which acts believers receive the benefits of his atonement; 2. That the recipient has, by faith, been vitally united with Christ, and received the benefits of his death, and will be raised with him in the likeness of his resurrection."[18]

James Boyce writes, "So far as [baptism and the Lord's Supper] are fitted to convey truth, or to impress duty, they are instrumental in regeneration. . . . But neither of them regenerates or confers regeneration."[19] Broadus writes, "baptism only represents regeneration and forgiveness like a picture. . . . The water signifies purification from sin, and the immersion signifies that we are dead to sin, and like Christ have been buried and risen again."[20]

That baptism is for believers only, as opposed to infant/child baptism before personal belief, has been a foundational Baptist belief as well.

---

13   Gill, "A Defence . . . of a Book," 177, emphasis original.
14   Gill, "The Ancient Mode of Baptizing," 198.
15   Fuller, "Practical Uses of Christian Baptism," 339, emphasis original.
16   Robertson, *Modern Scholarship and the Form of Baptism*, 3.
17   Pendleton, *Church Manual*, 64.
18   Graves, *The Acts of Christian Baptism*, 43.
19   Boyce, *Abstract of Systematic Theology*, 377.
20   Broadus, "A Catechism of Bible Teaching," 233.

After quoting various Scriptures, Dagg writes, "All these quotations from Scripture harmonize perfectly with each other, and incontrovertibly establish the truth, that repentance and faith are necessary qualifications for baptism."[21] Pendleton agrees, writing, "Faith is a trustful acceptance of Christ as the Saviour. . . . On a profession of this 'one faith' in the 'one Lord,' the 'one baptism' is administered. Baptism is therefore a profession of faith. . . . If we put faith before the Lord, and baptism before faith, we invert the inspired order."[22]

The baptismal ordinance belongs to the church, initiates a believer into the church, and provides access to the Lord's Supper. Fuller writes, "Is baptism requisite? If it be so, it must belong to the church to judge whether the candidate has been baptized or not."[23] Graves comments, "Christ has also appointed baptism to be the one and only rite of initiation into his visible churches . . . an organization not a church, though all its members were Christians, has no authority to administer the ordinances of Christ's house."[24] Pendleton echoes his comment on immersion, writing, "a believer in Christ is so exclusively the subject of baptism, that without such a subject there is no baptism."[25]

BAPTISM IN MULTISITE CHURCHES

Multisite advocates have said very little about baptism and its practice in multisite churches.[26] Mark Driscoll recounts a stirring example of an Easter Sunday multisite baptismal service. Following a message he preached via live feed that morning, each campus held a baptismal service where people could come forward for baptism. Each campus experienced examples of people coming to faith and being baptized, and their baptism was followed by sharing in the Lord's Supper with the church body.[27]

---

21 Dagg, *A Treatise on Church Order*, 70.
22 Pendleton, *Distinctive Principles of Baptists*, 113.
23 Fuller, "The Admission of Unbaptized Persons," 514.
24 Graves, *The Acts of Christian Baptism*, 6, 7.
25 Pendleton, *Church Manual*, 64.
26 Surratt, Ligon, and Bird, *A Multi-Site Church Road Trip*, 96. The authors include "rightly administered sacraments" in their list of requirements for biblical churches.
27 Driscoll and Breshears, *Vintage Church*, 128–29.

Gregg Allison considers baptism to be an initiatory rite into a local church and believes baptism is to be administered by the church itself following a credible profession of faith. He says the church leaders do not have to perform the baptism themselves, but they should oversee the process and make sure the celebration is done properly.[28] He makes no statement regarding the appropriate settings for baptism, as to whether it must be done before a gathering of the whole church, or if it can be done before a smaller group of the church.

Considering baptism's importance in the church, multisite churches need a method that is biblically faithful and practically applicable. This is especially important in congregational churches, which view baptism as an initiatory rite into a local body of believers.[29] In multisite churches, baptism must be conducted in a way that maintains the authority and verification of the local church, and it should be done in a way that maintains baptism's role as an initiation into the body of believers.[30] For a multisite church, that authority and initiation must be credibly extended to each campus through the leadership of the campus pastor, pastoral staff, and/ or elders. The authority and initiation must be verified by the representative church membership of that location. As has been shown above, the full gathering of the church is not necessary to verify a baptism and its validity, although, as Thomas White says, "Such an important profession should occur in front of as many members of the church as possible."[31] Therefore, while the whole church does not have to be present, baptism is still best conducted when a large number of the church can gather to validate and celebrate the baptism.

Therefore, multisite churches, like all churches, should place a high value on the public baptism of new believers. One option is to have baptism opportunities as a part of the church worship gatherings, as is typical of many churches with a built in or portable baptistry. These baptisms can, and should, be conducted at each campus as the new believer is being incorporated into that segment of the church family. Another option for

---

28   Allison, *Sojourners and Strangers*, 356, 363.
29   Nettles, "Baptist View," 25.
30   White, "What Makes Baptism Valid?," 112–13.
31   White, "What Makes Baptism Valid?," 113.

multisite churches that want to demonstrate the overall unity of the whole-church family is for multisite churches to have periodic whole-church worship and fellowship celebrations at which time new believers can be baptized before the whole church. Similarly, churches that use livestream can incorporate their baptismal celebration into the worship stream so all campuses can observe and celebrate the baptism together. Regardless of the model, the church must emphasize that baptism is an initiation into the church—both the campus and the whole church. For Baptist multisite churches, it must also clearly convey the symbolic meaning of identifying with Christ in his death, burial, and resurrection.

THE LORD'S SUPPER: BIBLICAL SUMMARY AND HISTORICAL PERSPECTIVES

Jesus initiated the Lord's Supper on the night of his betrayal as he gathered with his disciples over a meal. Matthew describes the scene in Matthew 26:26–28: "As they were eating, Jesus took bread, blessed and broke it, gave it to the disciples, and said, 'Take and eat it; this is my body.' Then he took a cup, and after giving thanks, he gave it to them and said, 'Drink from it, all of you. For this is my blood of the covenant, which is poured out for many for the forgiveness of sins.'"

The apostle Paul adds in 1 Corinthians 11:24–25 that Jesus instructed the disciples to take both the bread and cup "in remembrance of me." It is Paul, in verse 20 of this passage, who identifies this ceremony as "the Lord's Supper." This Supper, at a most basic understanding agreeable to all denominations, is "a sacred act of communion, remembrance, and thanksgiving."[32]

The Lord's Supper, as practiced by the early church, is described only a few times in the New Testament.[33] In 1 Corinthians, Paul provides the most detailed treatment of the subject, describing the process of the original Lord's Supper and how the church should act as they gather to share in the Supper (11:17–35). Paul also includes a brief description about

---

32   Armstrong, "Introduction," in *Understanding Four Views on the Lord's Supper*, 15. Many denominations believe it is more than this, but this is a foundational starting point for the discussion.

33   Hammett, *Biblical Foundations for Baptist Churches*, 278.

the shared, communal aspect of the Supper in 10:16–18.[34] The book of Acts also mentions "breaking bread" in the context of community gatherings of the church.[35] "Breaking bread" in Acts 2:42, 46, and 20:7, 11 have generally been understood to be references to the Lord's Supper, while the mention in 27:35 refers to an ordinary meal.[36] Everett Ferguson suggests that the terms are sometimes ambiguous, and the context must decide whether the Lord's Supper is in view. When Paul sat down to "break bread" in Acts 20:7–11, Ferguson states, the context signifies a normal meal. He says "broke bread" in Acts 2:46 is not as clear, and could be interpreted either way, but that the opposite is true of Acts 2:42. The language there shows "the breaking of bread" refers to a ceremonial meal.[37] F. F. Bruce writes that even the mention of "the breaking of bread" in Acts 2:42 cannot be absolutely determined lexically. However, he states the Lord's Supper is probably intended because the act of breaking bread is trivial, yet it is mentioned with great emphasis suggesting it was the significant part of the meal.[38] Quoting Rudolf Otto, he adds, "But it could only be significant when it was a 'signum,' viz., of Christ's being broken in death."[39] Andrew McGowan, commenting on Acts 2:42, says,

> We lack details of these elements, but one thing in particular is surprising relative to more recent patterns of worship: Christians met for meals. A distinctive meal tradition—here called the "breaking of bread"—was not a social event additional to worship, or a programmatic attempt to create fellowship among the Christians, but the regular form of Christian gathering. These assemblies . . . were of course the forerunners of what Christians have known as the Eucharist, Lord's Supper, Holy Communion, or Mass.[40]

---

34 Schreiner, "The Lord's Supper in the Bible," 139–42.
35 Acts 2:42, 46; 20:7, 11; 27:35. It is also used in Luke 22:19; 24:30, 35.
36 Armstrong, "Introduction," 13–14; Hammett, *Biblical Foundations for Baptist Churches*, 278; Moore, "The Baptist View," 36; Schreiner, "The Lord's Supper in the Bible," 138.
37 Ferguson, "The Lord's Supper and Love Feast," 29–30.
38 Bruce, *The Acts of the Apostles*, 132.
39 Otto, *The Kingdom of God and the Son of Man*, 315.
40 McGowan, *Ancient Christian Worship*, 19.

Schreiner notes the usual consensus that Acts 2 and 20 refer to the Lord's Supper, noting, "the breaking of the bread at the Last Supper clearly symbolizes Jesus' death, where the broken bread symbolizes the breaking of his body for the salvation and forgiveness of his people."[41] He says the house gatherings in Acts 2:42 and 46 point to a worship context, thus indicating a proper place to celebrate the Lord's Supper. He says Luke mentioning the circumstances of the gathering in Acts 20:7, "On the first day of the week, we assembled to break bread" (CSB), suggests a formal setting gathered on the day of Jesus's resurrection, where a celebration of the Lord's Supper would be warranted.[42]

Baptists view the Lord's Supper as a symbolic memorial of Christ's sacrificial death, and have generally believed it is to be given only to a person following his or her baptism. Their statements have echoed this belief throughout the centuries. An Anabaptist confession from 1524 states, "The Mass is not a sacrifice but a memorial of the death of Christ. . . . As often as such a memorial is celebrated, shall the death of our Lord be preached."[43] John Smyth writes in his *Short Confession* of 1609, "That the Lord's Supper is the external sign of the communion of Christ, and of the faithful amongst themselves by faith and love."[44] The Second London Confession acknowledges the Supper is for believers only, and also clarifies that it is a memorial, stating, "In [the Lord's Supper] Christ is not offered up to his Father, nor any real sacrifice made at all, for remission of sin of the quick or dead; but only a memorial of that one offering up of himself, upon the cross . . . once for all."[45] The BFM states, "The Lord's Supper is a symbolic act of obedience whereby members of the church, through partaking of the bread and the fruit of the vine, memorialize the death of the Redeemer and anticipate His second coming."[46]

Many in history have agreed with these confessional statements in their writing and preaching. J. L. Reynolds writes of the Lord's Supper,

---

41   Schreiner, "The Lord's Supper in the Bible," 138.
42   Schreiner, "The Lord's Supper in the Bible," 138–39. This book will work on the assumption that the breaking of bread in Acts 2 and 20 refer to the Lord's Supper.
43   Friedberger et al., *Eighteen Dissertations*, 20.
44   Smyth, *Shorter Confession*, 101.
45   Lumpkin, *Baptist Confessions of Faith*, 292–93.
46   "2000 Baptist Faith and Message," *Southern Baptist Convention*.

"It is simply commemorative, and might be styled a symbolic sermon on the death of the Redeemer."[47] Carroll confirms its purpose as a memorial to be shared by believers only, saying, "That this is bread and bread only, and wine and wine only; that it is not a means of grace; that there is no virtue in it; that it is merely a memorial, simply that, nothing more . . . and that it should not be given to people outside of the church, i.e., to individuals."[48] He also states its intended purpose, saying,

> The Lord's table; it speaks about the Lord, because all of its lessons are about the Lord, and the lessons are three-fold: lessons of the past; lessons of the present; lessons of the future. So far as it is of the past, it is Memory . . . so far as it is of the future, it is Hope . . . so far as it is of the present, it is the spirit of thankfulness, it is the spirit of faith, and it is the spirit of joy.[49]

There are requirements to participate in the Lord's Supper, the most important of which is to be a true believer, and the second of which is to have been baptized as a believer by immersion. Pendleton captures this belief, writing, "It would be vastly inconsistent for an impenitent sinner to sit down at the Lord's Table and professedly celebrate his death. . . . Impenitence is surely a disqualification for a place at the table of the Lord. Penitence is a qualification. . . . There is, however, a ritual qualification for the Lord's Supper. . . . Baptism is that qualification."[50]

Broadus agrees, saying, "Who ought to partake of the Lord's Supper? Those ought to partake of the Lord's Supper who have believed in Christ, and have been baptized, and are trying to live in obedience to Christ's commands."[51] Baptists have also agreed that the Lord's Supper belongs to a local church and is to be given under the authority of a local church.[52]

---

47   Reynolds, "Church Polity," 389.
48   Carroll, *The Supper and Suffering of Our Lord*, 20.
49   Carroll, *The Supper and Suffering of Our Lord*, 33.
50   Pendleton, *Ecclesiological*, 343, 346.
51   Broadus, "A Catechism of Bible Teaching," 233.
52   There is disagreement, even within Baptist circles, on how to determine which believers may participate in a local church's communion observance. There are three views, each of which adds an additional requirement for someone to participate in a Lord's Sup-

Pendleton writes, "As the Lord's Supper is a church ordinance it is not proper to administer it to persons in their individual capacity—for example to the sick at their homes."[53] Dagg writes, "The rite was designed to be social. . . . It could not serve as a token of fellowship between the disciples of Christ, if it were performed in solitude. . . . The rite should be celebrated by the church, in public assembly."[54] Carroll ties the requirements back to the Word of God, specifically Christ, stating, "It follows that if the Lord has a table, if the Lord instituted an ordinance, the Lord puts it where He wants it. The Lord prescribes the terms of admissions to it and nobody else."[55]

This brief analysis shows that the Lord's Supper is a memorial celebration of the sacrificial death of Christ on the cross.[56] It is to be a celebration of the death of Christ and its victory over sin on believers' behalf. It is to be observed by baptized believers in a gathering of the church body, under the authority of that local church.

---

per celebration. In open communion, the Lord's Supper is only restricted to believers. Believer's baptism is not required. Transient communion adds the requirement of believer's baptism. Close communion adds the requirement of membership in the specific local congregation that is celebrating the ordinance. This book will land in the middle, holding to the transient communion view. There is not enough space to provide a full argument for the case.

53   Pendleton, *Church Manual*, 90.

54   Dagg, *A Treatise on Church Order*, 212–13.

55   Carroll, *The Supper and Suffering of Our Lord*, 20.

56   Grace, "Early English Baptists' View of the Lord's Supper," 178. Some early Reformed Baptists accepted the spiritual presence view, believing Jesus was spiritually present in the elements. Yet they also stated it was a memorial and was not in any way a dispenser of grace (Allison, *Sojourners and Strangers*, 385). The London Confession of 1689 says, "Worthy recipients who outwardly partake of the visible elements in this ordinance also by faith inwardly receive and feed on Christ crucified and all the benefits of his death. They do so really and truly, yet not physically and bodily but spiritually. The body and blood of Christ are not present bodily or physically in the ordinance but spiritually to the faith of believers, just as the elements themselves are present to their outward senses." This shows an understanding of partaking spiritually in the body and blood of Christ. Yet, the confession also confirms, "In this ordinance Christ is not offered up to his Father, nor is any real sacrifice made at all for remission of sin of the living or the dead. It is only a memorial of the one offering Christ made of himself on the cross once for all" (Stan Reeves, ed., *The 1689 Baptist Confession of Faith in Modern English* [Cape Coral, FL: Founders, 2017], Article 30).

THE LORD'S SUPPER IN MULTISITE CHURCHES

Multisite church advocates have not addressed the Lord's Supper in great length.[57] Mark Driscoll writes that his church participated in the Lord's Supper in each worship service each weekend, including simultaneous communion celebrations at different campuses following a simulcast message. He also encouraged small groups to share the Supper in homes where they gathered.[58] This shows a perspective that the Lord's Supper is something that can be shared by the church gathered in part, but provides no comment on gathering the whole church for sharing in the Supper.[59]

In his discussion on the Lord's Supper, Gregg Allison emphasizes multiple times that communion should be reserved for whole church gatherings only. He writes the church should observe the Supper with "all its members" as "a united whole" and that "the Lord's Supper should be reserved for times when the entire church can gather together for its celebration." He adds, "An implication of my position is that those in sub-groups of the church. . . that are intended to be partial gatherings of the church's membership. . . should refrain from its observance."[60] It seems from this statement that Allison would recommend multisite churches to celebrate the Lord's Supper only in times when the whole church is gathered. However, in the same book, Allison describes his home church, Sojourn Church, as a multisite church "which distributes itself into weekly gatherings at five sites." About his church, he

---

57   Surratt, Ligon, and Bird, *A Multi-Site Church Road Trip*, 96. The authors include "rightly administered sacraments" in their description of biblical requirements for churches. Critics of multisite churches raise serious concerns about practicing the ordinances in multisite churches. These concerns will be considered in Part 3.

58   Driscoll and Breshears, *Vintage Church*, 122, 129. This book is not suggesting the Lord's Supper should be celebrated in small group gatherings outside of a worship assembly of the church.

59   Under Driscoll, Mars Hill held rare gatherings where it encouraged all campuses to come together. The last time they attempted this was in 2011, when they rented out Qwest Field to gather its nine campuses and an anticipated twenty thousand people for an Easter service. Under his leadership, Mars Hill Church grew to fifteen locations in five states, and had a weekly combined attendance of around thirteen thousand. While the idea of gathering people from such wide distances might be imaginable, it is not truly feasible (Cosper, "Who Killed Mars Hill?"; Tu, "Mars Hill Church to Hold Easter Service at Qwest Field"; Welch, "The Rise and Fall of Mars Hill Church.")

60   Allison, *Sojourners and Strangers*, 408.

says, "We promote this multisite structure for the very same reasons discussed above: preaching the gospel, *celebrating the Lord's Supper*, praying, giving, and the like."[61] He also mentions the church meets at various times in a local arena for the express purpose of gathering the whole church together. Even if it is assumed that the church shares communion at these whole-church gatherings, the church's stated purpose for multisite, specifically regarding celebrating the Lord's Supper, does not match Allison's viewpoint on how and when the Supper should be observed. More clarity would be appreciated regarding how Allison applies his view.[62]

Many multisite advocates, while not specifically addressing the Lord's Supper in multisite churches, do reveal that they consider it an acceptable practice to share the Lord's Supper in gatherings that are not gatherings of the whole church. J. D. Greear refers to house church gatherings where the Supper was celebrated together.[63] The authors of *The Multi-Site Church Revolution* (*MCR*) do not specifically reference the Lord's Supper, but they cite Aubrey Malphurs's book *Being Leaders*, where he describes city churches gathering in homes to celebrate the Lord's Supper.[64] Based on his reading of the new Jerusalem church's practice, Elmer Towns concludes that the early church only celebrated the Lord's Supper in homes, never in large gatherings.[65]

As churches move toward a multisite structure, they will have to carefully consider how they practice the Lord's Supper. The biblical account appears to show the early church celebrating the Lord's Supper in small groups as well as in gatherings of the whole church. This allows for

---

61 Allison, *Sojourners and Strangers*, 316, emphasis added.
62 Allison and Sojourn's multisite structure and descriptors has changed since he penned *Sojourners and Strangers* in 2012. As the House and Allison wrote *MultiChurch*, the church referred to its campuses as "churches." In *MultiChurch*, the authors say the church, a "multichurch," is a cooperative, "one church with multiple congregations or 'churches' in a set geographic area" (House and Allison, *MultiChurch*, 16). In an email from Brad House, he confirmed that Sojourn had transitioned to a collective of "interdependent churches," which technically takes them out of the true multisite category (Brad House, "Email Between Brad House and Dustin Slaton," August 5, 2020).
63 Greear, "A Pastor Defends His Multi-Site Church," 19.
64 Malphurs, *Being Leaders*, 24; Surratt, Ligon, and Bird, *Multi-Site Church Revolution*, 17.
65 Towns, *Today's Most Innovative Churches.*

flexibility in how the Supper is celebrated. However, if a church is to be faithful to the example of the early church, then whole church gatherings should also be a part of the church's ministry plan.[66] Celebrating the Lord's Supper should be a part of these whole church gatherings.

---

66   Gaines, "One Church in One Location," 2.

CHURCH MEMBERSHIP

A BIBLICAL VIEW AND PRACTICE of church membership is an essential health marker of any church. A basic definition of church membership is someone's "formal commitment to a local church."[1] Sadly, church membership and member participation has declined in the last fifty years, according to Mark Dever, who suggests that two thirds of the people on Southern Baptist churches' membership roles are non-attending members.[2] To reverse this trend, churches must return to biblical practices of membership. To do so, a proper understanding of biblical church membership must be in place; however, there is no specific Scripture passage that prescribes church membership as a requirement. Rather it is a conglomeration of various Scriptures in which participation in the church implies committed membership.[3]

Perhaps the clearest example of necessary committed membership is in 1 Corinthians 12–14. Paul describes the church as "the body of Christ," and the people within the church as "individual members of it." Thom Rainer says, "Members of a church comprise the whole and are

---

1   Merkle, "The Biblical Basis for Church Membership," 31–32.
2   Dever, "Regaining Meaningful Church Membership," 45.
3   Merkle, "The Biblical Basis for Church Membership," 32–33.

essential parts of it."[4] The Bible describes the church as a single "entity made up of multiple individuals," using descriptions such as families (Heb. 2:11), communities (Acts 2:41–47), a body and its parts (1 Cor. 12:12–31), and buildings (1 Peter 2:4–5). Believers are even said to be part of one another (Rom. 12:5).[5] A church should reflect these examples of unity.[6]

In addition to these descriptions of the church, the biblical expectation of membership is implied by the functions of the church. One function is accountability between church members and between members and their leaders. Membership is implied in Hebrews 13:17, where members are instructed to "obey your leaders and submit to them, since they keep watch over your souls as those who give an account." Without the commitment of membership to a local church, a Christian would not have an identified leader to which they should submit, and a pastor would not know for whom he is accountable.[7] This accountability feeds into church discipline, an aspect of a church so vital to its health that many, as shown in Part 1, have considered it a mark of a church. In Matthew 18:15–17, Jesus instructs the disciples to treat an unrepentant brother "like a Gentile and tax collector," meaning he is no longer considered a welcome part of their fellowship.[8] Paul is more explicit in 1 Corinthians 5:13 when he says to "remove the evil person from among you." The implication of these verses is that someone who was once a part of the group is being removed from the group.[9] Ed Stetzer says, "It is difficult to get around Scripture . . . when it talks about being brought into the body and also being put out of it."[10]

The ministry and mission of the church, an aspect of the church that cannot be delegated to any other organization, also implies membership.[11]

---

4   Rainer, *I Am a Church Member*, 11–12.
5   Dever, *The Church*, 4.1.
6   Stetzer, "Membership Matters."
7   Chandler, "Is Church Membership Biblical?"
8   Adams, *Handbook of Church Discipline*, 80. Also see Cheong, *God Redeeming His Bride*; Kimble, *That His Spirit May Be Saved*.
9   Merkle, "The Biblical Basis for Church Membership," 41–43.
10   Stetzer, "Membership Matters."
11   Dever, *The Church*, 4.3.

The spiritual gifts given to each individual by the Holy Spirit are given in order to be used within the community of believers (Eph. 4:11–13). Church members were added to the community of believers in Jerusalem, and the church in Antioch was instructed to send out Paul and Barnabas. These passages show the church identified people who were part of their groups, and they also commissioned, sent out, and supported people as representatives of their group.[12]

HISTORICAL PERSPECTIVES ON CHURCH MEMBERSHIP

Congregationalists have generally had strong views regarding church membership. Nathan Finn captures this clearly, writing, "Baptists affirmed a voluntary membership comprised of adult believers and organized around a covenantal ecclesiology."[13] More specifically, Hammett notes Baptists require members to be baptized believers, committed to—or covenanted with—the church body.[14] The BFM does not have a section on church membership but describes those who would be church members, stating, "A New Testament church of the Lord Jesus Christ is an autonomous local congregation of baptized believers, associated by covenant in the faith and fellowship of the gospel."[15]

The Second London Confession states, "The Members . . . of these Churches . . . are Saints . . . by calling, visibly manifesting and evidencing . . . their obedience unto that call of Christ."[16] Emphasizing the necessity of regenerate, baptized members, John Gill writes, "Such who are admitted into fellowship with a particular church of Christ, should be truly baptized in water, that is, by immersion, upon a profession of their faith."[17] In a very detailed description of these two requirements, B. H. Carroll says in a lecture,

---

12 Merkle, "The Biblical Basis for Church Membership," 44–49.
13 Finn, "A Historical Analysis of Church Membership," 66–67.
14 Hammett, "The Why and Who of Church Membership," 173–79.
15 "2000 Baptist Faith & Message," *Southern Baptist Convention*.
16 Lumpkin, *Baptist Confessions of Faith*, 286.
17 Gill, *Doctrinal and Practical Divinity*, 564.

Now I have given you the entrance qualifications to the church of Jesus Christ. The legal qualifications are redemption, justification, and adoption. The spiritual regeneration on the divine side and contrition, repentance, conversion, and faith, on the human side. Ceremonial, espousing him, confessing him before the church, and then being baptized in the name of the Father, Son, and Holy Spirit.[18]

Membership entails a commitment to the local church.[19] Gill writes,

Persons may hear the word aright, have faith, and profess it, and be baptized, and yet not be church-members; it is only mutual consent that makes them such: persons must propose themselves to a church, and give up themselves to it, to walk in it, in an observance of the ordinances of Christ, and duties of religion; and the church must voluntarily receive them in the Lord.[20]

A. H. Strong emphasizes the spiritual necessity and expectation that a believer join himself or herself to a church. He writes, "The church, unlike the family and the state, is a voluntary society. . . . As [regeneration] is mediated not by outward appliances, but by inward and conscious reception of Christ and his truth, union with the church logically follows, not precedes, the soul's spiritual union with Christ."[21]

Gill similarly points not only to the effects of such a commitment on the individual members, but on the glory of God as well. He writes, "A church thus confederated and united by consent and agreement, there are several duties incumbent on its members; which, both for their own

---

18   Carroll, "Qualifications for Church Membership," 31.
19   While most Baptist churches have a "church covenant," the aspect of covenantal responsibility has waned in the past century. Many ecclesiologists have called to a return to emphasizing church covenants as a means of greater commitment on the part of the members, and a greater ability to disciple and discipline on the part of churches. For more on this topic, see Lee, "Baptism and Covenant."
20   Gill, *Doctrinal and Practical Divinity*, 567.
21   Strong, *Systematic Theology*, 893.

comfort, credit, and edification, and for the glory of God, it is highly necessary to observe."[22] This language of commitment is often expressed in a church covenant, a set of beliefs and behaviors that a member agrees to and that binds the church together.[23] Church covenants have been a consistent part of churches in history. They are included in the New Hampshire Confession, which states, "A visible Church . . . of Christ is a congregation of baptized believers, associated by covenant in the faith and fellowship of the Gospel," as well as the BFM 2000, which uses almost the exact same language.[24]

These examples show membership has held a high value. It has been protected by the expectation that all members are believers and through the processes of baptism and the church covenant. A healthy church should prioritize these three elements to ensure its members are disciples of Jesus, seeking to hear his voice in their decision making, and in practicing the faith together.

CHURCH MEMBERSHIP IN MULTISITE CHURCHES

Multisite advocates have addressed membership in multisite churches, but membership has not received adequate attention.[25] Gregg Allison and Brad House consider membership "one of the most significant and often overlooked elements" in multisite churches.[26] The most in-depth analysis of membership in multisite churches is a Doctor of Education project by Nathan Reed on membership practices in large multisite churches.[27] He notes larger churches have a difficult time maintaining effective membership processes due to the overwhelming complexity of overseeing and shepherding large numbers of people. The churches

---

22   Gill, *Doctrinal and Practical Divinity*, 568.

23   Dever, *Nine Marks of a Healthy Church*, 172–75.

24   Lumpkin, *Baptist Confessions of Faith*, 365; "2000 Baptist Faith and Message." The BFM 2000 says, "A New Testament church of the Lord Jesus Christ is an autonomous local congregation of baptized believers, associated by covenant in the faith and fellowship of the gospel . . .".

25   Surratt, Ligon, and Bird, *A Multi-Site Church Road Trip*, 96. The authors include "regenerate church membership" in their list of requirements for biblical churches.

26   House and Allison, *MultiChurch*, 185.

27   Reed, "A Comparative Analysis of Church Membership Practices."

he studied had implemented effective strategies for incorporating new members into the membership and ministries of the church.[28]

In his ecclesiology volume, Allison notes one of the core aspects of a church is the "covenant relationship with God and . . . with each other."[29] For Allison, the church covenant joins the member to the church body. He writes, "Becoming a member, joining with others in the voluntary society called the church, does not ultimately constitute the church. Rather, it joins that member to an already existing reality, or it defines the constituents of that particular entity that has already been constituted a church by the Holy Spirit."[30]

This is similar to J. D. Greear's belief that what constitutes a church is the covenant relationship of the members.[31] Specifically regarding multisite membership, Allison and House identify the locus of an individual's membership as the whole church, not specifically the campus. However, the campus provides the physical place of entry into the church membership, and each individual is specifically identified with a particular campus. A specific campus's leadership and its campus members are responsible to provide the benefits and oversight of church membership, such as ministry, care, discipleship, discipline, baptism, and the Lord's Supper.[32] Mark Driscoll and Gerry Breshears are clear that membership at a multisite church is in the single church, but they also write, "Membership should be tied to the campus. People need to be committed to one campus at which they will be members, attend services, give generously, join a community group, and serve, and to which they will bring others." They describe multisite churches as an organization where the various members of the single church can participate in and take advantage of the various ministries at various campuses.[33]

---

28 Reed, "A Comparative Analysis of Church Membership Practices," 1–6, 95–157. Reed's church subjects were Bethlehem Baptist Church in Minneapolis, Minnesota, College Park Church in Indianapolis, Indiana, Long Hollow Baptist Church in Hendersonville, Tennessee, and The Village Church in Flower Mound, Texas.
29 Allison, *Sojourners and Strangers*, 123.
30 Allison, *Sojourners and Strangers*, 128.
31 Greear, "A Pastor Defends His Multi-Site Church," 19.
32 House and Allison, *MultiChurch*, 191–93.
33 Driscoll and Breshears, *Vintage Church*, 266.

As multisite churches consider membership, they must be intentional about making membership meaningful. Dever notes that intentional, meaningful membership—and especially regaining it once it has been lost—is both difficult and essential for all churches.[34] Multisite churches add an additional layer of complexity because their membership gathers in multiple locations instead of one. This is why it is essential to have the membership initiation process attached to the local campus.[35]

As noted previously, regenerate members are a primary component of healthy churches. John Hammett considers this a central imperative for the sake of church ecclesiology and the health of the church.[36] Churches need a process by which they can ensure their members have made a genuine decision for Jesus Christ. They key way to do this is to establish a process for assimilating new members into the church that clearly explains the gospel, salvation, church beliefs, ministry expectations, and other aspects of the church.[37] For multisite churches, this process can be contained at the local campus level only, or it can be a hybrid process where new members make their initial steps at a campus but go through new a member class with other new member candidates from all campuses.[38] Regardless of the process, it must be remembered that membership is in the whole church, not just the campus location.[39] Therefore, while the local campus might be the place where the member is initiated into the body, it is healthy for the rest of the church to be introduced to their new church family members. This could be accomplished, for example, by a church-wide email or by an online church directory.[40] Once a member

---

34   Dever, "Meaningful Church Membership," 46.
35   House and Allison, *MultiChurch*, 192.
36   Hammett, "Regenerate Church Membership," 27, 32–33.
37   Dever, "Meaningful Church Membership," 58; Warren, *The Purpose Driven Church*, 311–29.
38   House and Allison, *MultiChurch*, 192; Scroggins and Wright, "Building a New Church Culture."
39   House and Allison, *MultiChurch*, 191–92.
40   Dever, "The Practical Issues of Church Membership," 99. Dever suggests including a church directory. He does not, however, advocate it as a part of multisite churches because he is not an advocate of multisite. The church where I served as campus pastor used a weekly email newsletter to introduce new church members to the whole congregation.

is joined to the church and connected to a campus, he or she must be assimilated into the ministries of the church, both in receiving ministry and providing ministry.[41]

Congregational multisite churches must also be especially intentional about ensuring its members fulfill their role in the congregational leadership of the church.[42] Very often, the church body delegates responsibilities to groups of members, such as boards, teams, and committees, entrusting them to act on behalf of the whole body. The final authority, however, resides with the whole body.[43] In a multisite church, the whole body can delegate authority to groups that represent the whole church for churchwide responsibilities and to groups that represent the campuses for responsibilities of the individual campuses.[44] Still, there are times when the whole church needs to gather as one body for worship, fellowship, and decision making. A healthy multisite church must make this a priority.[45]

---

41   Dever, "Meaningful Church Membership," 60; Driscoll and Bershears, *Vintage Church*, 253–55.

42   Allison, *Sojourners and Strangers*, 316.

43   Garrett, "The Congregation-Led Church," 157–56.

44   House and Allison, *MultiChurch*, 44–72, 143–59.

45   Gaines, "One Church in One Location," 172; House and Allison, *MultiChurch*, 195. Allison and House make it clear that they think it is *wise* to gather as a whole, but it is not *required* in order to be considered a true church. They believe even multisite churches which never gather together can still be legitimately called one church.

CHAPTER 8

CHURCH DISCIPLINE

CHURCH MEMBERSHIP IS A FOUNDATIONAL element for church discipline, which is sadly absent from many of today's churches. The goal is to progress through steps of discipline in order to bring an erring church member to repentance and to restoration to the church community. The goal is never humiliation or public rebuke.[1] However, should the person refuse to repent and be reconciled, the Bible does call for their exclusion from the church family.[2] A healthy church must abide by a biblical understanding of church discipline.

The model of church discipline was established by Jesus in Matthew 18:15–20. This passage is "typically considered to be the most important and definitive text for church discipline."[3] In it, Jesus describes a four-step process with the goal being to restore a wayward brother or sister in Christ to the church. The first step is a private, face-to-face interaction between the offended party and the offender, with the hope of reaching reconciliation. If that is unsuccessful, the second step is bringing along two or three others who can fairly judge the issue, and hope to reach

---

1   Schreiner, "The Biblical Basis for Church Discipline," 106.
2   Carson, "Matthew," chap. 5.13.B.5; Osborne, *Matthew*, 686–87.
3   Norman, "Proper Church Discipline," 200.

reconciliation. The third step, if this is unsuccessful, is bringing the matter to the attention of the whole church for the sake of discussion and judging what could rectify the matter. Should this third step prove unsuccessful, the fourth step is removing the unrepentant member from the fellowship of the congregation.[4]

An equally important text for church discipline is 1 Corinthians 5:1–13, in which Paul describes discipline, in this case dealing with a sexually immoral relationship.[5] In Paul's description, his concern is not with restoration of the sinful member, but rather the member's spiritual cleansing, either through repentance or through the restoration to Christ after his death.[6] In this passage, Paul is also concerned with the purity of the church fellowship. He fears the sinful license could spread through the rest of the church.[7] Paul is not, however, totally unconcerned for the restoration of the sinful members. Galatians 1:6 and 1 Timothy 1:20 reveal Paul's concern and desire for restorative discipline.[8]

HISTORICAL PERSPECTIVES ON CHURCH DISCIPLINE

The effective practice of church discipline in many churches has waned in the past centuries, but it has historically been an essential aspect of church life.[9] Gregory Wills writes, "Baptists in the South practiced a thorough church discipline for about two hundred years. . . . But by 1950 only a fading memory of the practice remained. Southern Baptist churches had abandoned New Testament church discipline."[10] This

---

4   Davis, "Practical Issues of Church Discipline," 184–86.
5   Verbrugge, "1 Corinthians," 2.B.3.
6   Schreiner, "Biblical Basis for Church Discipline," 116–17.
7   Norman, "Proper Church Discipline," 207.
8   Schreiner, "Biblical Basis for Church Discipline," 117.
9   Norman, *The Baptist Way*, 64–65.
10   Wills, "Southern Baptists and Church Discipline," 179. In a 2019 *9Marks* blog post, Sam Emadi lists seven common modern objections to church discipline: (1) We cannot judge someone's heart, so how could we say they are not a Christian? (2) Jesus never turned anyone away. (3) No one is perfect. (4) People will not hear the gospel if they are not in church. (5) I have never heard of church discipline. (6) Church discipline will hurt the church's reputation. (7) We did not practice church discipline previously when our church was larger (Emadi, "7 Well-Meaning Objections to Church Discipline"). In a similar post, Paul Alexander lists additional common objections: (1) It is arrogant to

sad fact means that Southern Baptist churches, and churches of other denominations, are missing an essential element of what makes a church "a healthy church."[11] Albert Mohler considers the decline of church discipline as "the most visible failure of the contemporary church."[12] R. Stanton Norman describes discipline, stating, "Church discipline is the process by which a local church works to restore a professing Christian who falls into sin."[13]

Francis Wayland captured the tragedy of the loss of church discipline, even in the mid-1800s, writing, "The church discipline, which was formerly universal, could not now be carried into effect. The tide of worldliness, the love of gain, and the ambition of expense, which has been for some years, flowing over the Christian world, has overwhelmed us also."[14] Wills writes, "To an antebellum Baptist, a church without discipline would hardly have counted as a church."[15] While the BFM does not include any language regarding church discipline, previous Baptist confessions such as the Second London Confession and an addendum to the Philadelphia Confession have included church discipline as an essential aspect of a church.[16]

J. M. Pendleton voices the ultimate reason for church discipline, writing,

> The need of discipline in all its stages arises from the fact that here is a state of things in conflict with the will of God. Whatever is in conflict with his will tarnishes his glory. If then God is to be honored, and his glory promoted in the churches, discipline must be exercised to correct that which is in conflict with his will, and which obscures his glory. Our God is infinitely holy, and the neglect of discipline, when either personal or general

---

discipline. (2) It is divisive to discipline. (3) It is foolish to discipline. (4) It is unloving to discipline. (5) It is unholy to discipline. (6) It is hypocritical to discipline. (7) It is confusing to discipline. (8) It is unjust to discipline (Alexander, "8 Reasons").

11   Hammett, "Membership, Discipline, and the Nature of the Church," 27–28.

12   Mohler, "Church Discipline," 43.

13   Norman, "The Reestablishment of Proper Church Discipline," 207.

14   Wayland, *The Principles and Practices of Baptist Churches*, 138.

15   Wills, *Democratic Religion*, 12.

16   Lumpkin, *Baptist Confessions of Faith*, 286, 351–52.

offenses require it, virtually represents him as the patron of iniquity. Let the churches tremble at this though, and remember that the holy God they serve is also a jealous God.[17]

Gill identifies four purposes of church discipline: (1) the glory of God, (2) to purge the church, (3) to protect against false teaching, and (4) for the ultimate good of the disciplined individual.[18] Thus, church discipline is to be corrective and redemptive, not punitive.[19] Edward Hiscox writes, "It is therefore of the utmost importance that a correct spiritual discipline be strictly maintained. The neglect of it fills a Church . . . with evils which check the growth of piety, hinder the success of the Gospel . . . and reproach the Christian name."[20] Hiscox also points to the biblical commands of Jesus in Matthew 18 and Paul's commands in 1 Corinthians 5 as the guidelines for principles of discipline.[21]

These examples from history show that church discipline is an essential component of a local church. Biblical discipline is based on the commands of Jesus and is carried out in a way that preserves the unity of the church, the integrity of the gospel, and the glory of God, and seeks to restore a wayward member. These are vastly important aspects of church life. Mohler writes,

> The mandate of the church is to maintain true gospel doctrine and order. A church lacking these essential qualities is, biblically defined, not a true church. . . . At the end of the twentieth century, the great task of the church is to prove itself the genuine church revealed in the New Testament. . . . We must regain the New Testament concern for fidelity of doctrine, purity of life, and unity of fellowship. We must regain [church discipline].[22]

---

17   Pendleton, *Church Manual*, 143–44.
18   Gill, *Doctrinal and Practical Divinity*, 619–20.
19   Schreiner, "The Biblical Basis for Church Discipline," 105–13.
20   Hiscox, *The New Directory for Baptist Churches*, 164.
21   Hiscox, *The New Directory for Baptist Churches*, 173–80.
22   Mohler, "Church Discipline: The Missing Mark," 56.

If a church is to be a healthy church, it must preserve, or regain, effective, biblical church discipline.

CHURCH DISCIPLINE IN MULTISITE CHURCHES

Church discipline is a reality that multisite churches must work diligently to address. J. D. Greear acknowledges discipline is a difficult issue for multisite churches to address, writing in 2010 that one of their primary multisite questions is, "How do we best do membership and discipline in the multi-site model?"[23] Gregg Allison points out that some multisite churches choose to limit what aspects of church ministry they emphasize, including church discipline, in what he refers to as "ecclesiological circumcision." He says this lack of thought in the area of ecclesiology needs more thought and answers.[24] However, aside from Brad House and Allison, multisite advocates have been silent on the topic of church discipline when specifically discussing multisite models.

This is not to say they never address discipline in general terms. John Piper sees church discipline as a restorative measure in the church but also recognizes that there may come time for removal of a member from the church.[25] Matt Chandler concurs, noting church discipline's goal is restoration.[26] Allison believes church discipline is at the core of a church

---

23   Greear, "A Pastor Defends His Multi-Site Church," 23. Greear acknowledges that discipline is a part of their church process. In an endorsement of Jonathan Leeman's book *Church Discipline: How the Church Protects the Name of Jesus*, Greear writes, "This book is an outstanding, one-of-a-kind theological work. I believe this will be the definitive work on church discipline, and *our elders plan to use this work as our guide*" (emphasis added) (Greear, "Endorsement of *Church Discipline*").

24   Allison, "Theological Defense of Multi-Site," 10.

25   Piper, "Avoid the Unrepentant"; Piper, "The Leniency of Excommunication." Piper understands the painful necessity of practicing church discipline. He removed his own son, Abraham, from church membership because of his son's refusal to repent of sin and his public acknowledgment that he was not a believer (Graves, "Prodigal Children").

26   Chandler, "Wanderer / Restorer." Chandler's church practices discipline, and, due to an unfortunate event in 2015, is an example of the difficulty of correctly practicing church discipline. The Village Church apologized for making poor judgment in how it carried out church discipline against a member going through a marriage annulment. Chandler, himself, was placed on a disciplinary leave of absence in August 2022. In a social media post at the end of October 2022, he indicated he would be returning to The Village Church at some time, but as of the this moment, a date has not been identified ("Bylaws," *The Village Church*; Chandler, "Instagram Post from October 23, 2022"; Roys,

fulfilling its missional purpose, writing, "Church discipline serves to protect the actualization of the biblical vision of the church."[27] Mark Driscoll and Gerry Breshears describe church discipline as a necessary act of love toward Christ, the church, and the sinner, writing, "Because church leaders love the reputation of Jesus, love the entire church in which they serve, and love the sinner, dealing with sin is an art form that takes great courage, discernment, and wisdom."[28] Hammett, who is at least friendly toward multisite ministry, notes the importance of church discipline to the life and health of the church and the individual member.[29] David Platt and Jimmy Scroggins are examples of other multisite pastors who believe and practice church discipline in their churches.[30] These multisite advocates show church discipline is certainly a belief they hold to personally and in their churches, yet they do not address how church discipline works in a multisite context.

House and Allison, however, do discuss church discipline in a multisite context. Allison points out that church discipline is a vital aspect of a church's ministry and responsibility, and that multisite churches must take the matter seriously.[31] He suggests two models of multisite that deal with church discipline in different ways. The first model puts the responsibility of church discipline in the hands of the whole church gathered together, which "engages in accepting new members, *excommunicating sinful members through church discipline*, voting on official business, etc."[32] The second model seems to place the responsibility of church discipline in the hands of the members of a campus, although in his 2010 article, it is not perfectly clear. He writes, "The congregation—which exists at multiple sites—works with authority in . . . excommunicating sinful members through church discipline."[33] It appears Allison intends this statement to mean a campus's local membership has authority over discipline. *MultiChurch* provides a

"Matt Chandler Signals Imminent Return"; Silliman, "Matt Chandler Steps Aside"; Zylstra, Lee, and Smietana, "Former Member Accepts Acts 29 Megachurch").

27   Allison, *Sojourners and Strangers*, 181.
28   Driscoll and Breshears, *Vintage Church*, 165.
29   Hammett and Merkle, *Those Who Must Give an Account*, 1.
30   Platt, "The Four Steps of Restorative Church Discipline"; Scroggins, "Vintage Church."
31   Allison, "Theological Defense of Multi-Site," 10.
32   Allison, "Theological Defense of Multi-Site," 16, emphasis added.
33   Allison, "Theological Defense of Multi-Site," 16.

little more clarity, but is still not as definitive as would be preferred. The authors seem to indicate that carrying out discipline is the responsibility of the campuses, writing, "Although a multichurch has one united membership, both entrance into and exclusion from church membership is the responsibility of a particular congregation."[34] However, just a few pages over, they write about quarterly whole church gatherings, stating, "This could be a congregational meeting in which the business of the whole church is carried out along with *any exercise of church discipline*."[35] Thus, House and Allison leave some uncertainty about whether they believe church discipline should be the responsibility of the local campus where a member's primary attendance is located, or a responsibility of the whole church. Perhaps they intend for the whole church to simply ratify a decision made in the local congregation, because they do emphasize that any process of discipline must be clearly communicated throughout the whole church. They write, "In cases of church discipline, it is especially important that all the congregations communicate to enhance care for those who have been sinned against and to increase chances of reconciliation. This also prevents people from avoiding repentance by inserting themselves into another congregation."[36]

Multisite churches must be intentional about practicing church discipline in a biblical way. Jesus's model, presented in Matthew 18:15–20, serves as the guide for both multisite and single-site church leaders. In this model, the first two steps, the initial one-on-one encounter and the subsequent meeting with two or three witnesses, are the same regardless of church model. However, multisite leaders must decide how to deal with steps three and four, taking it before the church and removing the member from fellowship. Allison presents two options in his 2010 *9Marks* article. Both of these are feasible models, although his preferred model, more clearly described in *MultiChurch*, is the better option.[37] In it, the third step of restorative discipline in a multisite church is to present the matter to

---

34   House and Allison, *MultiChurch*, 191–92.
35   House and Allison, *MultiChurch*, 195, emphasis added.
36   House and Allison, *MultiChurch*, 192.
37   Allison, "Theological Defense of Multi-Site," 16; House and Allison, *MultiChurch*, 191–92.

the gathered body of the local campus for their judgment. They in turn will make the decision about removing the unrepentant member, and they too will be the ones to attempt to bring the member to restoration.[38] If the local campus must make the decision to remove the unrepentant member, that decision must then be communicated to the rest of the church.[39] An additional step in the process of removal, not suggested by House and Allison, but which would be wise for the sake of church unity on the matter, is to have the whole church ratify the decision of removing the member. This could be accomplished either through individual votes at each campus as they receive a report on the discipline, or by vote of the whole gathered church at a scheduled whole church gathering. This additional step preserves the unity of the whole church and reminds the whole body that the responsibility of church discipline is one which they share collectively.[40]

---

38   House and Allison, *MultiChurch*, 192–93.
39   House and Allison, *MultiChurch*, 192.
40   Mohler, "Church Discipline," 55–56. Mohler is writing of church discipline in general, not in a multisite context.

CHAPTER 9

CHURCH LEADERSHIP: CONGREGATION, ELDERS, AND DEACONS

IN CONGREGATIONAL POLITY, authority in the church is held by the congregation, and there are two offices that provide leadership to the body. Those two offices are elders and deacons.[1] Adherents to congregational polity find evidence throughout the New Testament. As in the previous section, they first point to Jesus's description of church

---

1 There are three common types of leadership structures in congregational churches: (1) congregation-led (democratic) churches, (2) single-elder-led churches, and (3) plural-elder-led churches. I will not comment on which model is the most biblical. For a discussion on this topic, see chapters 1, 3, and 5 in Brand and Norman, *Perspectives on Church Government*. I will, however, make the case that plural elder leadership is the best model for multisite churches.

There are also the common church government views of presbyterian polity, episcopal polity, and Erastian polity. For more on these forms see Daniel Akin, James Leo Garrett Jr., and James R. White's responses in chapters 2 and 4 of *Perspectives on Church Government: 5 Views*. Additionally, Wayne Grudem notes some churches reject the concept of a formal system of church government, but rather trust the Spirit to lead through a general consensus of the church body (Grudem, *Systematic Theology*, 936; cf. Fergusson, *A Brief Refutation of the Doctrine of Erastianism*, 3–4).

discipline in Matthew 18:15–20. This passage shows the final authority in a discipline situation lies with the local body of believers. First Corinthians 5:2 and 2 Corinthians 2:6 demonstrate this as well.[2]

The word used to identify the church, *ekklesia*, also implies the autonomy of a local church body. John Hammett writes, "There is no superior organizational level to which churches are accountable."[3] There is also evidence for local church autonomy in that most of the letters in the New Testament were addressed to churches, not their leaders.[4] Acts 6:3–6; 13:2–3; and 15:22 show the church choosing and commissioning its own leaders under the guidance of the Spirit, which, again, points to the authority of the church body to make decisions.[5]

Baptistic congregationalists see only two offices in the early church, and therefore, only accept two offices in the church body. The first office in the church is that of elders.[6] In the church, elders serve as shepherds of the church, teachers in the church, equippers of the church, and leaders of the church.[7] Their authority in the church "is never dictatorial, but with a humble spirit, open to the input of others and seeking to 'lead the church into spiritually minded consensus.'"[8] There is no set number of elders described in the New Testament, although it is clear that every church

---

2   Garrett, "Congregation-Led Church," 159–62, 167–70.
3   Hammett, *Biblical Foundations for Baptist Churches*, 146.
4   Hammett, *Biblical Foundations for Baptist Churches*, 147. The exceptions are 1 and 2 Timothy, Titus, and Philemon.
5   Garrett, "Congregation-Led Church," 162–67.
6   In this book, the term elder will be used in place of the New Testament terms *poimen* (pastor/shepherd), *episkopos* (bishop/overseer), and *presbuteros* (elder). Baptists see these terms used interchangeably in the New Testament, and therefore believe all three of them point to a single office. For an explanations of this topic, see chapter 1, "Defining a Pastor-Elder" in Cowen, *Who Rules the Church?*, 5–16. For arguments for multiple offices, see Peter Toon and L. Roy Taylor's chapters in Cowan, *Who Runs the Church?*, 19–41, 71–98.
7   Merkle, "The Biblical Role of Elders," 271–76. Some have suggested the New Testament church role of elder was based on the model of the Old Testament and adapted from the pattern of elders that was already present in the Jewish synagogue (Mappes, "The 'Elder' in the Old and New Testaments," 88–92). However, that is not a universally accepted conclusion. For potential issues with that conclusion, see Merkle, "The Scriptural Basis for Elders," 243–44.
8   Hammett, *Biblical Foundations for Baptist Churches*, 165, with a quote from Carson, "Church, Authority," 251.

should have at least one.[9] Scripture is also clear of the qualifications for elders, with lists in both 1 Timothy 3:1–7 and Titus 1:6–9.[10] Scripture also limits the role of elder to men.[11] Church history, while not infallible by any means, affirms this, as the office of elder has historically been limited to men. This conclusion has been agreed upon by major denominational groups throughout history until recently.[12]

Alongside the elder, the deacon is the second office in the church. Deacons and elders are designed to complement each other, with the elders being the leaders, and deacons filling the role of servant in the church. The qualifications for deacons are only given in Acts 6:3 and 1 Timothy 3:8–13. The qualifications of deacons are almost identical to that of elders, with the similarities being in the area of character, and differences in the area of gifts and calling.[13] Two distinguishing elements are evident. The first are the titles given to the two offices. *Episkopos* (bishop/overseer) indicates a role of leadership and authority, whereas *diakonos* (deacon/servant) indicates a role of service in the church. The second distinction is the qualification of being "able to teach," present in the qualifications for elders but absent from the qualifications of deacons.[14]

---

9 Akin, "The Single-Elder-Led Church," 25–27.

10 Merkle, "The Biblical Qualifications for Elders," 254–63. The qualifications taken from these two passages are a desire to serve, above reproach, the husband of one wife, self-controlled, sensible, respectable, hospitable, able to teach, not an excessive drinker, not a bully, gentle, not quarrelsome, not greedy, be able to manage his household competently, have his children under control, not a new convert, has a good reputation among outsiders, righteous, holy, disciplined, not arrogant, and not quick-tempered.

11 Geisler, *Systematic Theology*, 4:110–11, 202–5; Grudem, *Systematic Theology*, 937–44. This book does not have the space to provide a full discussion of the biblical role of women in ministry. For a good evaluation of both sides, see Beck, *Two Views on Women in Ministry*.

12 Schreiner, "Women in Ministry," 266–67. The Baptist view on this is clarified in the BFM 2000, which states, "While both men and women are gifted for service in the church, the office of pastor/elder/overseer is limited to men as qualified by Scripture." There is not time in this book to fully discuss both sides of the debate on women as elders. For more on this, a good source is the book cited above.

13 Merkle, "The Office of Deacon," 314–15. The qualifications for deacons are worthy of respect, not hypocritical, not drinking a lot of wine, not greedy, holding the mystery of the faith with a clear conscience, must be tested, blameless, husbands of one wife, managing their children and households competently, have a good reputation, full of the Spirit, wise, and have respectable wives who are not slanderers, are self-controlled, and faithful.

14 Hammett, *Biblical Foundations for Baptist Churches*, 194.

The primary role of the deacon is serving to "meet people's practical, material needs," and Acts 6:1–6 serves as a model for how deacons are to serve in the church.[15] This practical ministry is most often understood to be caring for those with needs in the church, but some conclude that descriptions of deacons in 1 Timothy 3:8–13 imply they could provide oversight of the church's finances and administration as well.[16] These passages lead many to conclude that the deacon's fundamental ministry is a spiritual ministry in support and encouragement to the ministry of the elders.[17] However, Gregg Allison points out that the text isn't so specific, and he notes that two of the men selected in Acts 6 as deacons, Stephen and Phillip, are later described "engaging in activities far removed from what is typically considered 'deacon work.'"[18] Therefore, the conclusion that there is a clear division between service ministry and "spiritual" ministry is not as explicit as often assumed.

Acts 6 describes deacons as men, and 1 Timothy 3:11 mentions deacons' wives, so the office has typically been limited to men.[19] However, that is not now, and has not historically, been the universally accepted standard.[20] In fact, even the BFM does not limit the office of deacon to men, which is a unique contrast to its requirement that only men can serve as an elder.[21]

HISTORICAL PERSPECTIVES ON CHURCH LEADERSHIP

The First London Confession of 1644, a confession of early English Baptists, gave the congregation the authority to choose officers, carry out discipline, and administer the ordinances without any other hierarchy above them. The officers identified were "pastors, teachers, elders, deacons," while the Second London Confession identifies only "bishops or elders and

15 Strauch, *The New Testament Deacon*, 70–75.
16 Grudem, *Systematic Theology*, 919.
17 Dever, *The Church*, 5.3.1.
18 Allison, *Sojourners and Strangers*, 242.
19 Norman, *The Baptist Way*, 121.
20 Hammett, *Biblical Foundations for Baptist Churches*, 201–3.
21 "2000 Baptist Faith and Message," *Southern Baptist Convention*. As with the office of elder, there is not enough space to allow for a full discussion of this topic. For a more complete discussion see Beck, *Two Views on Women in Ministry*.

deacons."[22] The New Hampshire Confession says "bishops or pastors and deacons," are the officers of the church, and the BFM 2000 says the officers are "pastors/elders/overseers and deacons," and that the "office of pastor/elders/overseers is limited to men." These last two confessions both state the church is "governed by [Christ's] laws," and the BFM 2000 adds the "congregation operates under the Lordship of Christ through democratic processes."[23]

J. L. Reynolds locates the authority within the local church in the hands of the members, writing, "The Baptists recognize only believers as the constituents of a gospel Church... and commit its government to its members." He further clarifies, "We believe that Jesus Christ is the head of the Church ... the only Lawgiver ... that the government is with the Church."[24] B. H. Carroll clarifies the location of the church's government is in the hands of only that local body, saying, "Each congregation is a complete temple in itself, and has final jurisdiction over all its affairs. This is the church, to which grievances must be told, and whose decision is final.... But a Baptist church cannot project or merge its sovereignty into a general body of any kind, nor delegate its powers. There is not and cannot be a Baptist federal body."[25]

Carroll believed, "The church is a pure democracy," although A. T. Robertson disagreed, writing, "A Baptist church is a practical democracy, not a pure democracy. The existence of pastors and deacons imposes limitations of leadership and service. This limitation is carried still further by various committees and other organizations for special classes."[26]

Commenting on the officers of the church, Pendleton writes, "Pastors and teachers, the same men, are the ordinary and permanent spiritual offices of the churches, while the office of deacon has special reference to the secular interests of the churches." Concerning the authority of the pastors, he adds, "The pastor is to rule in accordance with the law of Christ. No other kind of rule is legitimate or obligatory; but when he rules in accordance with the will of Christ, obedience and submission on

---

22   Haykin, "Historical Roots of Congregationalism," 38–40; Lumpkin, *Baptist Confessions of Faith*, 166–69, 287.

23   "2000 Baptist Faith and Message," *Southern Baptist Convention*; Lumpkin, *Baptist Confessions of Faith*, 365–66.

24   Reynolds, *Church Polity*, 86, 103.

25   Carroll, *Baptists and Their Doctrines*, 28.

26   Carroll, *Baptists and Their Doctrines*, 28; Robertson, "Our Baptist Democracy," 213.

the part of the members of the church are imperative duties."[27] Carroll emphasizes the distinctions between the two roles, writing, "The officers of the church are bishops and deacons, the first charged with spiritualities and the second with temporalities."[28] The requirements for elders and deacons are those found in 1 Timothy 3:1–18 and Titus 1:6–9.[29]

CHURCH LEADERSHIP IN MULTISITE CHURCHES

Multisite advocates have much to say about church leadership. Their focus is less theological, however, and more organizational.[30] In *The Multi-Site Church Revolution* (*MCR*), the authors discuss the importance of staffing structures that fit the particular multisite model a church chooses. They also discuss the importance of developing solid teams of leaders for the church, writing, "Finding, training, and deploying effective leaders are the keys to successfully building a church in more than one location."[31] When they talk about leaders, they refer to typical leaders that would be present in many church settings, such as directors, ministry leaders, and worship directors. However, the most important part of the leadership team in a multisite setting, according to *MCR*'s authors, is the campus pastor. They write, "The key to any new start-up is the campus pastor. This is the leader who will convey the DNA of the primary campus, recruit the core team, develop the new leaders, and carry on the ministry once the campus is launched."[32] The conclusion that the campus pastor is the most important staff member in the

---

27   Pendleton, *Church Manual*, 23, 27–28.
28   Carroll, *Baptists and Their Doctrines*, 33.
29   Gill, *Doctrinal and Practical Divinity*, 575–77, 604–5; Reynolds, *Church Polity*, 122; Strong, *Systematic Theology*, 919.
30   Surratt, Ligon, and Bird, *A Multi-Site Church Road Trip*, 96. The authors include "qualified leadership" in their list of requirements for biblical churches.
31   Surratt, Ligon, and Bird, *Multi-Site Church Revolution*, 133–43.
32   Surratt, Ligon, and Bird, *Multi-Site Church Revolution*, 144. Surratt, Ligon, and Bird's second multisite book, *A Multi-Site Church Road Trip*, has chapters on structure changes and leadership development that offer very little new content different from *MCR* aside from anecdotal content. Highlighting the importance of the campus pastor, this book also includes three sample job descriptions for campus pastors from three different multisite churches (Surratt, Ligon, and Bird, *A Multi-Site Church Road Trip*, 114–28, 186–97, 225–30).

multisite model is not unique, as many advocates make the same claim.[33] Because of the importance of this pastoral role, the literature often has key characteristics that are essential qualifications for a campus pastor. These characteristics usually include traits such as "High capacity leader . . . Team player . . . People magnet . . . Mobilizer . . . Multi-tasker . . . Communicator . . . DNA Carrier."[34] *MCR* describes the campus pastor with traits such as "buys into the church's vision and is loyal to its senior leadership . . . team player with strong relational skills . . . team builder who can reproduce vision . . . pastor, someone with a desire and heart to shepherd groups and individuals . . . flexible entrepreneur."[35] These descriptions, and others like them, consistently focus on organizational, leadership, and personality skills, and only occasionally include a nod to biblical leadership qualifications.[36] *Multi-Site Churches* misses the chance to include biblical qualifications in its twenty-two-page description of the campus pastor or its sixteen pages about developing leaders.[37] Gregg Allison suggests substituting skill traits in place of biblical qualifications is a major issue in the multisite movement, writing, "Substituting biblical qualifications for requirements such as these denies the sufficiency of Scripture and establishes a kind of leadership that fails to reflect biblical

---

33   Bird, "Campus Pastor as Key to Multisite Success"; Ligon, "What Makes a Great Campus Pastor?"; McConnell, *Multi-Site Churches*, 92–91; Morgan, "Hiring Campus Pastors"; Tomberlin, "What Makes a Great Campus Pastor?"

34   Tomberlin, "What Makes a Great Campus Pastor?"

35   Surratt, Ligon, and Bird, *Multi-Site Church Revolution*, 144.

36   Surratt, Ligon, and Bird, *A Multi-Site Church Road Trip*, 225–30. None of the three sample campus pastor job descriptions included in *MRT* from actual multisite churches include biblical qualifications of pastor/elders from 1 Timothy and Titus.

    Warren Bird's campus pastor report, "Campus Pastor as Key to Multisite Success," includes six sample campus pastor job descriptions. Only one of these mentions biblical qualifications, including "Meets the requirements of 1 Timothy 3:2–7 and Titus 1:6–9" (Bird, "Campus Pastor as Key to Multisite Success," 8).

    Taking the opposite approach, focusing on disqualifications, Daniel Im offers "10 Signs You Shouldn't be a Campus Pastor." Aside from "I don't want to preach," none of these reasons refer to lacking any biblical qualifications found in 1 Timothy or Titus (Im, "10 Signs You Shouldn't be a Campus Pastor").

37   McConnell, *Multi-Site Churches*, 89–126. McConnell identifies the two essential roles of a campus pastor as leading and shepherding, but does not provide any reference to biblical qualifications for the shepherd leader (94–98).

standards."[38] Sadly, the emphasis on deacons is even more paltry, if not non-existent.[39] Aside from one passing mention, neither *MCR* nor *A Multi-Site Church Road Trip* (*MRT*) even mention deacons, except in condescending passages that chastise a crotchety, penny-pinching deacon straw-man.[40]

The exceptions to this pattern, when specifically addressing multisite models, are House and Allison.[41] In their chapter on polity in *MultiChurch*, their first polity-shaping value is "Conviction," of which they write,

> Polity should be biblically grounded, theologically sound, wise, and faithful to God's character and his intention for the church. As noted earlier, Scripture has much to say about those who lead; therefore, governance should be the responsibility of those who meet the qualifications—the call, character, and competencies—as set forth in 1 Timothy 3:1–7 and Titus 1:5–9 (for elders) and 1 Timothy 3:8–13 (for deacons and deaconesses).[42]

---

38   Allison, "Theological Defense of Multi-Site," 9.

39   I have not been able to find a multisite advocate, aside from House and Allison, who specifically addresses deacons in a multisite context. Jim Tomberlin describes deacons as simply one of many options of "boards" who lead a church (Tomberlin, "How to Handle Governance in Multisite Churches").

40   Surratt, Ligon, and Bird, *Multi-Site Church Revolution*, 78, 98, 100, 102, 106; Surratt, Ligon, and Bird, *A Multi-Site Church Road Trip*. *MRT* does not include the word "deacon."

41   Driscoll and Breshears discuss the biblical requirements for elders and deacons, specifically discussing the 1 Timothy and Titus passages. This discussion in *Vintage Church* is in the general discussion of church ecclesiology. In their chapter on multisite churches, they do not discuss the qualifications of elders, but they do mention campus pastors and unpaid elders as essential roles when launching new campuses. It can be assumed they would expect these leaders to meet the same biblical qualifications, even though the discussion is not present in the multisite chapter (Driscoll and Breshears, *Vintage Church*, 65–77, 253–54).

42   House and Allison, *MultiChurch*, 148–49. In *Sojourners and Strangers* Allison mentions pastoral teams and describes the elder structure of Sojourn Church, but does not specifically mention the biblical qualifications of elders in his brief discussion of multisite churches. The same can be said of his *9Marks Journal* article, aside from the statement that concludes the previous paragraph. However, *Sojourners and Strangers* gives a very thorough discussion of the biblical qualifications of elders and deacons, which obviously is the foundation for how Allison views the expectations and qualifications for elders of multisite churches (Allison, *Sojourners and Strangers*, 211–47, 315–16; Allison, "Theological Defense of Multi-Site," 9, 16).

Only those who meet the qualifications of a pastor/elder are qualified to serve in that capacity in the church. This is why Christopher Kouba writes, "In order for a multisite campus to be a part of a biblical church model, campus pastors must meet and fulfill the biblical requirements of a pastor. . . . When churches make the decision to become a multisite church, they must start with the Bible to determine who they should consider for the role of campus pastor."[43] The emphasis on biblical qualifications informs the polity structure House and Allison suggest.[44] Their structure is one that is filled by men and women who meet the biblical qualifications of church leaders.[45]

The majority of multisite literature presents a top-down leadership structure. This means the senior pastor and his leadership team determine the direction of the church and make the majority of the decisions for the church.[46] This is not surprising, considering the trend of large churches becoming more dependent upon staff leadership. John Vaughn draws a correlation between church size and the transition to a staff-led church: "As a church grows beyond being a single cell organism and as organizational change occurs, an increasing shift in congregational polity evolves from congregational . . . to presbyterial . . . to Episcopal."[47] This explains why many descriptions of campus pastors include "loyalty" to the senior leadership as an essential qualification.[48] Scott McConnell notes

---

43   Kouba, "Role of Campus Pastor," 22, 39.

44   House and Allison, *MultiChurch*, 150–58.

45   Allison, "Theological Defense of Multi-Site," 16. Allison provides two models in his article, which he considers to be biblical models of multisite polity. House and Allison allow for women to serve in the role of deaconess. They do not specifically mention that the role of elder is limited to men, aside from using "he" when referring to the lead pastor. However, Allison is thoroughly clear in *Sojourners and Strangers* that the office of elder is limited to men (Allison, *Sojourners and Strangers*, 223–40).

46   Surratt, Ligon, and Bird, *Multi-Site Church Revolution*, 133–41; Surratt, Ligon, and Bird, *A Multi-Site Church Road Trip*, 114–28.

47   Vaughn, *Megachurches and America's Cities*, 84–85. Vaughn uses these terms as follows: (1) congregational: the church votes on decisions; (2) presbyterian: boards, teams and committees make decisions for the church; (3) episcopal: staff leaders are the primary decision makers for the church.

48   McConnell, *Multi-Site Churches*, 93, 98, 102–3; Surratt, Ligon, and Bird, *A Multi-Site Church Road Trip*, 151, 227; Surratt, Ligon, and Bird, *Multi-Site Church Revolution*, 144; Tomberlin, "What Makes a Great Campus Pastor"; Towns, Stetzer, and Bird, *11 Innovations in the Local Church*, 78.

that even those churches that maintain congregational polity still tend to locate most decision making power in the senior leadership, writing, "The senior pastor or leadership team is responsible for establishing the church's identity (both beliefs and vision), values, and expression."[49] He admits that in many of these churches, even decisions about core beliefs and values are made not by the congregation but by the leaders. Scroggins, himself the senior pastor of a large multisite church, acknowledges power becomes centralized in the senior leadership team, and specifically in the senior pastor.[50]

Heath Kahlbau says the tendency for senior pastors to become leaders of leaders rather than a leader of the congregation pulls the church away from congregational polity.[51] He suggests a polity form composed of lay elders serving alongside the paid staff and senior pastor in order to create levels of accountability between the staff and the congregation, and to create a greater connection between the senior pastor and his congregation.[52] This is similar to the multisite structure House and Allison have developed, which has various levels of elder leadership, both paid and non-paid, in various areas of leadership. They see in this elder-led model certain areas of authority held by the elders and certain authority held by the congregation. These two spheres of authority hold each other in balance for the good of the whole church.[53]

Few multisite advocates have highlighted the importance of congregational polity, tending more toward central leadership making the decisions for the church.[54] Mark Driscoll and Gerry Breshears define congregational

---

49   McConnell, *Multi-Site Churches*, 91.
50   Scroggins, "Interview with Heath Kahlbau," 250.
51   Kahlbau, "Is Anything New Under the Sun?," 169–70. Kahlbau admits this is a problem not only in multisite churches, but in large single-site churches as well.
52   Kahlbau, "Is Anything New Under the Sun?," 297–300.
53   House and Allison, *MultiChurch*, 91–92, 150–57.
54   Surratt, Ligon, and Bird, *Multi-Site Church Revolution*, 86. Throughout *MCR*, the authors give a picture of church leaders going through a process of convincing the church that multisite ministry is the future of the church. The picture is one of central leadership convincing the church to support what the leadership has already determined must be done. It seems to be a coercive strategy, rather than one defined by mutual submission and a final lean toward congregational authority. See also Gilbert, "What Is This Thing, Anyway?" 25–27. Gilbert reveals the struggle, noting that multisite churches tend to be a blend of various polity philosophies.

polity, but they do not advocate it. They prefer an elder-ruled style of governance.[55] McConnell's description of multisite development rests heavy on the leadership's planning and makes mention of the congregation only in supporting roles.[56] Multisite pastor John Piper makes clear the congregation is the "final authority in the church" under Christ, clarifying, "The congregation, and not the pastors or elders or deacons or bishops or popes, is the body that settles matters of faith and life." For Piper, however, this authority is not a decision-making authority. Rather, "the corporate authority of the congregation . . . puts doctrinal and moral boundaries around the [elder] leadership and holds it accountable to serve the good of the church." The body of elders "inspires and models and mobilizes and teaches and *persuades* and *points* the way in ministry and mission."[57] Thus, for Piper, congregational authority exists simply to choose the elders and define their calling and beliefs. The elders make the decisions in the church. House and Allison hold a similar view, although they describe the local congregation's members as holding oversight over certain decisions made by the elders, such as budget approval and large-scale changes in the

---

This author believes one reason the multisite literature as a whole does not make a strong case for congregational polity is that the literature is written to a broad (multi-denominational) audience, not simply a congregational audience. Therefore, they limit their discussion to general concepts, without delving into denominationally defined concepts such as polity.

55 Driscoll and Breshears, *Vintage Church*, 49–50, 65–74; Wax, "The Mars Hill Postmortem."
56 McConnell, *Multi-Site Churches*, 26–33. McConnell does quote Jim Carrie, a former staff member at Chartwell Baptist Church in Oakville, Ontario, who says, "We really want to empower our congregations to be fully congregational in that they have local decision-making rights and authority. We really want each congregation to have its own identity and yet still achieve success by working together." This is included as an example in a discussion of campus autonomy (76–77). McConnell makes no recommendation of a preferred level of campus autonomy. Jim Carrie no longer serves at Chartwell Baptist Church, and Chartwell, now Chartwell Church, is no longer a multisite church (Carrie, "Jim Carrie"; "Home," *Chartwell Church*).
57 Piper, "Who Are the Elders?," emphasis added. The context of this comment was a sermon from 1991, long before Bethlehem Baptist Church became a multisite church. Therefore, it reveals Piper's view on congregational authority but says nothing about that authority in the context of multisite churches. In the article, he clarifies, "The congregation, under Christ and by his word and Spirit, uses its authority to recognize and affirm leaders who God calls. And then the congregation puts those people in positions of leadership and voluntarily supports that leadership by learning from their teaching and following their initiatives."

church. They describe their multichurch polity as "elder-led, deacon- and deaconess-served, and congregation-affirming."[58]

For congregational multisite churches, whether democratically led or elder led, maintaining strong congregational polity as they add additional campus locations to their church will be a challenge.[59] As some multisite pastors have indicated, it is simpler to move toward a central leadership that makes the decisions for the church, and to have a church body that exists more as an empowering unit rather than an authoritative, decision-making body.[60] This is not solely an issue of multisite churches, but it is truly a challenge for all churches as they grow in membership.[61] Jonathan Leeman is correct when he concludes that when churches shift from one service or site to multiple services or sites, they "inevitably shift some degree or authority and responsibility upward onto the shoulders of the leaders, even if you maintain the same formal structure (congregational, elder-rule, etc.)."[62] However, the reality is that this is a size issue, not a site or service issue. The same struggle would be present in a single-site, single-service megachurch.

Given that the tendency of authority in multisite churches is to drift toward less congregational authority, multisite churches will have to intentionally create structures to retain congregational authority, regardless of their stated polity model. Dever acknowledges a congregation can determine how involved they will be in the general day-to-day decision making of the church, but that final authority always rests with the congregation.[63] Multisite churches must develop their structure to require the whole congregation to make decisions when necessary, but to also allow for campus-specific decisions to be made at the campus level.[64] In

58   House and Allison, *MultiChurch*, 157–58.
59   Frye, "The Multi-Site Church Phenomenon," 209–10; Hammett, "What Makes a Multi-Site Church One Church?," 106–8.
60   Piper, "Who Are the Elders?"; Scroggins, "Interview with Heath Kahlbau"; Wax, "Mars Hill Postmortem."
61   Garrett, "Congregation-Led Church," 190–92; Vaughn, *Megachurches and America's Cities*, 84–85.
62   Leeman, *One Assembly*, 4.1.
63   Dever, *Understanding Church Leadership*, 35–38.
64   House and Allison, *MultiChurch*, 157–58.

order to accomplish this, multisite churches will need to establish two levels of congregational authority and rule.[65] The first of these is the general authority of the whole church. In this realm, the church comes together to approve matters that pertain to the whole church, such as choosing and approving senior leadership, whole-church budgets, adding additional campuses, and anything else that is a part of the whole church's oversight. These decisions are best carried out at a whole church gathering, where the entire church family can discuss, pray, and vote their decision.[66] The second level is at the local campus level. At this level, the campus members make decisions on matters contained at their own location. This gives them ownership, authority, and accountability for matters happening at their own location.[67] These two levels of congregational authority are consistent with congregational polity in the same way a single-site church holds congregational rule. However, it delegates authority for decision-making in certain areas to groups of members within the whole body.[68]

---

65   These levels are for major decisions that require the voice of the whole church or local campus. This strategy is not recommending a purely democratic process, in which the church must gather for all decisions. This strategy can work with single and plural elder structures and can work with churches who empower committees and/or teams to make decisions in their ministry areas.

66   Allison, *Sojourners and Strangers*, 316; Allison, "Theological Defense of Multi-Site," 17–18; Frye, "Phenomenon," 215–16, House and Allison, *MultiChurch*, 157.

67   House and Allison, *MultiChurch*, 157–58.

68   Dever, *Understanding Church Leadership*, 36–37; Garrett, "Congregation-Led Church," 158; Grenz, *Theology for the Community of God*, 561. Dever, Garrett, and Grenz are not speaking directly about multisite churches. However, they allow for churches with congregational polity to invest leadership and decision-making authority in groups (committees) within the church. (To be fair, Dever *allows* for it but does not *prefer* it.) These groups, under the authority of the church, make decisions in their specific areas to carry out the ministry of the church in that area. This parallels the congregational multisite model presented, in that the whole church gives the campuses the authority to make decisions in their specific areas of ministry oversight.

CHAPTER 10

CORPORATE WORSHIP

KARL VATERS captures the value of corporate worship when he writes,

> I don't go to church to worship Jesus. I go to church to worship Jesus *with other people.* . . . I need to worship Jesus along with:
>
> - People I know
> - People I don't know
> - People who know me
> - People I share life with
> - People I share common beliefs with
> - People I disagree with
> - People who love me anyway
> - People I have to love anyway.[1]

Corporate worship, correctly practiced, is an essential component of a healthy church.[2]

---

1   Vaters, "If We Can Worship Anywhere, Why Go to Church?," emphasis original.
2   Gregg Allison notes, "We must consider that everything in which the church engages—singing songs of praise to God, reading and preaching the Word of God, educating children in the faith, giving, feeding the poor, baptizing, fellowship—if done as a

The descriptions of the early church's worship contain very little detail. Daniel Block writes, "The New Testament actually provides little instruction on formal corporate gatherings. . . . neither [Jesus] nor the apostles offer detailed counsel on how we should practice it, except to emphasize the ordinances of the Lord's Supper . . . and baptism."[3] Andrew McGowan acknowledges the sparsity of details and also warns of modern worshipers' tendency to "fill in the gaps" with their own notions and preferences when he writes,

> So these documents manifestly do not present a systematic description or prescription for Christian gatherings; they do assume various practices as available for assessment and critique. Reading the NT as a liturgical source thus requires some imaginative construction of these assumed practices; such construction must of course be accountable to the evidence for what actually took place, and appropriate critical attention must be given to how imagination tends to favor present experience and preferences.[4]

faith response in obedience to and adoration of God, is worship. As the church lives, moves, and breathes *coram Deo*, . . . it engages in worship" (Allison, *Sojourners and Strangers*, 425). He is correct in his analysis that everything the church does for God, led by the Spirit, it does in worship of God. However, when speaking of "worship" in this section, this book will be referring to the corporate worship gathering. As Grudem defines it, "I am using *worship* in a more specific sense to refer to the music and words that Christians direct to God in praise, together with heart attitudes that accompany that praise, especially when Christians assemble together" (Grudem, *Systematic Theology*, 1003).

Unfortunately, whereas corporate worship should be a unifying aspect of church life, in the past few decades, "worship wars" over music styles have created unhealthy divisions in many churches. Daniel Block identifies three negative outcomes of these conflicts that have permeated the church: (1) churches have split over worship styles, (2) churches form two different worship services to gratify two different preferences, and (3) churches adopt a contemporary style, marginalizing those that prefer a more traditional format. These negative outcomes, however, have not been universal. Many churches navigated the worship style challenge and came out on the other side unified and with a clear vision for the future (Block, *For the Glory of God*, 2).

3   Block, *For the Glory of God*, 6–7.
4   McGowan, *Ancient Christian Worship*, 10.

Worshipers must, therefore, seek to understand those details that are available in the Bible regarding proper worship.

The Bible is clear that God is the center of our worship. Jesus told the Samaritan woman that God seeks worshipers (John 4:23), and he also made clear to Satan that the Lord was the only one worthy of worship (Matt. 4:10).[5] Wayne Grudem notes, "Because God is worthy of worship and seeks to be worshiped, everything in our worship services should be designed and carried out not to call attention to ourselves or bring glory to ourselves, but to call attention to God and to cause people to think about him."[6] Anything that takes the focus of worship away from God becomes an idol and violates the first and second commandments (Exod. 20:3–6), as well as the Greatest Commandment (Deut. 6:5; Matt. 22:37–38).[7] As Jesus Christ is coequal with God the Father, as well as the Holy Spirit, he is worthy of the same worship the Father expects and receives from the church, as is evident in some of the New Testament doxologies (Rom. 16:27, 2 Peter 3:18).[8]

The Bible is also clear that corporate worship is an expectation.[9] The Pentateuch shows Israel was called to worship God corporately in the Old Testament (Exod. 3:12, 18; Lev. 23), and the Psalms are filled with references to corporate worship.[10] Psalm 68:26 commands the assembled Israelites to worship God, Psalm 105:1–6 commands proclamation of Yahweh's good works in the midst of the people, and Psalm 148:13 commands people to worship Yahweh together.[11] Colossians 3:16 shows the church was expected to worship together in the New Testament, and Hebrews 10:24–25 is a reminder

---

5   Boice, *Foundations of the Christian Faith*, 587.

6   Grudem, *Systematic Theology*, 1003–5.

7   Block, *For the Glory of God*, 29–30. Block acknowledges that worship of the Spirit is missing in the New Testament. "No one addresses the Holy Spirit in prayer, or bows down to the Holy Spirit, or serves him in a liturgical gesture. Put simply, in the Bible the Spirit is never the object of worship. . . . The Spirit drives the worship of believers yet does not receive worship. . . . In true worship, the persons of the Trinity may not be interchanged without changing the significance of their work" (50).

8   Akin, "The Person of Christ," 46–49.

9   Grudem, *Systematic Theology*, 1003–4.

10   Delitzsch and Keil, *Genesis to Judges 6:32*, 337–40; Jamieson, "Biblical Theology and Corporate Worship"; Wenham, *The Book of Leviticus*, 301, 306; Wilson, *Psalms, Volume 1*, 23–26.

11   VanGemeren, *Psalms*, II.Z.4–6, IV.P.1; V.PP.3; Wilson, *Psalms*, 944.

for the church to never cease gathering together.[12] Corporate worship will even be a part of the eternal future of the church (Rev. 5:13–14).[13] Paul assumes corporate gatherings will include, at least at times, the whole church gathered together in one place (1 Cor. 14:23).[14] Corporate worship is vital because "There are certain aspects of how we relate to each other and how we relate to God together that can only happen when" we come together.[15]

Worshiping God includes certain elements. The New Testament and church history demonstrate numerous aspects of worship that could be mentioned, but four items summarize the foundational elements of corporate worship: music and singing, preaching the Word, prayer, and observing the ordinances.[16] Colossians 3:16, where Paul instructs the believers to sing "psalms, hymns, and spiritual songs," shows the expectation of music and singing in the worship service, as do other examples in the New Testament church (Eph. 5:18–20) and in the eternal church (Rev. 5:8–10).[17] These musical expectations grew out of the Old Testament worship patterns and even the first-century patterns in the synagogues.[18] Music and singing is, perhaps, the aspect of corporate worship that most church members think of first when they hear the word "worship," yet McGowan writes, "Music was neither the most central or distinctive aspect of their gatherings."[19]

The second aspect of corporate worship, which took center stage in the New Testament church, is the preaching of the Word of God.[20] Block

---

12   Bruce, *The Epistle to the Hebrews*, 256–58; Manser, *Dictionary of Bible Themes*, Theme: 8624; Osborne, *Colossians and Philemon*, Col. 3:1–4; Pao, *Colossians and Philemon*, 247–50.

13   Boice, *Foundations of the Christian Faith*, 588.

14   Leeman, *One Assembly*, 6; O'Brien, "Church," 125; Slaton, "The Citywide Church," 7–10, 20–22.

15   Vaters, "Why Go to Church?"

16   Grenz, *Theology for the Community of God*, 492.

17   Aune, *Revelation 1–5*, 374; Bruce, *The Epistles to the Colossians, to Philemon, and to the Ephesians*, 380–81; McGowan, *Ancient Christian Worship*, 112–13; O'Brien, *The Letter to the Ephesians*, 394; Osborne, *Colossians and Philemon*, Col. 3:1–4; Osborne, *Revelation*, 264–66; Pao, *Colossians and Philemon*, 247–50.

18   Block, *For the Glory of God*, 230.

19   McGowan, *Ancient Christian Worship*, 111. Grenz writes music *was* the central aspect of worship in the Old Testament (Grenz, *Theology for the Community of God*, 493).

20   Grenz, *Theology for the Community of God*, 493; McGowan, *Ancient Christian Worship*, 72–74.

writes, "If corporate worship involves an audience with God, and true worship is the engaged response to God's revelation, then ensuring that divine communication occurs is a high priority."[21] In preaching a message grounded in the biblical text, the speaker establishes a living interaction involving God, the preacher, and the congregation" so that God may communicate his truth to the congregation, and the congregation can worship through responding to that truth.[22]

Proclaiming the Word and works of God was an essential part of worship in the Old Testament.[23] David encouraged teaching about God's works in Psalm 96:2–3, and reading the rediscovered copies of the Law led to revival in the days of King Josiah of Judah (2 Kings 23:1–3).[24] Preaching was central in the New Testament church.[25] The early church was devoted to listening to the apostles' teaching (Acts 2:42), and Paul was clear about the authority of God's word for "teaching, rebuking, correcting and training in righteousness" (2 Tim. 3:16, NIV).[26] The early church used the scriptures in preaching, teaching, reading (1 Tim. 4:13), and even singing (Eph. 5:19).[27]

The third foundational element of corporate worship is prayer.[28] E. M. Bounds writes, "Prayer is perfectly at home in the house of God. It is no stranger, no mere guest; it belongs there. It has a peculiar affinity for the place, and has, moreover, a Divine right there, being set, therein, by Divine appointment and approval."[29] In worship, prayer can and should take the same form as it does in times of personal prayer. It should include praise, thanksgiving, confession, and requests.[30] Solomon's prayer at the dedication of the temple in 1 Kings 8:12–61 is a lengthy example of corporate prayer

21   Block, For the Glory of God, 169.
22   Robinson, Biblical Preaching, 21.
23   Grenz, Theology for the Community of God, 493.
24   Hobbs, 1, 2 Kings, 73; VanGemeren, Psalms, IV.G.1.
25   McGowan, Ancient Christian Worship, 74–75.
26   Liefeld, 1 and 2 Timothy, 279–81; Schnabel, Acts, 172, 177–80.
27   Block, For the Glory of God, 188–89; Liefeld, 1 and 2 Timothy, 166; O'Brien, Letter to the Ephesians, 394–95.
28   Grenz, Theology for the Community of God, 494.
29   Bounds, The Necessity of Prayer, 61.
30   Block, For the Glory of God, 215; Grenz, Theology for the Community of God, 494–95; Sproul, Does Prayer Change Things? 14.4.

in the Old Testament.[31] In the New Testament, descriptions of the church's corporate prayer are in the book of Acts. Acts 1:14 says they were continually united together in prayer, as does Acts 2:42. Acts 4:23–31 is a lengthy corporate prayer or praise and petition that results in a powerful move of the Spirit.[32]

The final of the four aspects of corporate worship is observing the ordinances of baptism and the Lord's Supper. As the biblical grounds for the ordinances have been discussed previously, the case will not be made here. However, a brief discussion of the ordinances in relation to corporate worship is appropriate. Nowhere in the New Testament is baptism described in the context of a corporate gathering of the church. The multitudes converted on the day of Pentecost are assumed to have baptized *en masse*, apparently by the current members of the church (Acts 2:41), which would entail a corporate baptism. However, the example of the Ethiopian eunuch also exists, where he was baptized in the presence of Philip alone. Other examples reveal baptisms of groups by apparent groups of believers, thus something closer to a corporate baptism. Thomas White affirms that while he cannot be dogmatic about a baptism taking place in a worship service, "The gathered believers should see the person's baptism and accept him or her into fellowship. It is a church ordinance. Thus, baptism must be associated with a local church."[33] The Lord's Supper, however, is specifically linked to corporate gatherings of the church (Acts 2:42; 1 Cor. 10:15–17). John Armstrong writes, "There is no real doubt about this simple historical fact—through the centuries this meal has been *the central and characteristic action of the church at worship.*" He adds that the Lord's Supper is not a private meal, but rather is intended to be observed corporately.[34] Thus, it is apparent that the ordinances were practiced by the early church in corporate ways, always with the Lord's Supper, and often with baptism.

---

31 Block, *For the Glory of God*, 205; Hobbs, *1, 2 Kings*, 3, 88.
32 Block, *For the Glory of God*, 213–14.
33 White, "What Makes Baptism Valid?," 112–13. See also Grudem, *Systematic Theology*, 984.
34 Armstrong, "Introduction," in *Understanding Four Views on the Lord's Supper*, 15–16, emphasis original.

HISTORICAL PERSPECTIVES ON CORPORATE WORSHIP

While churches in history have enjoyed different modes of worship, biblical principles have permeated their thoughts. John Gill notes the importance of worship as an extension of one's own personal attitude of worship. He writes, "Internal worship requires our first attention, it being of the greatest moment and importance; external worship profits little in comparison of that; if the heart is not engaged in worship bodily exercise is of little advantage, that being only the form without the power of godliness."[35]

Charles Spurgeon notes there is freedom in worship, saying, "We believe that any form which true worship takes is a form which the Lord Jesus Christ not only tolerates, but sanctions, if His Spirit is there."[36] Whatever the form, worship has consistently included preaching, singing, prayer, and the ordinances, as indicated by Wayland, writing, "Again, our notion of worship is simply this. We meet together on the Sabbath to offer up to God, each one for himself, the sacrifice of prayer and praise, and to cultivate holy affections by the reading and explanation of the word of God, and by applying its truth to our own souls."[37]

As has been shown, biblical preaching should hold a central place in the corporate worship of the church. W. A. Criswell writes, "But the sermon is the center of the Christian worship of Jesus. This is according to the Word of God."[38] E. C. Dargan, in agreement, writes, "[Preaching] is an established institution of the Christian religion; as such it is a function of worship."[39] Spurgeon believes, "In fact, there is no worship of God that is better than the hearing of a sermon."[40] This is not to suggest that Spurgeon did not promote other aspects of worship. He emphasized prayer and singing as well, saying,

---

35 Gill, *Doctrinal and Practical Divinity*, 346.
36 Spurgeon, "The Lord with Two or Three," 52.
37 Wayland, *The Principles and Practices of Baptist Churches*, 125.
38 Criswell, *Criswell's Guidebook for Pastors*, 34.
39 Dargan, *The Art of Preaching in the Light of Its History*, 16.
40 Spurgeon, "The Blessing of Public Worship," 36–37.

Let others do as they may, as for us, we worship Him, we believe in the reality and power and usefulness of prayer, and,
therefore, in the light of day, before all men, we gather together
to pray. . . . As we are members of one mystical body, it is but
right that we should, as members of that one body, worship
together, lifting up the joyous song in tuneful harmony, and
blending our supplications around our common mercy seat.[41]

John Broadus emphasized balance, saying,

There is a disposition to underrate the importance of public
worship; to think only of the preaching. . . . What I wish to
say is, wherever that may be true, let us consider whether we
ought not to take more interest in our worship, in the reading
of God's Word for devotional impression, in solemn, sacred
song and in humble prayer to God, in which we wish the hearts
of the whole assembly to rise and melt together.[42]

Edward Hiscox, emphasizing the importance of corporate singing,
writes, "The power and influence of sacred song in worship are not understood and appreciated as they ought to be."[43] A. T. Robertson shows
the value and importance which Baptist place on ordinances in worship,
saying, "Let baptism preach. . . . The second ordinance preaches much
the same message as that of the first, the death of Christ."[44]

The core elements of worship are preaching, singing, prayer, and the
ordinances. Churches have freedom to design worship services as fits the
personality of the church and culture, but these four aspects are essential.[45]
They will be a part of the worship strategy of a healthy church.

---

41 Spurgeon, "The Blessing of Public Worship," 32–33.
42 Broadus, "Worship," 25.
43 Hiscox, *The New Directory for Baptist Churches*, 238.
44 Robertson, "The Spiritual Interpretations of the Ordinances," 213–14.
45 The ordinances, while a part of worship, may not be a part of every worship service. In
     addition, some churches may not be able to baptize in a worship center. Wherever they
     baptize, the opportunity should be a time of brief corporate worship (Criswell, *Criswell's
     Guidebook for Pastors*, 204–5).

CORPORATE WORSHIP IN MULTISITE CHURCHES

Rick Warren considers worship to be the church's primary purpose, and he builds his strategy for church growth with this as his foundational purpose.[46] Warren, like many multisite advocates and practitioners, discusses the practical aspects of conducting corporate worship, but spends little time considering the ecclesiological aspects of corporate worship.[47] *MCR* focuses on the aspects of worship style variation throughout the book. The only place with any description of what a corporate service should include is in a definition of terms page, which says, "*Worship service*: Christ-centered community that usually includes singing, praying, and preaching. It happens regularly, usually weekly. Also known as a celebration, service of divine worship, worship experience, and sometimes simply 'church.'"[48] The only aspect of corporate worship that receives much attention is preaching, and the focus remains on the practicalities of deciding how the message will be delivered, by video or by live teaching.[49] *MRT* is hardly better. In a chapter on internet campuses, it describes how the various elements of worship are still present in online worship services, while the rest of the book gives little consideration to the vital aspects of biblical corporate worship in multisite churches' campuses.[50] Scott McConnell discusses video and live preaching as an important decision for churches. He also acknowledges that preaching and music

---

46   Warren, *Purpose Driven Church*, 103.

47   Warren, *Purpose Driven Church*, 103, 185–203, 223–306. See also Surratt, Ligon, and Bird, *A Multi-Site Church Road Trip*, 96. The authors of *MRT* include "preaching and worship" in their list of requirements for biblical churches.

48   Surratt, Ligon, and Bird, *Multi-Site Church Revolution*, 18, 28. Another place where multiple aspects of worship are mentioned, not discussed or promoted, is in a description of National Community Church's services: "The church even plays with its setting, such as using popcorn boxes to receive the offering. But the location does add more fun to worship, prayer, preaching, and receiving Holy Communion in a place used for entertainment the rest of the week" (72).

49   Surratt, Ligon, and Bird, *Multi-Site Church Revolution*, 29–42, 163–69. The authors include a list of pros and cons to video preaching. Summarized, the pros are: (1) focuses on excellent sermon delivery, (2) makes it easier for church to expand to more sites, and (3) helps develop new leaders. Summarized, the cons are: (1) technological issues disrupt the worship environment, (2) preachers can make comments that are distracting to other sites, and (3) aspiring teachers have little opportunity for developing their gifts.

50   Surratt, Ligon, and Bird, *A Multi-Site Church Road Trip*, 90–96.

in corporate worship are two aspects of multisite that help build unity in the church. Teaching on the same topic, and even singing the same song, creates a sense of unity across the sites.[51]

Mark Driscoll and Gerry Breshears note one of the traits of a biblical church is that the church, as a "worshiping community," should gather regularly to hear preaching and to worship. They suggest each campus of a multisite church should adopt a musical style it prefers in worship, and the local leaders of the worship should make the decisions regarding the music at their campus. The authors are adamant that biblical preaching is the central aspect of the worship service and also agree the Lord's Supper should be practiced during worship.[52]

In *MultiChurch*, Brad House and Gregg Allison highlight the importance of worship in the church as an opportunity to display the image of God and present themselves as the united body of Christ.[53] They also include it in the various categories of ministry as they discuss how ministry happens in multisite churches. They discuss how decisions about the forms of corporate worship services are made in the various multisite models. They do emphasize the centrality of the preaching, and how multisite campuses are able to contextualize their preaching and music as they have more autonomy from central authority.[54] They also include a section on unity within the church, highlighting ways a multisite church can maintain unity, even while divided across multiple locations. They recommend a periodic gathering with worship and the ordinances, as well as any church business that may be pertinent to the whole church.[55]

Allison's ecclesiology provides the best worship analysis from a multisite advocate. In it, he says, "Worship must be God-centered . . . must

---

51   McConnell, *Multi-Site Churches*, 78–85, 204–6.
52   Driscoll and Breshears, *Vintage Church*, 39–40, 90–96, 122, 128, 253. Mars Hill Church celebrated the Lord's Supper in each service each week. The church regularly celebrated baptism as a part of the worship service, although the authors do not specifically require baptism to be conducted as a part of a service.
53   House and Allison, *MultiChurch*, 99–100.
54   House and Allison, *MultiChurch*, 52, 56–57, 59, 64, 66, 68, 71, 160.
55   House and Allison, *MultiChurch*, 94, 195. The authors make this recommendation, even though they "believe that the weekly gathering of local congregations in multisite models meets the biblical admonition to assemble" (94).

take place in Christ . . . must be by—empowered by and flowing from—the Holy Spirit."[56] He lists praise, preaching the Word, and observing the ordinances as vital aspects of the corporate worship experience.[57] Allison makes the case that a single church can legitimately meet for worship in more than one location, thus being a multisite church. He cites the examples of the church in Corinth and the Jerusalem church's meeting practices recorded in Acts 2. The church in Corinth is said to have gathered in three different homes (Acts 18:7–8; 1 Cor. 16:15), which stands in contrast to the described "whole church" gatherings (Rom. 16:23; 1 Cor. 14:23). Citing an article, Allison writes, "Importantly, 'each of the home-based groups included only parts of the church, i.e., a subset of its membership.'"[58] The passage in Acts 2:42–46 describes a church meeting in various homes "for the purposes of teaching the Word, edification, the Lord's Supper, prayer, giving, and the like."[59] These actions show that the church was meeting in groups in various homes, and the groups were performing the functions of corporate worship.[60] "Such distributed meetings were still the church of Jerusalem."[61]

As churches enter into a multisite model, they must carefully consider how they will maintain the integrity of corporate worship. As with any church's corporate worship, there are foundational aspects of corporate worship to which churches must adhere. Worship must include music that glorifies God. Songs should declare the worth of the Savior with the foundational truth of the Scripture informing the content of the words. Music that simply appeals to the emotions or preferences of the congregation is not biblical worship.[62] Biblical preaching must be central to every corporate

---

56   Allison, *Sojourners and Strangers*, 426.
57   Allison, *Sojourners and Strangers*, 425–27. Allison clarifies in a later section that biblical preaching is "intimately tied" to the church's worship of God (433).
58   Allison, *Sojourners and Strangers*, 313. Allison cites Button and Van Rensburg, "The 'House Churches' in Corinth," 14.
59   Allison, *Sojourners and Strangers*, 313.
60   Slaton, "Discovering Evidence of Multisite *Ekklesia*," 12–22.
61   Allison, *Sojourners and Strangers*, 313.
62   Block, *For the Glory of God*, 236–45. There is debate about what can and cannot be included in a worship service. Those who ascribe to the regulative principle believe the Scripture outlines what is acceptable for worship and what is not. Even within the regulative camp, there are extremes and differences of opinion. Those who follow the

worship service at every location. Multisite churches can facilitate this either by providing biblical preaching by video or by developing a strong teaching team working together to develop and deliver biblical messages regularly.[63] Time for prayer must also be included in worship services. In corporate prayer, the worshipers "express their oneness with each other and with Christ," and reveal to one another their individual and corporate dependance upon the Savior.[64] Churches must make intentional efforts to highlight prayer in their services, ensuring it is not simply included as an afterthought or to allow for transition time.[65] Finally, the ordinances must be observed in corporate worship at the campus locations. These ordinances are commanded by Christ and are best observed as a part of the corporate worship experience.[66] As the members of a particular campus evangelize the lost, they need to see the new believers baptized in obedience to Christ and incorporated into the fellowship of the church in the Lord's Supper.[67]

The most obvious issue that multisite churches must address is how to maintain the unity of the whole church when it is dispersed across multiple campuses. Corporate worship is a foundational unifying element of the local church because it is the primary place the church gathers together.[68] Therefore, for a church to be "one church," there must be times when the

---

normative principle suggest a church is free to use elements in worship so long as it is not forbidden in worship. Some allow this to lead them to far extremes as well. A good discussion that provides a balanced view of the regulative principle is the July-August 2013 edition of *9Marks Journal*. A brief resource for a balanced view of the normative principle is in *For the Glory of God* by Block ("Is Scripture Enough?," *9Marks Journal*; Block, *For the Glory of God*, 2–3, 7, 29, 41, 2, 99, 118, 122, 190, 282, 296).

63 McConnell, *Multi-Site Churches*, 78–85; Scroggins and Wright, "How Family Church Does Multisite"; Surratt, Ligon, and Bird, *Multi-Site Church Revolution*, 163–72.

64 Block, *For the Glory of God*, 218.

65 Rainer and Howe, "Seven Ways Churches Make Prayer Central." Rainer's seven recommendations are: (1) They stress the priority of prayer. (2) They have a designated time of corporate prayer with clear guidelines. (3) They share stories of answered prayers. (4) They provide prayer guides in the worship folder/bulletin. (5) They have visible manifestations of prayer. (6) They pray to send people out from the worship services. (7) They have people pray during and before the worship services.

66 Hammett, *Biblical Foundations for Baptist Churches*, 261–62.

67 Akin, "The Meaning of Baptism," 79; White, "A Baptist's Theology of the Lord's Supper," 140–42, 152–53. These authors are writing on baptism and the Lord's Supper respectively, but are not writing in reference to multisite churches.

68 Grenz, *Theology for the Community of God*, 490–91.

whole church is gathered together. Grant Gaines, who is not a multisite advocate, maintains that "a multisite church must be 'characterized' by campus-wide gatherings in order to claim to be a single church."[69] His conclusion is correct, and multisite churches must be intentional about creating whole church gatherings where the smaller units at the campuses can come together as the whole corporate body for worship.[70] In doing so, they should incorporate all aspects of the corporate worship experience, including praise, proclamation of the word, prayer, and observing the ordinances.[71]

---

69   Gaines, "One Church in One Location," 2.
70   This expectation inherently eliminates the logical possibility that a multisite church's reach could extend beyond a reasonable day-trip driving distance. Multisite literature such as *MCR* and *MRT* allow for multisite church campuses to exist "in the same region, or in some instances, different cities, states, or nations" (Surratt, Ligon, and Bird, *Multi-Site Church Revolution*, 18). Churches that extend beyond a reasonable driving distance effectively divide the congregation into units that cannot meet corporately for worship, and are thus illegitimately called "one church" (Gaines, "One Church in One Location," 2). Thus, in order for a church to perform the necessary biblical function of whole church gatherings, they must be limited to a region or smaller, and must have periodic whole church gatherings (House and Allison, *MultiChurch*, 17).
71   Allison, *Sojourners and Strangers*, 316; Allison, "Theological Defense of Multi-Site," 17–18; Frye, "The Multi-Site Church Phenomenon," 229–30.

CHAPTER 11

DISCIPLESHIP

DISCIPLESHIP IS NOT ONLY AN EXPECTATION of believers, but, as George Ladd points out, discipleship is a privilege of following Christ.[1] Discipleship for the believer is the intentional act of becoming a committed follower of Christ, welcoming to oneself the privileges, joys, and costs of following him.[2] The church's responsibility in discipleship can be seen in the Great Commission (Matt. 28:18–20). Jesus commanded his own disciples to go out into the world to create more disciples and teach these new believers all that Jesus had taught them in his three-year ministry. This shows the necessary pattern of one follower of Jesus helping develop other believers.[3] Paul continues this emphasis saying the purpose of his preaching and evangelism is to create believers who are mature in Christ (Col. 1:28).[4] Stanley Grenz describes it as follows: "Discipleship as patterning our lives after Jesus means that Jesus' model and teaching become the standard by comparison to which we evaluate our innermost

---

1   Dever, *Nine Marks of a Healthy Church*, 213–14; Ladd, *A Theology of the New Testament*, 235.

2   Manser, *Dictionary of Bible Themes*, 8114–17.

3   Allison, *Sojourners and Strangers*, 441; Grenz, *Theology for the Community of God*, 504.

4   Allison, *Sojourners and Strangers*, 441; Warren, *The Purpose Driven Church*, 106.

attitudes and our outward actions."[5] The process of discipleship was never intended to be accomplished alone. In other words, true discipleship does not happen with one isolated person seeking to become more like Christ. Discipleship happens when one (or more) believer helps another (or many) believers become more like Christ.[6] Paul provided a model of this in 2 Timothy 2:2, in which he describes four levels of discipleship and leadership development: come, grow, disciple, and multiply.

HISTORICAL PERSPECTIVES ON DISCIPLESHIP

Baptists throughout history have not emphasized the term "discipleship" to great lengths, but they have talked about the processes of instruction, growth, and sanctification. E. Y. Mullins says of believers, "All Christians are men in the making," and, "Sanctification is a life process."[7] John Gill refers to discipleship as "growing in grace," writing, "There is such a thing as growing in grace, in the grace of faith, and abounding in hope and love, and increasing in the knowledge of divine things."[8] Showing that spiritual growth is a process, Gill adds,

> Though sanctification is imperfect, it is progressive, it is going on gradually till it comes to perfection; this is clear from the characters of the saints, who were first as little children, infants, new-born; are in a state of childhood, and by degrees come to be young men, strong and robust, and overcome the evil one, and at length are fathers in Christ, 1 John ii.13,14.[9]

Mullins points to the church's part in the growth process, writing, "The means of instrumentality of sanctification is chiefly the truth of the gospel. . . . The truth is learned through all the means of grace, in the

---

5   Grenz, *Theology for the Community of God*, 292.
6   Gallaty, *Rediscovering Discipleship*, 35–38, 78–91; Grenz, *Theology for the Community of God*, 293.
7   Mullins, *Talks on Soul Winning*, 52; see also Mullins, *The Christian Religion in its Doctrinal Expression*, 422.
8   Gill, *Doctrinal and Practical Divinity*, 150.
9   Gill, *Doctrinal and Practical Divinity*, 150.

church, in preaching, in Christian fellowship, in temptation and trial, in suffering, in Christian conquest, in the performance of daily duty."[10]

James Boyce writes much about sanctification and identifies the church community as one of God's means of sanctification, writing, "The associations of believers in church relations, is another of the means ordained by God for the increase of individual spiritual life and consequently sanctification."[11] W. A. Criswell points to the Sunday school ministry as a place of discipleship, stating, "Outside the preaching services themselves, the most important activity in the church concerns the teaching, visiting, soul-winning ministry of the Sunday School. . . . This is our primary instrument of visitation, soul-winning, and Bible teaching."[12] Edward Hiscox includes a similar sentiment, writing,

> It is likely that, so far as the local congregation is concerned, next to preaching the Gospel . . . the Sunday-school is to be ranked in importance as an evangelical agency. . . . The influence of Sunday-school is threefold: The direct influence on the pupils in storing their minds with religious knowledge, forming their characters to virtue and moulding . . . their hearts to good morals.[13]

In a description from the mid-1800s, John Dagg highlights the importance of multi-generational discipleship. He says,

> Besides the public ministrations of the word, other means of promoting religious knowledge ought to receive the attention and support of the churches. The study of the Bible ought to be encouraged, whether by individuals, by Bible classes, or by Sunday schools. It is a great fault if the work of instructing is

---

10   Mullins, *The Christian Religion in its Doctrinal Expression*, 423.

11   Boyce, *Abstract of Systematic Theology*, 420.

12   Criswell, *Criswell's Guidebook for Pastors*, 176.

13   Hiscox, *The New Directory for Baptist Churches*, 257–58. Hiscox's other two influences of Sunday schools are (1) "The indirect influence on the homes of the pupils . . ." and (2) "The reflex influence on officers and teachers . . ."

entirely given up to the young. Let the heads which have grown gray in the service of the Lord, bow with pleasure to impart instruction to the opening minds of the rising generation, and sow in this promising soil the seed which will produce a rich harvest, when the gray-haired instructor shall have gone to his eternal reward. Let the circulation of good religious books and periodicals publications be promoted, and a spirit of religious inquiry be fostered in every proper way. Let men be taught, both by the words and the deeds of those who claim to be Christ's, that religion is the chief concern.[14]

While the processes may look different today, the basic biblical form of life-on-life teaching and training remains the same. A healthy church must include an intentional system of discipleship in order to grow believers to maturity.

DISCIPLESHIP IN MULTISITE CHURCHES

In multisite literature, discipleship is not discussed in depth but is still considered an essential aspect of a multisite church. In *The Multi-Site Church Revolution* (*MCR*) the authors tie discipleship to the heart of multisite ministry, saying, "The purpose of becoming a multi-site church is to make more and better disciples by bringing the church closer to where people are."[15] They again emphasize this purpose, saying the potential cost of not going multisite is "the cost of not gaining ground in obedience to Jesus's command to make disciples."[16] They also include discipleship as a health marker for churches and imply in their concluding paragraph that multisite is the primary answer for seeing the Great Commission accomplished. They write, "If we are truly to go into all the world and make disciples of all the nations, we can no longer hold on to the comfortable thought of being a

---

14   Dagg, *A Treatise on Church Order*, 271–72.
15   Surratt, Ligon, and Bird, *Multi-Site Church Revolution*, 18. They emphasize this in *A Multi Site Church Road Trip* as well, writing, "Multi-site is about the two-thousand-year-old challenge of reaching people and making disciples, just with a different wrapper on the package" (18).
16   Surratt, Ligon, and Bird, *Multi-Site Church Revolution*, 97.

church that meets in one location under one room. . . . We have to open our doors to other churches that may be more effective at reaching the lost and making disciples than we are."[17]

In *MCR*, however, they say nothing about the discipleship process or biblical considerations of the discipleship ministries in multisite churches. It is not until their next book, *A Multi-Site Church Road Trip (MRT)*, that they address some questions about discipleship in multisite churches, but they say very little about discipleship processes or biblical considerations.[18]

Brad House and Gregg Allison list discipleship as one of the ministries of a multisite church. They believe that regarding ministry in general, the multisite strategy allows for contextualization of the ministries at each campus. Discipleship, they add, is one area where the church reveals, and teaches, what it means to be in relationship to God the Father and Jesus Christ.[19] Allison is clear in *Sojourners and Strangers* that discipleship is an essential ministry of the church. He notes that while many areas of ministry feed into the discipleship process, the ministries of Christian communication and Christian community are the two primary means of discipleship. He makes the case that multisite models help one church accomplish its discipleship goals through campus multiplication more effectively than traditional church planting. As for practical methodology, he writes that the local campus's leadership is responsible for the discipleship process at its own location.[20] This is consistent with *MultiChurch*'s description of discipleship responsibilities.[21]

Other multisite practitioners have discussed discipleship in general terms, although not usually in the context of multisite churches specifically.

---

17   Surratt, Ligon, and Bird, *Multi-Site Church Revolution*, 200. *MCR* says the Great Commandment (Matt. 22:37–39), the Great Commission (Matt. 28:18–20), and the Great Charge (1 Peter 5:1–4) are the "primary motive[s]" behind multisite approaches (10).

18   Surratt, Ligon, and Bird, *A Multi-Site Church Road Trip*, 95–96, 206–7. In regard to internet "campuses," they answer the question, "How do you know that disciples of Jesus Christ are actually being made?" Their answer is that people are going through discipleship "processes," including baptism, giving, serving, inviting friends, and evangelism (95). Later they address multisite critics' charge that multisite fails to make disciples. Their answer is, essentially, that multisite can do as good a job as any other model of church (206–7).

19   House and Allison, *MultiChurch*, 99–100, 160, 164.

20   Allison, *Sojourners and Strangers*, 315–16, 441–47.

21   House and Allison, *MultiChurch*, 155–58.

John Piper defines a disciple as "a follower of Jesus, one who embraces him as Lord and Savior and Treasure."[22] He lists many examples of how the Bible describes the process of developing believers, adding, "Every Christian should be helping other believers grow to more and more maturity. . . . And every Christian should be seeking to get help for themselves from others to keep on growing. . . . And every church should think through how all of these kinds of biblical disciple-making find expression in their corporate life.[23]

J. D. Greear says, "Disciple making is . . . the key component of Jesus's Great Commission, and it ought to be the standard by which we judge every ministry in the church."[24] Daniel Im provides some insightful reasons why a multisite church can effectively develop disciples. These are practical reasons, but he does not provide biblical considerations.[25] Jimmy Scroggins notes one key to effective disciple-making in the church is a culture of disciple-making that is "mediated through leadership over time."[26] This points to the responsibility of leadership within the church to develop the discipleship culture they want to see active throughout

---

22   Piper, "What Is Discipleship and How Is It Done?" These remarks are made in reference to discipleship in general, and not to multisite churches.

23   Piper, "What Is Discipleship and How Is It Done?" The biblical examples Piper lists are (1) Titus 2:4—Older women are to train younger women. (2) Second Timothy 2:2—Paul trained Timothy to train others to train others. (3) Ephesians 6:4—Fathers are to train their children. (4) Matthew 28:20—Missionaries are to teach the nations everything Jesus commanded. (5) Hebrews 3:13—All Christians are to exhort each other every day to avoid sin and to stir each other up to love and good works. (6) First Peter 4:10—All Christians are to use their gifts to serve others. (7) Acts 18:24–26—Priscilla and Aquila, on the spur of the moment it seems, explained the way of God more accurately to Apollos.

24   Greear, "How to Judge the Success of a Church." In this article, he describes discipleship as "Life on life. Real friendship. Hard conversations. Intentionally missional. . . . As you go through the normal rhythms of life, invite someone to travel alongside you and read the Bible together along the way. Let the pressures of life, God's Word, and the Holy Spirit carry the heavy load. You'll be amazed at the results."

25   Im, "Multi-Site Churches and Discipleship." Im concludes, "In multi-site churches, there are greater opportunities for discipleship, since multi-site churches": (1) "Bring together the strengths of a large church . . ."; (2) "Mobilize a larger number of volunteers . . ."; (3) "Allow for a multi-level leadership pipeline for individuals discerning a call to ministry . . . "; (4) "Help individuals engage in missional community within a closer geographical area." He adds that the disciple-making problem in churches today is not a multisite church issue, but "a larger issue in North American churches."

26   Scroggins and BSCNC Communications, "Q&A: Jimmy Scroggins."

the whole church. He says in one of his podcast episodes that "disciples that make disciples" is one of the five strategies in Acts that should be a cornerstone of a church's ministry.[27]

Earl Ferguson, writing the first research thesis on the multisite topic, concludes, "The multi-site church is a faithful, effective, practical, and productive expression of Christ's challenge to make disciples." His conclusions are the most specific in identifying why multisite churches are specifically preferable for creating disciples. Of a multisite model, he first says, "It is faithful in that it is true to the New Testament pattern with its emphasis on celebration and cell groups while focusing on people." Second, he adds, "It is effective in that it holds the potential to produce healthier, strong bodies of believers more quickly and more efficiently than traditional methods." Third, he says, "It is practical in the sense that it allows for the synergy and effectiveness of a large and proven staff and carries with it the values of an already successful church." Finally, he says, "It is productive in that it takes the good news of the gospel out of the four walls we call a sanctuary and into the apartments, homes, and work-places of people who have needs."[28]

Effective discipleship can take place at a multisite church, just as at a single-site church, so long as intentional processes are in place. Rick Warren says, "Spiritual growth begins with commitment, is a gradual process, involves developing habits, is measured by five factors, is stimulated by relationships, and requires participations in all five purposes of the church."[29] Whether a multisite church takes the same approach as Warren or develops their own process, the key factor is having a process of spiritual growth, and this process must be reproducible at each campus.[30] The simplest, most efficient, and most accountable method for this is having an effective small group ministry in place at every location. Robby Gallaty, a multisite pastor, writes, "The disciples of Jesus understood that

---

27   Scroggins and White, "Five Free Strategies for Church Growth."
28   Ferguson, "The Multi-Site Church and Disciplemaking," 35. This is similar to *MCR's* conclusion at the end of the book (Surratt, Ligon, and Bird, *Multi-Site Church Revolution*, 200).
29   Warren, *Purpose Driven Church*, 334–38.
30   Driscoll and Breshears, *Vintage Church*, 252–54.

discipleship happens in community, as a group."[31] Multisite churches that have a strategy of small groups will be the most effective at providing discipleship opportunities and discipling relationships. As people are assimilated into their groups, they will have a connection point that will help them develop as biblical disciples.[32]

---

31 Gallaty, *Rediscovering Discipleship*, 144–51.
32 Books on discipleship abound. An essential classic on what it means to be a disciple is Bonhoeffer, *The Cost of Discipleship*. A great resource on practices for developing disciples is Ogden, *Discipleship Essentials*. Finally a good new resource for church discipleship ministry is English, *Deep Discipleship*.

CHAPTER 12

PRAYER

IN HIS CLASSIC BOOK ON PRAYER, Andrew Murray writes,

> And of all the traits of a life *like Christ* . . . there is none higher
> and more glorious than conformity to Him in the work that
> now engages Him without ceasing in the Father's presence—
> His all-prevailing intercession. . . . it is only when the Church
> . . . gives herself up to this holy work of intercession that we
> can expect the power of Christ to manifest itself in her behalf.[1]

He adds again, "Who can say what power a Church . . . could develop and exercise, if it gave itself to the work of prayer day and night for the coming of the kingdom, for God's power on His servants and His word, for the glorifying of God in the salvation of souls?"[2] Sadly, prayer is something that has been significantly lacking in today's church.[3] It is an indictment on the church, and a great challenge it must face, that something so essential to its very nature is something that is often ill

---

1   Murray, *With Christ in the School of Prayer*, 9–10.
2   Murray, *With Christ in the School of Prayer*, 112.
3   Helopoulos, "Pastor, Include More Prayer in Your Church Service."

represented in its ministries.[4] Much has already been said about prayer, specifically in the setting of the corporate worship service. This section will briefly address prayer as a ministry of the church.

Prayer among God's people is not only a New Testament reality but an Old Testament one as well. The prayer practices of the leaders and corporate community present in the Old Testament were the foundation for the practices of the early church.[5] One essential aspect of corporate prayer is the necessity of a prayerful leader. Jesus prayed for and modeled prayer for his disciples (Matt. 6:5–13; John 17:6–26), the apostles considered prayer one of their two essential ministries (Acts 6:4), and Paul told the young pastor Timothy that prayer was a primary concern (1 Tim. 2:1–8).[6] The early church prayed as a part of establishing new churches (Acts 14:23), prayed over important actions (Acts 13:3), and prayed in times of great need (Acts 12:5, 12). They prayed for those within the church (Acts 8:15, 17), for leaders in the church (Acts 6:6), and for those outside the church (1 Tim. 2:1–3).[7] The New Testament church included prayers of praise (Col. 1:3), thanksgiving (Acts 5:41), confession (James 5:16), and requests (Acts 4:27–30).[8] Prayer was foundational to everything the early church did, setting the standard for how the church of today should function as well.

HISTORICAL PERSPECTIVES ON PRAYER

History has many examples of people of prayer and has highlighted the importance of prayer in the church. Charles Spurgeon emphasized the importance of private and corporate prayer, saying, "Yet, though we pray in the closet, though we get into such a habit of prayer and are so full of the spirit of prayer that we can pray anywhere, yet it is well to go and mingle with others."[9] He said elsewhere about praying with others

---

4   Grenz, *Prayer*, 1.
5   Hamilton, "A Biblical Theology of Corporate Prayer."
6   Schofield, "The Bible and Church Prayer," 276–79.
7   Booth, "The Place of Prayer in the Early Church," 285–87.
8   Block, *For the Glory of God*, 215; Grenz, *Prayer*, 23–30; Grenz, *Theology for the Community of God*, 494–95; Smith, "The Aspects, Varieties, and Kinds of Prayer," 83–89; Sproul, *Does Prayer Change Things?*, Chapter 14.4.
9   Spurgeon, "The Blessing of Public Worship," 31–32.

outside the church, "The hour of prayer is the hour of need, the hour of opportunity, the hour of desire, the hour when you can come together."[10] John Broadus identifies the core aspects of prayer, writing, "He who leads a great congregation in prayer, who undertakes to express what they feel, or ought to feel, before God, to give utterance to their adoration, confession, supplication, assumes a very heavy responsibility."[11]

A. T. Robertson compares the church gathering to pray to the disciples' prayer in the upper room, saying, "It is certain that this attitude of united prayer is essential for a spiritual revival for any church and for any age."[12] This points to the power of prayer, something Criswell speaks of, writing, "But if a church is to be filled with the flame of the Holy Spirit of God, it comes through the intercessory prayer of his people. He comes in no other way."[13] William Carey credits prayer with powerful effects, writing, "The most glorious works of grace that have ever taken place have been in answer to prayer."[14] W. A. Criswell attributed revival to a prayerful people, writing,

> A revival will be blessed in proportion to the unity of effort and intercession that we pour into it. We agree in believing God will give us a revival. We agree in feeling the necessity for revival. We agree in regard to the importance of revival. We agree to the measures that are essential to the promotion of a revival—our own devotion, our own praying, our own intercession. The church must be agreed. We will not have revival without it.[15]

These quotations are just a small sample of historic statements that demonstrate that prayer has been held dear by believers, and that show that they attribute the success of the church's ministries to its people's commitment to prayer. Thus, even today, the effectiveness of a church

---

10   Spurgeon, "The Lord with Two or Three," 51.
11   Broadus, *A Treatise on the Preparation and Delivery of Sermons*, 527–28.
12   Robertson, *Jesus as a Soul-Winner and Other Sermons*, 103.
13   Criswell, *Prayer / Angelology*, 16.
14   Carey, "An Enquiry into the Obligations of Christians," 50.
15   Criswell, *Prayer / Angelology*, 63.

can be tied to the prayerfulness of its people.[16] A healthy church will be committed to being a praying church.

PRAYER IN MULTISITE CHURCHES

Multisite literature includes prayer as an essential aspect of a multisite church and includes it in the processes for launching a new campus. *MCR's* "Should Your Church Go Multi-Site?" diagnostic tool includes prayer as one of the key factors to consider, stating, "There is widespread and prayerful agreement that now is the time to launch a new site or venue."[17] The authors include prayer in the initial stage of launching a new campus, labeling it the "prayer and investigation" stage.[18] Throughout the book, they encourage "prayerfully" considering the multisite church model.[19] These examples show the authors value prayer as a part of the multisite process. However, they say little about prayer as a ministry of the church, except to mention it as one of many ministries.[20]

In *MultiChurch*, Brad House and Gregg Allison include prayer as a ministry of the multisite church. They specifically mention prayer as an essential responsibility of the lead pastor and local campus pastors. They include some theological considerations in their discussions, noting prayer is a place where the church thanks God for who he is, what he has done in them, and what he has made them as the body of Christ.[21] Allison, in his ecclesiology, identifies two general categories of prayer that should be a part of a church: prayers toward God and prayers for people. He encourages

---

16   Floyd, *How to Pray*, 243–45.
17   Surratt, Ligon, and Bird, *Multi-Site Church Revolution*, 57. *MRT* also encourages a similar set of questions that a church should "prayerfully" answer (Surratt, Ligon, and Bird, *A Multi-Site Church Road Trip*, 40).
18   Surratt, Ligon, and Bird, *Multi-Site Church Revolution*, 87.
19   Surratt, Ligon, and Bird, *Multi-Site Church Revolution*, 97. They encourage the same throughout *MRT* (Surratt, Ligon, and Bird, *A Multi-Site Church Road Trip*, 40, 185).
20   Surratt, Ligon, and Bird, *Multi-Site Church Revolution*, 33, 39, 72; Surratt, Ligon, and Bird, *A Multi-Site Church Road Trip*, 40, 88, 171. In a report on multisite, Warren Bird includes "places to post a prayer" as a primary ministry of an internet campus (Bird, "Multisite Church Scorecard").
21   House and Allison, *MultiChurch*, 84, 99–100, 155, 160. Prayer isn't specifically mentioned under the campus pastor section, but it is included under the lead pastor section. The campus pastor, however, is described as having "gifts and abilities that allow them to fulfill the duties of a lead pastor of a church."

prayers of thanksgiving, praise, and request as a part of worship toward God.[22] He also encourages prayers of intercession for spiritual growth, tangible needs, physical healing, guidance, boldness, and clarity in sharing the gospel, as well as thanksgiving on behalf of other members.[23] Mark Driscoll and Gerry Breshears highlight the importance of a prayer ministry in the church, identifying it as a ministry of love. They write, "In the life of the church, prayer is to be naturally woven throughout the entire life of God's people. . . . In summary, a loving church is filled with innumerable spoken and unspoken prayers, continually prayed out of love for God and people."[24] They, like House and Allison, also highlight the importance of prayerful leaders.[25]

Other multisite advocates have spoken, in general terms, about the importance of prayer in churches. Ed Stetzer and Mike Dodson mention prayer as one of three key ingredients in a church that seeks to overcome a pattern of decline and see revitalization.[26] Thom Rainer notes prayer is a core element of healthy churches and says intentional prayer is the key missing health ingredient in many churches.[27] He suggests ways a church can develop effective prayer ministries, and in doing so, increase the overall health of the church.[28] John Piper says the power of the church to accomplish the Great Commission mandate is found in prayer.[29] Ronnie Floyd, a former multisite pastor, highlights the importance of the pastor visibly and publicly leading the church in prayer.[30] Matt Chandler believes prayer should be a vital part of the worship service of the church, and often leads his church, corporately, in seasons of focused prayer.[31] All of these examples show that these multisite leaders, like many of their

---

22   Allison, *Sojourners and Strangers*, 427, 447.
23   Allison, *Sojourners and Strangers*, 447–48.
24   Driscoll and Breshears, *Vintage Church*, 207–8.
25   Driscoll and Breshears, *Vintage Church*, 97.
26   Stetzer and Dodson, *Comeback Churches*, 68–71.
27   Rainer and Howe, "Pastoral Leadership, Prayer, and Church Health."
28   Rainer, "Five Example of Effective Prayer Ministries." The five effective ministries are: (1) Prayer over the facilities, (2) Senior adult/retirees guided prayer ministries, (3) Worship service prayer ministry, (4) Prayer over guest cards, and (5) 24/7 prayer ministry.
29   Piper, "No Prayer, No Power."
30   Floyd, *How to Pray*, 247–48.
31   Chandler, "He Hears: How to Pray."

single-site counterparts, value the necessity of corporate prayer and ministries of prayer.

A multisite church must make prayer an essential part of the ministry plan of the church. This motivation must start with the senior pastor, and his staff must carry the same burden into their own areas of ministry.[32] In addition to prayerful leadership, a "prayer ministry" is a good next step, as it can effectively permeate a church with motivation and accountability for prayer.[33] In multisite churches, the prayer ministry should have two levels. The first level of prayer should highlight prayer needs of general interest to the whole church, such as seasonal prayer emphases, whole-church ministry focuses, or service events that the whole church will participate in. The second level provides a prayer ministry at each campus to highlight needs specific to that campus, such as personal needs among campus members, campus-specific ministries, campus-specific events, or staff needs. In having two separate levels of prayer ministry, the church can maintain unity across the whole church while also allowing for specificity in prayer through the campus prayer ministry.

In addition to a prayer ministry, a multisite church must create opportunities for the church to pray with the whole church in mind in order to maintain the unity of the whole church.[34] One way of doing this is to have campuses pray for one another. As a campus corporately prays for another campus, it helps maintain unity across the whole church, reminding the body that they are one church participating in the same mission.[35] Another way is to emphasize prayer times that happen simultaneously across multiple congregations, or highlighting and praying for the ministries of the various campuses.[36] Finally, the periodic times of whole church worship should have a significant amount of time for the whole gathered body to pray together, as was the pattern of the early church.

---

32   Floyd, *How to Pray*, 248.
33   Helms, "Church Prayer Ministries and Prayer Rooms," 342–46.
34   House and Allison, *MultiChurch*, 195–96.
35   McConnell, *Multi-Site Churches*, 206.
36   House and Allison, *MultiChurch*, 196.

CHAPTER 13

EVANGELISM AND MISSIONS

EVANGELISM AND MISSIONS ARE ALSO ASPECTS of a healthy church.[1] Evangelism happens when a believer shares the gospel with an unbeliever, while missions happens when a believer takes the gospel to someone in a different culture.[2] Thus, missions is actually a subset of the evangelistic mission of the church.[3] Lewis Drummond says, "The church's responsibility of sharing the message of salvation rests right at the center of her ministry."[4]

The mandate of evangelism and missions can clearly be seen in Jesus's final words recorded in Acts 1:8. These words are specific about the local and cross-cultural dimensions of the disciple's mission. Believers are to witness to their own city and neighbors, as well as to every other part of the globe.[5]

---

1   For a good explanation of the difference between evangelism and missions, see Piper, "Differentiating Between Evangelism and Missions."
2   Manser, *Dictionary of Bible Themes*, 8424; Piper, "Differentiating Between Evangelism and Missions."
3   The term "mission" refers to the evangelistic task of the church, i.e., "the mission of the church," and/or the evangelistic responsibility of individual believers, i.e., "living on mission." This term is equal to evangelism (Manser, *Dictionary of Bible Themes*, 7948; Raymond, "Living on Mission Means Living on Purpose").
4   Drummond, *The Word of the Cross*, 9.
5   Bock, *Acts*, I.B.1:8

In the Bible, evangelism, from the Greek root *euangelion*, means sharing "good news."[6] The commands around evangelism include preaching the good news of Jesus, being a witness about Jesus, and making disciples of Jesus.[7] Evangelism, while in the New Testament referring to the good news of Jesus, has its roots in the Old Testament redemptive mission of Israel. Genesis 3:15, often called the *protoevangelium*, is understood by evangelical scholars to be the "first good news," foreshadowing the coming of one who would defeat the serpent.[8] Genesis 12:1–3 begins to unfold the story of redemption through the promises to the lineage of Abraham.[9] The Psalms declare over and over that God's call is to all nations (Pss. 2:8; 47:9), and the prophets predict the coming Messiah who will be a redeemer not just for Israel but for all people (Isa. 11:10; 49:6; Jonah 4:10–11).[10] In the book of Acts, it is evident that the disciples' primary daily goal was the task of evangelism. Peter's message on Pentecost is the first recorded time following Jesus's ascension the disciples began sharing the good news of Jesus. From this beginning point, the church used many different methods of sharing the gospel, including mass evangelism and preaching (Acts 14:8), house-to-house witnessing (Acts 5:42), personal evangelism (Acts 8:26–38), as well as evangelism by written accounts (Luke 1:1–4; John 20:31).[11]

As evangelism continued, the missionary movement took shape. Beginning with the persecution from Saul in Acts 8, the church began taking the gospel to the Gentile nations (Acts 8:1, 4; 11:19–21). These first "missionaries" were simply Christians who were moving from one place to another and shared the gospel along their way.[12] Yet, this was the fulfillment of Christ's command to take the gospel outside the Jewish community to all nations. The words Jesus used, *panta ta ethne*, indicate that the gospel was to go to

---

6   Strong, *The New Strong's Concise Dictionary of Bible Words*, 2098.
7   Reid, *Introduction to Evangelism*, 8–10.
8   Gow, "Fall," 3.
9   Reid, *Introduction to Evangelism*, 27.
10   Piper, *Let the Nations Be Glad*, 167–75.
11   Terry, *Evangelism*, 24–26. These categories are generalized from Terry's more specific categories, which include: (1) mass evangelism, (2) public preaching, (3) house-to-house witnessing, (4) evangelistic campaigns, (5) personal witnessing, (6) public debate, (7) lay evangelism, (8) literary evangelism, (9) church planting, and (10) home Bible studies.
12   Piper, *Let the Nations Be Glad*, 94.

all people groups, not simply countries.[13] This means Jesus's intention was literally that his disciples would cross every cultural barrier with the message of the gospel. The church eventually understood this command and embraced the call to reach the nations by sending missionaries on evangelistic church planting missions. Citing the church at Antioch commissioning and sending Paul and Barnabas for their first missionary journey (Acts 13:2–3), Grenz writes, "So began the great advance of the gospel into the wider Roman world. This incident reminds us that the believing company encourages, dedicates, commissions and supports those who carry the good news to the unevangelized."[14] He also highlights the responsibility of the church as God's voice in the world, writing, "The role of the church as God's agent in the sending of messengers is especially evident in the calling of missionaries."[15]

This analysis of the biblical expectation and the example of the early church shows that evangelism is an expectation of any healthy church. Not only that, churches are expected to take the gospel not just to their own people, but to other nations as well. Evangelism and cross-cultural engagement with the lost are essential components of a healthy church.

HISTORICAL PERSPECTIVES ON EVANGELISM AND MISSIONS

A concern for non-believers has been a hallmark of Protestant believers. An early confession from the sixteenth century speaks about public evangelism, stating, "That such as yet see not the truth, may hear the public doctrine and prayers of the church, and with all meekness are to be sought by all means."[16] A leadership position in early English Separatist Baptists was called a "Messenger." One such messenger, Thomas Grantham, writes in 1674 that his responsibility was "to preach the Gospel . . . where it is not known; to plant churches where there is none; to ordain Elders . . . in churches remote, and to assist in dispensing the

---

13   Piper, *Let the Nations Be Glad*, 161–67.
14   Grenz, *Theology for the Community of God*, 424.
15   Grenz, *Theology for the Community of God*, 423–24.
16   Lumpkin, *Baptist Confessions of Faith*, 94. This quote from "A True Confession" is presented here in modern spelling. The original spelling can be seen in the work cited.

holy Mysteries."[17] This common position in those days shows an early concern for evangelism and missions.

Noting a call to evangelism both near and to the nations, Andrew Fuller says,

> We are, doubtless, warranted and obliged, by this commission, to embrace any opening, in any part of the earth, within our reach, for the imparting of the word of life to them that are without it . . . the work of spreading the gospel is ordinary, and not confined to any single age. . . . We pray for the conversion and salvation of the world, and yet neglect the ordinary means by which those ends have been used to be accomplished . . . the command of the Saviour . . . is that we go, and preach it to every creature.[18]

William Carey, a pioneer of missions, writes concerning the Great Commission, "This commission was as extensive as possible, and laid them under obligation to disperse themselves into every country of the habitable globe, and preach to all the inhabitants, without exception, or limitation."[19] Francis Wayland emphasizes "missions" at home, writing,

> A large missionary field is spreading abroad on every side, in the immediate vicinity of our very churches. What are we doing to supply these perishing souls with the word of life? . . . Have believers any right to settle down at their ease, enjoying the privileges of the sanctuary, while their fellow-men are perishing around them in heathenish darkness?[20]

Like Carey and Wayland, A. T. Robertson calls for more missionaries, and he assigns the duty of calling them to the pastors. He says, "One thing

---

17   Grantham, quoted in *The Baptist Heritage: Four Centuries of Baptist Witness*, 78–79. By "Mysteries," Grantham means the ordinances of baptism and the Lord's Supper.
18   Fuller, "God's Approbation of Our Labours," 186–88; Fuller, "Instances, Evil, and Tendency of Delay," 148.
19   Carey, "An Enquiry into the Obligations of Christians, 26.
20   Wayland, *The Principles and Practices of Baptist Churches*, 162–63.

is certain: If all the pastors at home were real missionaries, there would be no lack of support of the work abroad."[21] Of course, missions has not been simply limited to social service. It has centered on the gospel, as Robertson makes clear, writing, "Christianity leads to brotherly love in its noblest expression of service to hospitals, orphanages, asylums, community chests, and all other forms of social helpfulness. But these things are the expression of Christianity, not the gospel itself."[22]

Evangelism has been seen historically as the responsibility of the whole church. John Dagg shows this, writing, "It is our duty to labor fruitfully and preservingly to bring all men to the knowledge of truth. . . . This commission requires us to preach the gospel to every creature; and we ought to be foremost in obeying it."[23] The first paragraph of L. R. Scarborough's classic *With Christ After the Lost* says,

> The most gigantic undertaking God has laid out for Christian men is to lead lost souls to Jesus Christ. . . . In this saving program he requisitioned all the powers of his triune deity, and he calls for the co-operation of every saved man. Christ emptied himself in sacrificial libation on God's altar to redeem us, and God requires us to offer to him our best and our all in witnessing to others of this redeeming grace.[24]

George Truett also points out that evangelism should be a ministry of the whole church, stating, "How shall we save our churches? My fellow Christians, there is one sure way, and that is that our churches be great life-saving stations to point lost sinners to Christ. The supreme indictment that you can bring against a church, if you are able in truth to bring it, is that such church lacks in passion and compassion for human souls."[25]

He emphasizes this is best accomplished by individuals performing personal evangelism. He says, "The supreme method for winning the

---

21   Robertson, *Jesus as a Soul-Winner*, 26.
22   Robertson, *Jesus as a Soul-Winner*, 107.
23   Dagg, "The Duty of Baptists," 199.
24   Scarborough, *With Christ After the Lost*, 2.
25   Truett, *A Quest for Souls*, 67.

world to Christ is the personal method, the bringing of people to Christ one by one. That is Christ's plan."[26] Others emphasize the need of training so evangelism and missions could be accomplished. Broadus says, "I know of no art of social life more needful to be cultivated in our time and country than the art of skillfully introducing religion into general conversation."[27] Mullins emphasizes training and discipleship for evangelism, saying, "Perhaps the best qualification for presenting clearly the truth that one knows is to have a clear grasp of the truth itself. The soul winner needs to be able to state the saving truths of the gospel in the clearest possible manner. . . . Nothing is more important for the soul winner and personal worker than a clear grasp of the saving message of the Gospel."[28]

These statements show that evangelism is a central component of all churches. A concern for the lost and a desire to share the gospel with them must be focal points of healthy churches. This concern should demonstrate itself in training believers in sharing the gospel and sending them out locally and abroad to evangelize, perform gospel-centered mission work, and plant churches. These reproducing activities are hallmarks of a healthy church.

EVANGELISM AND MISSIONS IN MULTISITE CHURCHES

In multisite literature, evangelism is assumed to be a primary motivator of churches who are using the multisite model. In *MCR*, the authors describe an "increase in evangelism" as a product of churches using multisite ministry.[29] They write, "The multi-site ride has most often been about opportunities—reaching more people with the gospel, developing more leaders, and influencing other churches."[30] Most of their references are to evangelism only as a category of ministry or a church value when telling a story of a certain multisite church.[31] Missions is never mentioned

26   Truett, *A Quest for Souls*, 57.
27   Broadus, *Sermons and Addresses*, 5.
28   Mullins, *Talks on Soul Winning*, 14–15.
29   Surratt, Ligon, and Bird, *Multi-Site Church Revolution*, 17, 197–98.
30   Surratt, Ligon, and Bird, *Multi-Site Church Revolution*, 66.
31   Surratt, Ligon, and Bird, *Multi-Site Church Revolution*, 34, 53.

aside from a category of ministry, or as a multisite church story.[32] In *MRT*, there is a brief discussion of mission strategy related to multisite churches. The authors recommend an international campus as an avenue for missions, suggesting international multisite churches will "transform approaches to missions."[33]

Brad House and Gregg Allison claim the multisite church helps a church contextualize the gospel in a way that helps them reach their specific neighborhood. They specifically speak about the church members as bearers of the image of God and witnesses of his grace, saying, "The church is image-bearer, and the church is the body of Christ. . . . This truth should be sung and prayed through the church's worship, proclaimed in its pulpit, displayed by its discipleship, and expanded through its mission." This reference shows that the authors consider evangelism and pointing to the reality of Christ as a central aspect of the church. They also make clear their understanding that the church must take the gospel both locally and globally, indicating an understanding of the importance of missions.[34] Allison notes the mission of the church is to spread the gospel locally and worldwide, writing, "Thus, the church engages in its work of sharing the good news, propelling itself in obedience to the Word of God, and being propelled by the Holy Spirit, into the uttermost parts of the earth to fulfill its mission until the Lord's return."[35] Specifically about multisite churches, he says the purpose of multisite is "city-reaching," a church seeking to impact its whole city with the gospel.[36]

Mark Driscoll and Gerry Breshears describe a "missional church" as a church that engages in evangelism and contextualizes the gospel so those in their community can respond to it. A church is not only concerned with its own location, but a missional church also calls, trains, and sends out missionaries into other cultures, whether those different cultures are

---

32   Surratt, Ligon, and Bird, *Multi-Site Church Revolution*, 33, 64. The authors suggest find-
      ing money in the missions budget with which to fund launching a multisite campus
      (102, 107).
33   Surratt, Ligon, and Bird, *A Multi-Site Church Road Trip*, 144, 219.
34   House and Allison, *MultiChurch*, 17, 62–63, 65, 67, 99–100, 140–41.
35   Allison, *Sojourners and Strangers*, 440.
36   Allison, "Theological Defense of Multi-Site," 14, 16.

in the same area or around the world.[37] J. D. Greear is a strong proponent of evangelism and missions. He writes, "Members need to learn to share the gospel, without the help of a pastor, in the community, and start ministries and Bible studies—even churches—in places without them. Churches must become discipleship factories, 'sending' agencies that equip their members to take the battle to the enemy."[38]

Greear's church, The Summit Church, engages in evangelism, church planting, and missions, and has a goal of planting one thousand churches by 2050.[39] John Piper is famously known for writing, "Missions exists because worship doesn't." His point is that God is ultimate, and the worship of God by as many people as possible is the ultimate driving force behind missions.[40] Thus, for Piper, the church engages in missions for the sake of God's glory. He also emphasizes that, like the early church, evangelism is the responsibility of the whole church.[41] Jimmy Scroggins's passion for church-wide evangelism led him to develop the "3 Circles" evangelism tool.[42] He says for a church to develop a healthy evangelistic passion, it takes time, and it must start with the leader.[43] His church uses multisite as an avenue for reaching more people with the gospel by contextualizing campuses to fit the demographics of their various neighborhoods and communities. They do the same through their church planting efforts.[44]

These examples show that spreading the gospel is at the heart of multisite ministry. As in any church, the church-wide passion for evangelism and missions is tied to the leadership, and this passion must be communicated frequently and clearly.[45] In a multisite church, the emphasis on evangelism and missions at the campus level typically parallels the

---

37   Driscoll and Breshears, *Doctrine*, 312–13 Driscoll and Breshears, *Vintage Church*, 222–33.

38   Greear, *Gaining by Losing*, 28.

39   Shellnut, "J. D. Greear Transformed His Church Through Missions."

40   Piper, *Let the Nations Be Glad*, 17.

41   Piper, "Inspired by the Incredible Early Church."

42   Austin, "The Origin of the '3 Circles.'"

43   Scroggins, "10 Ways to Build an Evangelistic Culture."

44   Scroggins and Wright, "Autonomous Launch"; Scroggins and Wright, "How Family Church Does Multisite."

45   Scroggins, "Build an Evangelistic Culture."

emphasis from the original campus and whole-church leadership.[46] Thus, in order for a multisite church as a whole to excel in evangelism and missions, the founding leadership and body must initially excel in evangelism and missions, or they must develop that passion. At the campuses, the campus pastor and local leadership must emphasize the same focus of evangelism and missions, reiterating the goals of the church.[47]

Multisite churches have the benefit of having a local presence in more than one location. Thus, the opportunity for contextualized evangelism and local missions can be embraced by the various campuses.[48] Each campus can engage its own community with the gospel and make a significant impact in its own backyard.[49] Multisite churches can also purposely place locations in cross-cultural situations as an intentional aspect of their missions strategy.[50] Whatever the strategy, the essential responsibility of multisite churches, as with all churches, is to maintain a focus on evangelism and missions in order to participate in the commission of taking the gospel to all peoples. Evangelism and missions must not be only a program of the church. They must be central to the church's culture.[51]

---

46   Bird and Walters, "Multisite Is Multiplying."
47   McConnell, *Multi-Site Churches*, 91–100.
48   House and Allison, *MultiChurch*, 64.
49   Allison, "Theological Defense," 16.
50   Ahlen and Thomas, *One Church, Many Congregations*, 78–79; Surratt, Ligon, and Bird, *A Multi-Site Church Road Trip*, 59, 79–80. Because of the wide range of international cultures that have found their way into U.S. cities, a missions strategy of cross-cultural campus planting or church planting can take place within the same city. While not international missions, this "diaspora missiology" is a viable way to impact international cultures, as many international residents currently in the U.S. will one day return to their people (Garrett, "The Next Frontier," 23).
51   Newton, "Your Church Can Reach the Nations," 20.

CHAPTER 14

STEWARDSHIP

A HEALTHY CHURCH MUST MANAGE its resources well and must also teach its members about handling their resources biblically. Biblical stewardship is concerned with more than money.[1] R. C. Sproul says, "Fundamentally, stewardship is about exercising our God-given dominion over His creation, reflecting the image of our creator God in His care, responsibility, maintenance, protection, and beautification of His creation."[2] Ben Gill says stewardship is rooted in a biblical worldview and can only be fully appreciated with an understanding of the self-revealed, personal God of the Bible. He writes,

> Only a biblical theism provides the adequate theological context for a doctrine and practice of personal stewardship. Thus, stewardship belongs to the category of revealed religion. An adequate understanding of stewardship rests upon the

---

1   Writers and pastors often refer to stewardship of "time, talent, and treasures," meaning we are to manage our time wisely, use our abilities productively, and utilize our money and resources wisely for the glory of God. This section on stewardship will only consider stewardship of physical resources and will not discuss stewardship of talent and time (Jamieson, "Giving Time, Talents, and Treasures"; Reardon, "Stewardship Is More than Giving Money").

2   Sproul, *How Should I Think About Money?*, 6.

principle that God is self-disclosed in the Word and without that disclosure there could be no comprehension of life as a steward. . . . Anything less than a revealed responsibility of stewardship fractionalizes stewardship on the basis of self-interest.[3]

Stewardship in the Bible begins in the garden of Eden, where God commands Adam to manage the creation he had given them. He tells him in Genesis 1:28 to "be fruitful, multiply, fill the earth, and subdue it," and in 2:15 to "work it and watch over it."[4] God alone, as the owner of all things prior to the creation of man and after, has the right to give stewardship of the earth and its resources.[5] From this beginning point of creation, the Bible continually reiterates that everything belongs to the Lord (Deut. 10:14; Job 41:11; Ps. 24:1). Scripture is also clear that people are to act as stewards, or managers, of the resources God gives them (Matt. 25:14–30; Luke 16:1–13; Rom. 14:12). Eventually there will be a time when the managers must give an account for their management of God's resources (Rom. 14:4, 12; Heb. 4:13).[6]

Jesus had much to say about how people use their money. In fact, one third of Jesus's parables dealt with how people handle their possessions.[7] He recognized that money has the potential to pull a believer's affections away from God if he or she loves it more than he or she loves the Lord (Matt. 6:24; Luke 18:18–30).[8] Jesus knew that money can lead to pride and other forms of sin (Matt. 6:1–4).[9] He also realized that the manner in which someone uses money can demonstrate his or her love for God and love for others (Luke 10:25–35; 19:2–10; 21:1–3).[10] Jesus upheld the tithe, continuing the Old Testament practice, which predated the Mosaic law (Matt. 23:23).[11]

---

3   Gill, *Stewardship*, 4.
4   Sproul, *How Should I Think About Money?*, 4–5.
5   Gill, *Stewardship*, 7.
6   Alcorn, *Managing God's Money*, 14–16, 21–31.
7   Hawkins, *Money Talks*, 8.
8   Edwards, *The Gospel According to Luke*, 16.7; Turner, *Matthew*, 197–98.
9   Driscoll and Breshears, *Doctrine*, 374–75.
10 Edwards, *The Gospel According to Luke*, 9.5, 17.2, 18.2.
11 Alcorn, *Managing God's Money*, 122; Gill, *Stewardship*, 60–63. This book takes the po-

The members of the early church modeled generosity in their giving. Acts 2:44–45 and 4:32–35 show the believers in Jerusalem were generous with their possessions and money in order to provide for those who had need.[12] These examples highlight the individual generosity of Christian believers, who, out of their own resources, gave to the church in order to support the ministry of the church. Paul refers to the generosity of the Gentile churches in providing for him and for ministry to other Christians (Rom. 15:25–29; 2 Cor. 9:1–15; Phil. 4:10, 15–19).[13] These acts Paul mentions highlight the generosity and stewardship of a church body, coming together to support the work of the ministry, even ministry happening outside the church. Generosity is a hallmark of Christian faith, and it is rewarded by God. Paul makes clear that God rewards those who, by faith, give generously to God's work. Paul writes,

The point is this: The person who sows sparingly will also reap sparingly, and the person who sows generously will also reap generously. Each person should do as he has decided in his heart—not reluctantly or out of compulsion, since God loves a cheerful giver. And God is able to make every grace overflow to you, so that in every way, always having everything you need, you may excel in every good work. (2 Cor. 9:6–8)[14]

HISTORICAL PERSPECTIVES ON STEWARDSHIP

Early confessions speak of giving, often regarding providing support for pastors. The First London Confession states, "They that preach the Gospel . . . should live on the Gospel."[15] Likewise, pastors have commented on giving and generosity, such as Fuller, who writes, "They might have said, We have enough to do to provide for our own houses. . . . But feeling,

---

sition that believers are still expected to tithe, but that is not a universally held belief. For a brief analysis of the views on either side of this debate see Barcley, "The Bible Commands Christians to Tithe"; Schreiner, "7 Reasons Christians Are Not Required to Tithe." For a more in-depth discussion see Croteau, *Perspectives on Tithing*.

12   Bock, *Acts*, 2.C.1, 2.E.1.
13   Guthrie, *2 Corinthians*; Kruse, *Paul's Letter to the Romans*; Osborne, *Philippians*, 12.
14   Guthrie, *2 Corinthians*, 3.C.
15   Lumpkin, *Baptist Confessions of Faith*, 166.

as they did, for the afflicted and necessitous, especially for those of the household of faith, they would deny themselves many comforts for the sake of being able to relieve them."[16]

Similarly, John Gill writes, "Brotherly love demands such a conduct in church-members to their brethren in distress; for, how dwelleth the love of God in such, who, having a portion of worldly things, shuts up their bowels of compassion from their brethren in need?"[17] Churches have taught that believers are simply stewards of that which belongs to God, and these resources are to be used for his purposes. Frank Leavell writes, "Stewardship is, then, administering that which belongs to another for the benefit of the owner. . . . Christian stewardship, as taught in the New Testament, means that the Christian holds that which he possesses as God's, to be used for God."[18]

The Protestant church has a long history of organized giving. William Carey, who formed the first mission society with Andrew Fuller, provides a stewardship plan to enable churches to engage in ministry more effectively, writing, "If congregations were to open subscriptions of one penny or more per week, according to their circumstances, and deposit it as a fund for the propagation of the gospel, much might be raised this way. By such simple means they might soon have it in their power to introduce the preaching of the gospel into most of the villages in England."[19]

Similarly, B. H. Carroll suggests a stewardship plan, saying, "First, no church can adjust herself properly to so many and such varied financial obligations without confusion of mind as to their number and relative merits, unless she adopts and conforms to a system formulated in wisdom

---

16   Fuller, "Alms-Giving and Prayer," 575.
17   Gill, *Doctrinal and Practical Divinity*, 570.
18   Leavell, *Training in Stewardship*, 5–6.
19   Carey, "An Inquiry into the Obligations of Christians," *Treasuries from the Baptist Heritage*, 54. In 1801, a clerk in his third year at the East India Company, a lucrative job in England, could expect to earn around £50 annually (Boot, "Real Incomes of the British Middle Class," 643). Thus, the £0.52 given toward missions annually would represent approximately 1 percent of their annual income. This would, of course, represent a higher percentage for those with lower paying jobs. Comparatively, someone with an annual income of $50,000 today would give $500 annually if giving an equal percentage. SBC individuals give much less than that. Using 2018/2019 numbers, SBC members gave an average of $31.82 per person ($462,299,010/14,525,579) ("Fast Facts," *Southern Baptist Convention*).

and thoughtful provision."[20] Carroll also encourages cooperative giving to organizations for the purpose of missions.[21]

These examples show that wise stewardship has been consistently advocated for in church history. Wise church leaders have encouraged giving and wise management of the funds that members entrust to the church. That giving, as a returned portion of the resources God provides members, is to be used in fulfilling the mission of the church. A healthy church will steward God's resources in this way.

STEWARDSHIP IN MULTISITE CHURCHES

Multisite advocates regularly speak about finances when discussing multisite churches, particularly in the area of financial costs of moving to a multisite model. *MCR* includes a chapter devoted to the expenses of multisite ministry. The authors conclude, "Most churches opening their first off-site campus will invest between $50,000 and $150,000."[22] They include many ideas for financing the project, with the goal of not just funding a new campus but of helping to keep the church in a financially stable situation. Both *MCR* and McConnell provide budgeting plans churches can use to think through the costs of moving in a multisite direction.[23] Understanding the balance of stewardship and trusting God to do the impossible, Scott McConnell writes, "The experience of these multi-site churches is that they step out in faith in many ways, but as [one church] demonstrates they also are not reckless or naïve in terms of finances. . . . You must plan and plan responsibly. But also watch for God to use finances to indicate his direction."[24]

MCR's authors, along with other writers and practitioners, see multisite as wisely stewarding the finances and resources they have

---

20 Carroll, *Saved to Serve*, 40.
21 Carroll, *Saved to Serve*, 43–44.
22 Surratt, Ligon, and Bird, *Multi-Site Church Revolution*, 96–110. Research conducted by Leadership Network eight years after *MCR* was published showed average start-up expenses, based on size and model, between $46,000 and $1,465,000, with an average of all sizes and models coming to $145,000 to begin a new campus (Bird, "Multisite Scorecard," 14).
23 McConnell, *Multi-Site Churches*, 42–46; Surratt, Ligon, and Bird, *Multi-Site Church Revolution*, 106–10.
24 McConnell, *Multi-Site Churches*, 41.

been provided, claiming the cost of going multisite is less than the cost of growing larger in one location.[25] Brad House and Gregg Allison, however, conclude the claim of financial savings is a multisite myth. They write, "Multisite and multichurch are complex models, and organizational complexity costs money."[26] They claim the overall financial expense goes up with the level of centralized control in a multisite church. The model House and Allison recommend is one where central operations receive lower amounts of financial control in order to keep as many financial decisions as possible in the hands of the local campus leadership. This keeps resources, and responsibility, in the hands of the people making the gifts.[27]

Multisite writers have not discussed teaching stewardship or developing biblical stewardship in the context of multisite churches, but some of them have discussed biblical stewardship separately. Mark Driscoll and Gerry Breshears advocate joyous giving on the part of individuals as an act of love toward God and others. They add that both individuals and churches recognize all they have comes from, and belongs to, God.[28] In *Doctrine*, they devote a lengthy chapter to the topic of stewardship and specifically address stewardship in churches. They expect churches to demonstrate financial accountability in their financial practices and expect the same from their leaders. They also say churches should give generously to outside ministries and should train their members on how to live financially responsible and generous lives.[29]

Allison encourages giving in *Sojourners and Strangers*. He uniquely mentions that the individuals of the church, and the church as a whole, must demonstrate genuine generosity. He notes the terrible fate Ananias and Sapphira received after trying to seek credit for artificial generosity (Acts 5:1–11). Genuine generosity flows out of the heart of a people who

---

25 Ferguson, "The Multi-Site Church"; Greear, "A Pastor Defends His Multi-Site Church," 20–21; Piper, "Treasuring Christ Together as a Church on Multiple Campuses"; Rainer and Howe, "Why Smaller Churches Are Going Multisite"; Surratt, Ligon, and Bird, *Multi-Site Church Revolution*, 88, 99.

26 House and Allison, *MultiChurch*, 175.

27 House and Allison, *MultiChurch*, 176–83.

28 Driscoll and Breshears, *Vintage Church*, 208–9.

29 Driscoll and Breshears, *Doctrine*, 399–402.

understand the generosity God has shown to them in Christ. Thus, Allison says, individuals should give to the church in times of plenty and in lean times for the work of the church now and in the future. Church leaders should encourage sacrificial giving by the members, and those same leaders should be financially responsible for the offerings the members provide, as they use the money for ministry. Allison specifically highlights three areas of special importance in a church's financial responsibilities: (1) financially support the pastor, (2) care for church members, and (3) help for the poor.[30]

These discussions of stewardship in churches, and biblical stewardship in general, provide a good foundation upon which to base a system of biblical stewardship for multisite churches. Multisite churches, like all churches, must have a system of financial accountability and responsibility in place in order to maintain integrity in its practices. This system must have levels of oversight to ensure money is properly handled and resources are used in the areas of ministry they were intended to be used.[31] Poor financial management, or worse, illegal action, not only hurts the church but the reputation of Christ himself.[32] Good financial stewardship on the part of church leadership, both corporately and individually, models stewardship for the church members.[33] Multisite churches, like all churches, should also teach biblical stewardship and provide resources for their members to grow in their ability to give.[34] This is something that comes from the leaders of the church and must be a topic preached on by the pastor. Pastors should not be silent about money and stewardship.[35] Stewardship, whether practiced well or practiced poorly, is a spiritual issue, revealing the heart of an individual. A church that struggles financially

---

30   Allison, *Sojourners and Strangers*, 449–59.
31   Allison, *Sojourners and Strangers*, 451; Malphurs, *Advanced Strategic Planning*, 255–82. Much more detail could be included to describe a good model, but that is beyond the necessary information for this section. For more details on a good structure, see Malphurs's chapter cited above.
32   Allison, *Sojourners and Strangers*, 451.
33   Driscoll and Breshears, *Doctrine*, 400.
34   Alcorn, *Managing God's Money*, 234–37; Driscoll and Breshears, *Doctrine*, 400–401.
35   Alcorn, *Managing God's Money*, 233–40; Bryant and Brunson, *The New Guidebook for Pastors*, 175–78.

likely has people whose hearts are not fully devoted to their Lord, or has leadership whose hearts are focused on the wrong motivation.[36]

All churches must deal with the decisions of budgeting and financial management. They must decide budgets for ministries and allocate funds accordingly. This takes wisdom and discernment on the part of church leadership. Four primary areas of budget concern are missions, ministries, staffing, and facilities.[37] While every church must develop and manage a budget, a multisite church adds in the complication of either managing multiple budgets (one from each campus) and a central budget, or managing a single budget that resources multiple locations. Both are complex structures.[38] While each campus may provide different amounts of funds to either a central budget or their own budget, it is essential to ensure members and campuses are financially invested in supporting the mission of the church.[39] Healthy multisite churches must have the goal of biblical stewardship by each individual, each campus, and as a whole church.

---

36   Whitney, *Spiritual Disciplines for the Christian Life*, 140–46; Whitney, *Spiritual Disciplines Within the Church*, 118–27.
37   Bryant and Brunson, *New Guidebook for Pastors*, 174–75; Malphurs, *Advanced Strategic Planning*, 264–68..
38   House and Allison, *MultiChurch*, 58–72; Surratt, Ligon, and Bird, *Multi-Site Church Revolution*, 106.
39   Bird, *Multi-Site Scorecard*, 13–14; House and Allison, *MultiChurch*, 157–58, 182–83.

CHAPTER 15

COMMUNITY

HEALTHY CHURCHES HAVE HEALTHY expressions of biblical community. Church leaders and writers frequently speak of the importance of community. Donald Whitney writes, "Emotionally healthy people crave community. God made us with that desire, and we seek to satisfy it in societies of all sorts."[1] Randy Frazee argues, "We were designed by God physically, emotionally, and spiritually to require community for our health and well-being."[2] Jerry Bridges writes, "Spiritual fellowship is not a luxury but a necessity, vital to our spiritual growth and health."[3] These authors and more highlight the importance of community, but it is not always clear what community includes. Even these authors interchange words and phrases such as *fellowship, small groups, community groups*, and others, which can lead to confusion in the conversation.[4]

---

1   Whitney, *Spiritual Disciplines Within the Church*, 147.
2   Frazee, *The Connecting Church 2.0*, 26.
3   Bridges, *True Fellowship*, 76.
4   Bridges, *True Fellowship*, 13, 181–89; Frazee, *The Connecting Church 2.0*, 149–50; Whitney, *Spiritual Disciplines Within the Church*, 148–49. In this book, "community" will be the operative word to refer to the concept of small groups, fellowship (other than a mere "fellowship event"), and church life together. Other terms will be used only when speaking about a specific practice of community, e.g., when referring to small group as a specific ministry model.

The example of the early church can help set a clear path for true biblical community.

The word *fellowship* is a common term in churches. Many churches have a "fellowship hall," which is a large room dedicated to hosting events, often involving meals, where the church comes together in celebration to enjoy one another's company.[5] However, there is more to the biblical idea of community than simply infrequent socializing.[6] When pastors and writers speak of biblical community, the word they are most often referring to in the Scriptures is *koinonia*. *Koinonia*, in the Greek, means "fellowship, communion or sharing together." It "refers to the community or fellowship of Christian believers participating together in the life of Christ as made possible by the spirit. This foundational shared participation in turn indicates the basic characteristics of the Christians' life together as a community of disciples."[7]

John Hammett points out, "Fellowship is expressed in the common life and intimate relationships believers share in the church."[8] Paul uses *koinonia* to describe the relationship between Jesus and his followers.[9] This fellowship/community with Christ must be present in a believer's life through the power and presence of the Holy Spirit before he or she can experience true community within the church. Stanley Grenz writes, "In mediating to us fellowship with God, the Spirit also brings us into community with one another and with all creation . . . through conversion the Spirit brings us to participation within a community, the disciples of Jesus and the new creation of God."[10]

The foundational passage for definitions of community is Acts 2:42–47, which says,

> They devoted themselves to the apostles' teaching, to the
> fellowship, to the breaking of bread, and to prayer. Everyone

---

5   Hammett, *Biblical Foundations for Baptist Churches*, 232–34.
6   Bridges, *True Fellowship*, 15, 181–89.
7   Grenz, Guretzki, and Nordling, *Pocket Dictionary of Theological Terms*, 7.
8   Hammett, *Biblical Foundations for Baptist Churches*, 232–33.
9   Whitney, *Spiritual Disciplines Within the Church*, 149.
10 Grenz, *Theology for the Community of God*, 439; cf. Hammett, *Biblical Foundations for Baptist Churches*, 233; Hellerman, *When the Church Was a Family*, 222.

was filled with awe, and many wonders and signs were being performed through the apostles. Now all the believers were together and held all things in common. They sold their possessions and property and distributed the proceeds to all, as any had need. Every day they devoted themselves to meeting together in the temple, and broke bread from house to house. They ate their food with joyful and sincere hearts, praising God and enjoying the favor of all the people. Every day the Lord added to their number those who were being saved.[11]

Bridges identifies four categories that summarize how the early church practiced community: (1) community relationship, (2) partnership, (3) communion, and (4) sharing material possessions.[12]

Community relationships emphasize the personal connections that are established by those within the community. An emphasis on community relationships can be seen in the frequency of the church gathering together. Acts 2:42 and 46 say the believers were "devoted" to their community, emphasizing the value they placed on these relationships. Other episodes in Acts reveal this devotion as well (Acts 4:32; 5:12, 14; 12:12), and passages in the epistles also emphasize the commitment to community relationships (1 Cor. 16:19; Philem. 1:2; 1 John 1:3).[13] These relationships show that the early church was committed to participating in the community together, not as isolated individuals.[14]

Partnership emphasizes the community aspect of sharing together in a common mission.[15] This community partnership can be seen in the Acts 2:42–47 passage, as well as in the other descriptions of the newly developing church (Acts 4:23–37; 5:12–16; 6:17). Paul emphasizes this often, referring to his cohort as "partners" for the sake of the gospel, including the struggle of carrying out the mission of evangelism (2 Cor. 8:23; Phil. 4:3;

---

11   See also Bridges, *True Fellowship*, 13–14; Hammett, *Biblical Foundations for Baptist Churches*, 233; Whitney, *Spiritual Disciplines Within the Church*, 148.

12   Bridges, *True Fellowship*, 22–23.

13   Bridges, *True Fellowship*, 13–14; Gardner, *1 Corinthians*, 16:19–21; Still, *Philippians and Philemon*, 175–76.

14   Grenz, *Theology for the Community of God*, 480–81.

15   Bridges, *True Fellowship*, 17.

Philem. 1:17).[16] He also referred to the Gentile believers as partners in the community of Christ (Eph. 3:6).[17] Thus, partnership in a common mission and common circumstances was an essential part of early church community.[18]

Being a community emphasizes the spiritual unity that is present in the community of believers. Acts 2:42 shows the spiritual hunger that was present in the new church, and that gathering in community is where that spiritual hunger was satisfied.[19] The epistles continue this emphasis on spiritual development as an aspect of community life. Paul says for the believers to let the words of Christ be present "among" the community, teaching and worshiping together (Col. 3:16).[20] The writer of Hebrews says the gathering of the community is a place to encourage and challenge one another in the pursuit of Christ (Heb. 10:24–25).[21] Thus, it is apparent that community is expected to provide and encourage spiritual growth within the church family.[22]

Sharing material possessions is a final aspect of biblical community. This is a challenging aspect of community in an individualistic culture such as the United States, but it seems to have been a natural inclination in the early church.[23] Again, Acts 2 serves as evidence. Verses 44–45 show the believers sharing their material possessions with one another, and Acts 4:34–37 provides more evidence that this was a common practice.[24] In fact, it was such an important aspect of the early church life that some were even willing to try to gain a reputation for such generosity through deceit.[25] Generosity was a hallmark of the church communities in the New Testament, as seen in comments throughout Paul's letters (Rom.

16   Guthrie, 2 Corinthians, 3.B.3; Osborne, Philippians, 12; Still, Philippians and Philemon, 170–78.
17   Thielman, Ephesians, 6.A.
18   Grenz, Theology for the Community of God, 481–82.
19   Bridges, True Fellowship, 18–20.
20   Osborne, Colossians and Philemon, 4.3.2.2.
21   Cockerill, The Epistle to the Hebrews, 3.A.1.
22   Whitney, Spiritual Disciplines Within the Church, 155–56.
23   Hellerman, When the Church Was a Family, 145–47.
24   Bock, Acts, 2.C, 2.E.
25   Alcorn, Managing God's Money, 135–37.

15:25–29; 2 Cor. 9:1–15; Phil. 4:10, 15–19).[26] This aspect of community builds dependence and trust between the believers, indicating they can, and should, depend on one another in times of need.[27]

HISTORICAL PERSPECTIVES ON COMMUNITY

Churches throughout history have valued fellowship within the church body. Thomas Helyws's confession from 1610 acknowledges the importance of the church community, stating, "That one and every member of the congregation should know one another in order that they may offer each other all gifts of fraternal charity, in mind as well as in body."[28] Similarly, John Gill writes,

> The relations that members of churches stand in to each other oblige to love; being fellow-citizens of the same family, are brethren to each other, and make one fraternity, or brotherhood which they should love. . . . Mutual love is an evidence of being the disciples of Christ. . . . It is this which makes communion in a church-state delightful and comfortable as well as honourable.[29]

When writing about those things that create a true gospel church, Benjamin Keach writes that believing members are

> not only united by the Spirit, to Christ the Foundation . . . but also to one another in sincere Love . . . and Affection . . . in the sweet Union . . . and Concord . . . that ought to be in the church. . . . To sympathize with the Afflicted . . . succour . . . the Tempted . . . and Relieving . . . the Poor . . . and Distressed. . . . Rejoicing with them that Rejoice . . . and Mourning . . . with them that Mourn . . . bear one another's Burdens . . . and so fulfill the Law of Christ.[30]

---

26 Guthrie, *2 Corinthians*, 3.C; Kruse, *Paul's Letter to the Romans*, 4.C.2; Osborne, *Philippians and Philemon*, 12.
27 Allison, *Sojourners and Strangers*, 451.
28 Helwys, "Confession of Faith of the True English Church," 62.
29 Gill, *Doctrinal and Practical Divinity*, 569.
30 Keach, *The Glory of a True Church, and Its Discipline Display'd*, 85–87.

A. H. Strong identifies the source of Christian fellowship as first having fellowship with Christ, writing, "Fellowship with each other is the effect and result of the fellowship of each with God in Christ. . . . Here is a unity, not of external organization, but of common life."[31] Andrew Fuller, writing on the biblical example of communal conduct, writes,

> They are described as keeping up a close communion with one another. . . . You may be sure their conversion was edifying, or it would not have been recorded. They might have occasion to reprove, to admonish, to counsel, to exhort, to encourage, to instruct. Such a state of things is necessary, especially in evil times. The more wicked the world, the more need of Christian fellowship.[32]

Fellowship provides resources for spiritual growth and spiritual provision, as well as physical resources when needed. A healthy church will have a healthy display of biblical community among its members. It will also include fellowship, or cooperation, among like-minded churches. Article XIV of the BFM states,

> Members of New Testament churches should cooperate with one another in carrying forward the missionary, educational, and benevolent ministries for the extension of Christ's Kingdom. Christian unity in the New Testament sense is spiritual harmony and voluntary cooperation for common ends by various groups of Christ's people. Cooperation is desirable between the various Christian denominations, when the end to be attained is itself justified, and when such cooperation involves no violation of conscience or compromise of loyalty to Christ and His Word as revealed in the New Testament.[33]

---

31   Strong, *Systematic Theology*, 807.
32   Fuller, "Fellowship of God's People in Evil Times," 442.
33   "The 2000 Baptist Faith and Message," *Southern Baptist Convention*.

Healthy churches will be prepared to work together with other churches of like faith in order to strengthen the larger group of believers in a certain vicinity.

COMMUNITY IN MULTISITE CHURCHES

Multisite literature references community in multisite churches, generally when discussing small group ministry. *MCR* says small groups are one way churches can maintain unity across campuses, as they provide an opportunity for teaching that is consistent across all campuses.[34] The authors also frequently mention small groups when discussing ministries of a church.[35] Their main contribution, when considering the aspect of biblical community as described in the previous two sections, is the suggestion to use small groups as a leadership development medium. This sees the small group as a part of a process of discipleship and growth happening organically in the community of the church.[36] They also quote a pastor who indicates small groups function as a pathway into the community of the church, a place to make lasting connections.[37] This shows the importance of community in linking people to the church family. They highlight the importance of small groups as "each site's relational glue, the muscle for doing ministry, and a primary context for leadership development."[38]

Brad House and Gregg Allison emphasize the importance of seeing the church as the body of Christ, a group of people "interdependent and [who] thus act together in concert."[39] Spirit empowered unity, they say, is vital to the health of a multisite church, as is collaboration. They write, "The whole body, with all its diverse parts working, is linked and bound together, collaborating fully as it extends and deepens itself in love through the grace of Christ."[40] They understand community development as a function of community groups and say, "Multichurch community

---

34   Surratt, Ligon, and Bird, *Multi-Site Church Revolution*, 16, 36–37.
35   Surratt, Ligon, and Bird, *Multi-Site Church Revolution*, 35–37, 39, 76, 145. This is also true of *MRT*.
36   Surratt, Ligon, and Bird, *Multi-Site Church Revolution*, 149.
37   Surratt, Ligon, and Bird, *Multi-Site Church Revolution*, 149.
38   Surratt, Ligon, and Bird, *Multi-Site Church Revolution*, 176.
39   House and Allison, *MultiChurch*, 99.
40   House and Allison, *MultiChurch*, 102–4, 107–9.

is rooted in both relationship and location, and discipleship is fostered by relational and spatial proximity."[41] Thus, for House and Allison, community is tied to the campuses, and it is the responsibility of the campus leaders to develop it.

House has much to say about community in a separate book, appropriately titled *Community*. He discusses community as follows:

> We have been reconciled through the blood of Jesus to be a community that exalts him. As we work from that vision, we can be a community that allows the gospel to saturate our lives and fulfill our purpose to make disciples and worship Jesus. Community groups that are steeped in the gospel will grow in their understanding of who they are in Jesus and will be more inspired to proclaim his excellencies and share the good news.[42]

House sees community as an essential component of the church, one developed by purposeful community groups, and without which the church cannot be what it is intended to be.[43] Allison, in his ecclesiology, highlights the community-building aspects of celebrations and tragedies, as the body of the church "relies on and builds strong community life and fosters discipleship."[44]

As a pastor, J. D. Greear understands community as an essential outworking of the church's mission. He says community fosters service inside and outside of the church, standing with fellow members and others, care for people in their time of need, real-life connections that are deep and meaningful, and a heart for evangelism and missions.[45] Likewise, Mark Driscoll and Gerry Breshears tie members' ability to fulfill their role in

---

41   House and Allison, *MultiChurch*, 188.
42   House, *Community*, 2.4.20. House says much more in detail about community that what can be espoused here.
43   House, *Community*, 2.1.1.
44   Allison, *Sojourners and Strangers*, 446–47. Allison mentions community groups and small groups as a part of a church's education and disciple making strategy, but not necessarily as a community-building ministry (443).
45   Greear, "Gospel."

the church to being connected in community.[46] Emphasizing the mutual dependence of believers in community, they write, "Practically speaking, loving fellowship means that people live life together devoted to being a community of people to depend on when times are tough and to rejoice with when times are good."[47] Highlighting the importance of community for helping one another persevere in faith, John Piper comments, "I totally believe in eternal security. . . . I have also said that this keeping, this divine keeping, is a community project in which God uses people. . . . So our exhorting one another every day is one of the instruments, one of the means, by which God keeps us in Christ to the end of time."[48] Dave Ferguson says small groups are the essential component for spiritual growth in the church and that they need to include Bible study, service, and relationships.[49]

In multisite churches, like all churches, community is an essential part of the health of the church. Community helps believers recognize who they are in Christ and who they are in the church. Community helps believers take responsibility for their growth and the growth of their fellow church members. Community gives believers a place to belong and helps believers take ownership of the mission of the church. Community helps the church demonstrate the glory of God as it fosters, encourages, and enables true unity.[50] While this community is essential in all churches, Robert Shelby concludes community development is a struggle for multisite churches due to the separation between the various campuses. He says community may develop at the campuses, but overall community of the whole church is difficult without a very intentional effort by the church leaders.[51] Therefore, multisite churches must develop an intentional process of creating on-campus community and whole-church community.

Community happens best in small groups, which is why most of the writing around "community" often centers around small group

46   Driscoll and Breshears, *Doctrine*, 333–35.
47   Driscoll and Breshears, *Vintage Church*, 200.
48   Piper, "The Danger of Deserting Community."
49   Ferguson, *The Big Idea*, 2.3.
50   House, *Community*, 1.1–3.
51   Shelby, "One Church with Multiple Locations," 111–12.

ministry.[52] Small groups allow for personal connections that are essential for fostering the benefits of community in believers.[53] Multisite churches can employ the same principles of biblical community as single-site churches in order to develop effective community among its members in small groups. The means of community-developing small group ministries is getting believers into groups where they can grow closer together, build on their common faith, and grow into a cohesive unit that journeys through life together.[54] A multisite campus is simply an extension of that goal and places the community-building small groups in a closer proximity to the neighborhoods where the campus's members live. It also puts these communities, which have hopefully developed a missional outlook, closer to their own neighbors and coworkers, giving a great opportunity for the groups to make an evangelistic impact in the community.[55]

To facilitate community on the various campuses, multisite churches will have to be intentional about coordinating their training and curriculum programs. While these kinds of discipleship processes are not the only aspect of small groups they are an essential element, and they are a means by which the church can communicate the expectations for community development through the small group ministry.[56] The reality is, member isolation is a problem that must be addressed in any size church, whether multisite or single-site.[57] Having the church gathered in one location is no guarantee that community will develop more naturally, or that the whole church will be more connected.[58] Multisite churches,

---

52 Stetzer, "4 Reasons Small Groups are Vital to Your Church's Health." For example: Frazee, *The Connecting Church 2.0*; House, *Community*; Howerton, *A Different Kind of Tribe*; Mosley, *Connecting in Communities*.
53 House, *Community*, 2.2.
54 Mosley, *Connecting in Communities*, 58–66, 74–77.
55 Greear, "A Pastor Defends His Multi-Site Church," 21–22.
56 Ferguson, *The Big Idea*, 2.4; Surratt, Ligon, and Bird, *Multi-Site Church Revolution*, 16, 36–37.
57 Ferguson, *The Big Idea*, 2.1.1.
58 Throughout the process of writing this book, I was serving as a campus pastor in a multisite church. While I was a campus pastor, our central campus location had a weekly small groups attendance of more than two thousand, and even with a strong small group ministry, people still often felt disconnected from true community. As the campus pastor at a much smaller campus, with weekly groups attendance of around

like all churches, must emphasize healthy, vibrant small groups across all campuses that provide the connections, development, and missional partnerships they need.

---

one hundred, I often communicated with attendees of the larger campus who said they had considered attending at the satellite location because they assumed community would happen more naturally at the smaller campus. This, in some ways, was true, as most members at the smaller campus, both long time members and newer members, say there is a "family feel" to the membership. The difference, however, is the culture of the two campuses, which is vastly different. Campus size is no guarantee of community.

A BIBLICAL ECCLESIOLOGY FOR MULTISITE CHURCHES

THE PRECEDING CHAPTERS DESCRIBED in detail how multisite churches can structure their church leadership, organization, and ministries in a way that is true to biblical guidelines. This short chapter simply compiles the aspects of a healthy multisite church into one concise summary that will prove useful as a quick reference tool for future use.

PREACHING

Multisite churches must ensure the Word of God is preached with quality and with faithfulness to the text. This must be a priority whether the preaching is in person or via video. In churches that choose to use video teaching, the preaching pastor must be intentional to communicate in ways that do not alienate the non-live campuses. All messages must be text-driven and faithful to the original meaning of the text as the Word of God.

THE ORDINANCES: BAPTISM AND THE LORD'S SUPPER

Multisite churches must practice the ordinances in a way that is faithful the Word of God. For Baptist churches, Baptism must be by immersion and should be administered to believers only, as a symbolic and celebratory representation of their identity in and with Christ in his death, burial, and resurrection. It should be performed under the authority of the church and supervision of church leaders as an initiatory rite into the church family. In multisite churches, baptism should join a believer to the whole church family but should also identify and join them to a specific campus for assimilation into the campus ministries and campus body. Baptisms in multisite churches should, therefore, be administered under the oversight of campus leadership, as representatives of both the campus leadership and the whole church leadership.

In multisite churches, the Lord's Supper should be celebrated as a memorial and celebration of the sacrifice of Jesus Christ on the cross, representing his broken body and shed blood. The Lord's Supper is for believers only and should be administered by the church leaders under the authority of the church. It should be celebrated both in local campus worship services and in periodic whole church gatherings.

CHURCH MEMBERSHIP

Multisite churches must emphasize the importance of membership in their churches. They must be intentional about developing a membership assimilation process by which someone joins the church and that clearly explains the new member's connection to both the whole church and the local campus. The membership process should ensure the candidate is a believer who has been baptized in accordance with Jesus's commands and the Bible's pattern. It should also explain the church covenant and clearly identify the church's expectations of members.

CHURCH DISCIPLINE

Churches, in general, need to recover a biblical practice of church discipline, and this is no less true of multisite churches. Discipline in the church should be practiced according to Jesus's model provided in Matthew 18. It should have the goals of correcting and restoring the sinning member, as well as preserving God's glory in the church and world. Multisite churches will need to establish a discipline process that locates the initial responsibility of discipline at the campus level, but that retains final authority, or oversight, in the whole body of believers. The process of communication in church discipline must also be clear so a whole church, in all its locations, can be aware of the church's disciplinary action.

CHURCH LEADERSHIP: CONGREGATION, ELDERS, AND DEACONS

Multisite churches must be careful to maintain a biblical church leadership organization. Even with multiple sites, and regardless of the specific form of polity, final authority must rest in the gathered body of the whole church. The church may entrust leadership authority in specific ministry staff positions, lay leadership roles, ministry teams and committees, or some other group, but those groups or individuals hold no authority over the church itself. Likewise, the campus congregations will have authority over their campus specific ministries, but the final authority over matters pertaining to the whole church remains with the whole church. There is no authority, other than Christ, over the church.

Elders and deacons must meet the qualifications described in 1 Timothy 3:1–7 and Titus 1:6–9. Elder leadership, whether single or plural, is given its position and authority by the church, and holds no authority that supersedes the church. Elders are to lead in the roles they have been assigned by the church. Local campus congregations have oversight over the local elders, as the local elders provide leadership to that location. However, lead elders of a campus (campus pastor) will also receive leadership from the senior leadership of the whole church. The deacons of the church should be selected and approved by their local campus and should serve that campus.

CORPORATE WORSHIP

Multisite churches should ensure biblical corporate worship is taking place each week at each of their campuses. Corporate worship should have its primary focus on amplifying the glory of Jesus Christ. Corporate worship should include preaching God's Word, congregational singing, corporate prayer, and celebrating the ordinances. Preaching should glorify God, be biblically based, be delivered with clarity, and have application that is accessible to the congregation. Singing should include music that is presented well and glorifies and praises God with truth and clarity.

Churches should include both individual and corporate times of prayer, and should emphasize prayers of praise, thanksgiving, confession, and requests. The celebration of the ordinances should be done in a way that symbolically magnifies the sacrifice of Jesus Christ and exhibits believers' participation in his death, burial, and resurrection.

In multisite churches, these elements of corporate worship should be consistent across all campuses, even as they are contextualized to fit the various locations. The worship may be the same, or similar, across all campuses, or it can vary based on the context of the congregation. Even with contextualization, these four aspects of worship can be consistently emphasized.

DISCIPLESHIP

Multisite churches should emphasize discipleship across all their campuses. Discipleship ministries can serve the church as a unifying aspect of the church ministries, as the discipleship program can, in large part, be the same across multiple campuses. Discipleship serves as the growth program of the church and is a place where leadership development can take place. A healthy multisite church will use a form of small group ministries to ensure members have a group of people to whom they are connected and with whom they can grow in their faith.

PRAYER

All churches need a strong prayer ministry. This is another ministry that can be a unifying ministry in a multisite church. Multisite churches need prayer ministries with two levels. The first level creates a prayer ministry for the whole church to pray for whole church ministries and needs. This helps unify the campuses and the various prayer groups. The second level in the prayer ministry is the local campus prayer ministry or prayer team, which emphasizes campus-specific prayer needs as well as helps to communicate the whole church needs to its campus.

EVANGELISM AND MISSIONS

Multisite churches must emphasize evangelism and missions in their churches. Both should be encouraged by the senior pastor as well as the rest of the church leadership. These two ministries will only be successful if the pastor is a champion for evangelism and missions. At the campus level, the campus pastor must encourage his own members to be evangelistic in their daily lives, and he should also provide information, direction, and encouragement for missions opportunities. Multisite churches can have missions opportunities at the campus level, as well as missions opportunities that the whole church participates in together.

STEWARDSHIP

Multisite churches must develop a strategy for emphasizing and practicing biblical stewardship. Church leadership must be bold in teaching on biblical stewardship and calling members to give according to biblical principles. Multisite churches, like single-site churches, must practice financial stewardship of the funds they are provided by members. There must be a budget for the whole church and for each campus, and the funds must be used with accountability to promote and accomplish the goals of the church.

COMMUNITY

Multisite churches must develop a strategy for fostering community in the church. In many ways, the multisite model assists in this process naturally by placing the members in smaller initial groups, the campuses, than they would be if they were all gathered at one location each week. Still at each campus, there must be intentional processes in place to get members connected in small groups so they can begin developing meaningful relationships with other people. Through these relationships, members will find the care and support they need as a member of the church body. Community groups are tied to a specific campus, and they help members have a connection to a specific campus, where they can also participate in ministry, missions, and evangelism.

PART 3

ANSWERING CRITIQUES OF MULTISITE CHURCHES

MATT CHANDLER WROTE A BRIEF ARTICLE in the 2010 *9Marks Journal* on multisite churches and stated, "Most of the criticism [of multisite churches] we found focused almost entirely on these methodological differences rather than on the issues involved in the entire philosophy of multi-site churches. . . . The theological and philosophical criticism we did find was both limited and weak."[1] Since that time, multisite critics have responded with some valid questions that multisite advocates need to address. Most critics have been pointed, but cordial, in their critiques, while others have taken the opportunity to be condescending toward multisite.[2] The multisite response has been minimal, with the most consistent and thorough response coming from Gregg Allison, both on his own and in collaboration with Brad House. In their work *MultiChurch*, House and Allison admit the critics raise important questions. They wrote the book believing the multisite church movement (MCM)

---

1   Chandler, "Clouds on the Horizon," 32.
2   Straightforward but cordial: Leeman, "Twenty-Two Problems with Multi-Site Churches"; White, "Nine Reasons I Don't Like Multi-Site Churches." Condescending: Anyabwile, "Multi-Site Churches Are from the Devil"; Jamieson, "Historical Critique of Multi-Site."

had aged to the point at which deeper reflection could be accomplished. They state, "Having reached a certain level of permanence and normality, it is now time to evaluate the churches, leaders, members, and ministries this movement has spawned."[3] To this end, they wrote their book, answering some of the critiques and providing their view of the best future for multisite churches.

Still, more can be said to answer some of the specific critiques of multisite churches. That is the goal of Part 3.[4] It will combine responses from multisite advocates into a cohesive defense of the model and will also consider biblical and historical precedents to see if they provide validation for the model. It will reveal areas where multisite critics have targeted a stereotype that does not reflect the full range of multisite churches, and it will also concede areas where the critiques are warranted. In these situations, the chapters will provide recommendations for multisite churches moving forward.

---

3   House and Allison, *MultiChurch*, 11.

4   Jonathan Leeman's critique, "Twenty-Two Problems with Multi-Site Churches," provides the most complete list of critiques of multisite models. It lists most of the questions raised by other critics in their most basic form. Therefore, Leeman's twenty-two problems will serve as the basic outline of this Part 3, and other critiques will be aligned with his statements. A few additional critiques, not on Leeman's list, are also included. It would be impossible to answer every nuanced critique from every writer (Leeman, "Twenty-Two Problems with Multi-Site Churches").

CHAPTER 17

CRITIQUES OF SPECIFIC MULTISITE MODELS

MANY CRITIQUES ARE LEVIED AGAINST what can only be described as a stereotypical multisite church. This stereotype is the large multisite church with numerous locations consisting of hundreds or even thousands of members, and big-name preachers communicating via video feeds into all its campuses, which are basically reproduced franchises of the original location.[1] Some of the critiques of this stereotype have merit, but they are not actually critiques of the whole MCM. They actually critique only a segment of certain models within the movement. Thus, their valid questions do not actually address the MCM as a whole. This chapter will consider these critiques and demonstrate how other multisite models provide corrections.

---

1   White and Yeats, *Franchising McChurch*, 151–206. Consider the multisite examples included in *The Multi-Site Church Revolution*'s introductory chapters. In many ways, they fit the stereotypical mold (Surratt, Ligon, and Bird, *Multi-Site Church Revolution*, 15–42). This model is not inherently flawed. If the described model fits the context of the church, it could be a valid expression of multisite church.

CRITIQUES OF THE SINGLE-PREACHER MODEL

One area of concern in multisite churches is their use of a single preacher across multiple venues.[2] This is often the senior pastor and/ or teaching pastor of the church, and he is often the primary preacher because of his strong communication abilities.[3] This critique often includes three subcategories of criticism: (1) the church is built around the celebrity status of the senior pastor and will likely not survive a pastoral succession; (2) the church limits the development of pastors in the area of preaching because fewer pastors have the opportunity to preach; and (3) the teaching cannot connect to the audience because it is coming from a screen.[4] This critique, and its subpoints, are valid concerns for multisite churches that use video feeds as the primary method of preaching at the satellite campuses. While many examples exist, North Coast Church in Vista, California is one church that is often cited as a prime example of this model.[5] North Coast has nine campuses and four microsites, many of which offer multiple worship styles and worship times.[6] Almost all of

2   Surratt, Ligon, and Bird, *Multi-Site Church Revolution*, 30–36, 163–72.

3   Anyabwile, "Multi-Site Churches Are from the Devil"; House and Allison, *MultiChurch*, 160–61; Hyatt, "Contribution to 'Multi-Site Churches Are Here'"; Leeman, "Twenty-Two Problems with Multi-Site Churches"; Stetzer, "Multisite Evolution"; White, "Nine Reasons I Don't Like Multi-Site Churches," 49–50; White and Yeats, *Franchising McChurch*, 151–56.

4   Anyabwile, "Multi-Site Churches Are from the Devil"; House and Allison, *MultiChurch*, 160–61; Hyatt, "Contribution to 'Multi-Site Churches Are Here, and Here, and Here to Stay'"; Leeman, "Twenty-Two Problems with Multi-Site Churches"; Stetzer, "Multisite Evolution"; White, "Nine Reasons I Don't Like Multi-Site Churches," 49–50; White and Yeats, *Franchising McChurch*, 151–56. This section addresses critiques 3, 4, 8, 13, 14, 16, 19, 20, and 22 of Leeman's twenty-two critiques.

5   Surratt, Ligon, and Bird, *A Multi-Site Church Road Trip*, 101–4; Surratt, Ligon, and Bird, *Multi-Site Church Revolution*, 30–33.

6   Surratt, Ligon, and Bird, *A Multi-Site Church Road Trip*, 101–13; Surratt, Ligon, and Bird, *Multi-Site Church Revolution*, 15–16, 30–31, 73–75, 80, 90, 99, 103–5; White, "Nine Reasons I Don't Like Multi-Site Churches," 49; "Campuses, Service Times, Locations," *North Coast Church*. Microsites are locations that do not offer a full menu of church ministries, where people gather for community and to watch the video feeds of the messages. Their current locations are in California, Ohio, Mexico, and Hawaii. Each full campus offers multiple worship options. As an example, the Vista Campus offers seven different worship styles and sixteen total worship services in those combined options. Of those only four are listed as having live preaching: three North Coast Live, and one Venue en Espanol.

        Microsites are also similar to micro-churches. A micro-church is functional church community, usually of around fifty or fewer attendees. A micro-campus is a

these services receive the same message, preached by one of the three teaching pastors, and delivered by video feed.[7] The three criticisms listed above will be addressed in the following sections.

Celebrity Pastors and Pastoral Transition

The implosion of Mars Hill Church in Seattle, Washington, following the resignation of its extremely popular senior pastor, Mark Driscoll, validates the concerns over churches that are built on the celebrity of a single pastor.[8] Churches of all kinds with such a popular leader, multisite or not, will struggle to navigate a leadership transition. So much dependence on a single person creates a situation where a large portion of a church's identity can suddenly depart, leaving the church without a clear leader and identity.[9] Celebrity pastoral leadership is not a multisite issue; it is a church issue. Even the early church struggled with comparing popular pastors, as evidenced in 1 Corinthians 1:11–17, and examples such as Charles Spurgeon show that celebrity pastors have been present long before the advent of technology and the instant digital access of today.[10]

While multisite churches are not the only churches that must face this issue, multisite churches that are so highly dependent on one leader compound the issue by having multiple locations affected by that one

---

campus of around fifty or fewer attendees. North Coast's microcites have grown out of small group ministries and in settings reaching a certain affinity group ("Campuses, Service Times, Locations," *North Coast Church*). For more on micro-churches, see Johns, *Micro Church*; Sanders, *Microchurches*; Sanders, *Underground Church*; Vincent, *The Micro-Church Revolution!*

7   "Teaching Pastors," *North Coast Church*.

8   Cosper, *The Rise and Fall of Mars Hill*; Van Skaik, Osborne, Phelps, and Rogers, "Pastor Mark Driscoll's Resignation"; Wax, "The Mars Hill Postmortem"; Welch, "The Rise and Fall of Mars Hill Church."

Mars Hill Church experienced significant loss in membership and giving due to Mark Driscoll's departure. As a result, Mars Hill closed its doors less than two months after Driscoll's resignation, releasing eleven of its fifteen campuses as autonomous churches and closing the other four. A local pastor commented, "We don't have anything in church history this apocalyptic, as far as a behemoth like Mars Hill—not only a city but national and international voice—collapsing in a two-month period" (Zylstra, "Seattle Reboot"; see also "Local Churches Update," *Mars Hill Church Archive*).

9   White, "The Single-Elder Led Church," 85–86.

10   Nieuwhof, "The Pros and Cons of a Celebrity Pastor Culture."

leader.[11] Churches with such a high-profile pastor must be wise in preparing for transition. Saddleback Church, with thirteen locations in Southern California as well as four international locations, is an example of a church that has prepared for the transition of not only the senior pastor but all high-profile positions. Saddleback has gone through a process of incrementally handing off leadership responsibilities, raising up and empowering new leaders, reorganizing, and intentionally staggering the retirements of certain leaders to make sure the church continues to thrive through all the major transitions. This includes moving to live teaching at its campuses and dispersing more leadership to campus leaders. The process began in 2009 and was completed with the retirement of senior pastor Rick Warren in August 2022.[12] Saddleback's example shows that a multisite church can navigate leadership transition in a healthy way.

Developing New Preachers

The critiques that video preaching prohibits the development of new teaching pastors is a valid concern. Thankfully, there is an alternative to this model that is already in place in many multisite churches. It provides a solution to the critiques levied against the single-teacher model and actually creates a training ground for developing preachers. While some churches do benefit from a "celebrity" pastor, not all multisite churches depend on the teaching, charisma, and "up-front leadership" of a single pastor.[13] MCR includes in its multisite models the "Teaching-Team Model," which "allows churches to extend their reach by leveraging a strong teaching team across multiple venues and sites."[14] They add, "Many multi-site churches feature on-site preaching delivered by a team of teaching pastors. *Most of those*

---

11   House and Allison, *MultiChurch*, 60–61; Leeman, "Twenty-Two Problems with Multisite Churches"; White, "Nine Reasons I Don't Like Multi-Site Churches," 50; White and Yeats, *Franchising McChurch*, 152.

12   Hernandez, "Pastor Rick Warren's Final Saddleback Church Sermon; Laura, "Pastor Rick Warren Is Well Prepared"; "Locations," *Saddleback Church*; Warren, "News and Views."

13   Leeman acknowledges that his critiques are given with a video-feed church in view, and that some of his critiques do not apply to multisite churches with live teaching at each location (Leeman, "Twenty-Two Problems with Multi-Site Churches").

14   Surratt, Ligon, and Bird, *Multi-Site Church Revolution*, 36–37.

have one regular preacher for each site. Other churches have their preachers rotate between sites."[15] House and Allison identify local-campus preaching as a strength of their Federation through Collective models, because it "enhances the church's ability to contextualize the gospel and provide more effective leadership at the local level."[16] Jimmy Scroggins says local preaching is effective in creating a contextualized ministry that matches the community surrounding each location. He points to the leadership structure of his multisite church as one that extends the leadership of the senior pastor through the local campus leaders to create a synergistic system that is based on one vision and shared through united and empowered leadership. The local leadership has the authority to contextualize, innovate, and even communicate necessary changes back up the chain of leadership.[17] Matt Chandler believes his church's practice of multisite actually led to a greater ability to raise up new pastors and leaders. He also concludes that live preaching is "one of the more powerful contextual pieces" of the multisite strategy.[18] J. D. Greear points out the multisite model actually helps disperse members' primary "connection" to their pastor, from one man for the whole church to one man for a segment of the church, and that local preaching helps in a pastoral transition. He writes, "If our church has ten thousand attenders, we believe that it would be better to have ten campuses of one thousand, who identify with ten campus pastors, rather than one campus of ten thousand who identify only with the one."[19]

Connecting with the Church Congregation

The critique that a pastor on screen is unable to connect with the people in the room is also a valid concern. Leeman writes, "Multi-site is anti-incarnational: it divides the Word from flesh. . . . Members receive the Word of God from a disembodied man on a screen. . . . A multi-site church separates the ministry of the Word from the ministry of deeds." Furthermore, "The pastor of a large church has difficulty knowing all

---

15   Surratt, Ligon, and Bird, *Multi-Site Church Revolution*, 37, emphasis added.
16   House and Allison, *MultiChurch*, 61–72.
17   Scroggins and Wright, "How Family Church Does Multisite."
18   Dever, Leeman, and Chandler, "On Multi-Site Churches."
19   Greear, "A Pastor Defends His Multi-Site Church," 22.

his members, but he can at least have some sense of the room in which he's preaching. Both of these are impossible by definition in a multi-site church that employs video-preaching."[20] This concern is valid. The disconnect of on-screen preaching became an obvious reality to thousands of pastors during the COVID-19 pandemic, as they took to live-streaming their services to share the Word with their congregation. The audience feedback they were used to receiving was suddenly gone.[21] Throughout the history of the church, except for very recently, the preaching medium was one of real-time interaction between an in-person preacher and his congregation. This in-person medium allowed for what Haddon Robinson and Jerry Vines say is one of the most important aspects of the physical preaching art: eye contact. Robinson writes, "Eye contact probably ranks as the single most effective means of nonverbal communication at your disposal."[22] Vines similarly states, "Eye contact is an extremely important psychological aspect of the preacher-audience dynamic and must be understood to communicate effectively."[23] Video preaching removes that, and any other personal, physical connection. No matter the quality of an on-screen preacher, in his speaking, movements, stories, and so forth, he cannot fully recreate the live experience. Live preaching solves this problem and regains the personal connection between preacher and audience.

In-Person Preaching Is a Solution

These considerations show that a multisite church built around a single pastor, and the potential landmines that surround such a structure, are not inherent problems of all multisite churches. Rather these are problems that result in the elevation of one person at the expense of expanding leadership across multiple leaders in multiple locations.[24] One solution to this problem is to employ a leadership structure that uses pastors at each campus to provide live, in-person teaching during

---

20   Leeman, "Twenty-Two Problems with Multi-Site Churches."
21   Roach, "COVID-19's Lasting Changes," 30–32.
22   Robinson, *Biblical Preaching*, 211.
23   Vines and Shaddix, *Power in the Pulpit*, 362.
24   Greear, "A Pastor Defends His Multi-Site Church," 22; House and Allison, *MultiChurch*, 78–84.

the majority of campus gatherings.[25] Many examples exist that use this model to disperse leadership and create a culture of connection between the man preaching, the message preached, and the congregation receiving the message. It can help multisite churches in pastoral transition and also benefits the church by developing the preaching gifts of new pastors.[26]

VIDEO PREACHING PAIRED WITH LIVE MUSIC SHOWS SINGING IS VALUED MORE THAN PREACHING

Leeman offers another critique that is similar to those in the previous section but warrants separate consideration. He suggests video preaching minimizes the value of preaching when paired with live, on-campus, in-person music. He writes,

> Multisite churches which use video preaching unwittingly communicate that singing is more significant for Christian growth and closer to the heart of worship than hearing God's preached Word. . . . A church wouldn't dare import the music, it's thought. People need to engage with a live band. People need their music authentic, personal, enfleshed. But preaching? Apparently it can be imported from afar.[27]

This critique raises a legitimate question. However, Leeman's critique actually conflicts with another statement in which Leeman acknowledges the true reason behind multisite churches using a video message from an exceptional speaker, writing, "Now, to give the multi-site and multi-service process a little credibility, God clearly gives some preachers greater gifts than others. . . . And faithful churches should look for ways to allow their home-run hitters to make the best use of their gifts and hit as many home-runs as possible."[28]

---

25   House and Allison, *MultiChurch*, 81–83.

26   "FBC Windermere: Teaching Pastor—Specs Updated"; "Resource Library," *TVC Resources*; Scroggins and Wright, "How Family Church Does Multisite."

27   Leeman, "Twenty-Two Problems with Multi-Site Churches." This section addresses critique 7 of Leeman's twenty-two.

28   Leeman, "The Alternative Case," 52.

Obviously Leeman is not making the case for video-feed preaching, or for multisite churches for that matter. But what he does do is undermine the argument he made above. What he actually reveals in this quote is that the real reason many multisite churches use video preaching is because they value the preaching ministry so much that they want to put their "best man" on the screen to do the job. While this book is not making the case that video preaching is preferable, this section is included to show that although the critique raises a valid concern, its conclusion is questionable. The above section, which highlighted the value of a live preacher, provides the solution to the critique. Multisite churches that include both live preaching and live music eliminate the risk of communicating that one is valued more than the other, as both are important aspects of a well-rounded worship service.

MULTISITE CHURCHES BUILD AND MAINTAIN A CHURCH ON THE IDENTITY OF A BRAND

Another critique, which is more of a critique of a certain multisite model rather than the whole MCM, is that multisite churches promote a brand as the identity of the church in much the same way companies like McDonald's or Chick-fil-A expand their reach on the credibility of their brand name. Leeman writes, "To the extent that a multi-site church relies on brand identity to reach unbelievers, to that same extent they are building Christianity on their brand identity."[29] Summarizing *Franchising McChurch*'s critique on multisite branding, he writes, "It's not Christ's kingdom they want to see expanded; it's their franchise brand. . . . Multi-site churches focus on independent kingdoms rather than on God's kingdom."[30] This concern is not without warrant. Some multisite churches do promote a brand identity across their ministries and consider the uniformity of their brand as an essential draw for reaching more people. Life Church, a multisite church with forty-five locations spread across eleven states, details their belief in brand identity, writing,

---

29   Leeman, "Twenty-Two Problems with Multi-Site Churches." This section addresses critiques 4 and 6 of Leeman's twenty-two.
30   Leeman, "Book Review: *Franchising McChurch*," 59.

We've found that multi-campus works best when every campus feels like the main campus. We create this feeling by replicating the experience down to the second across locations and then being intentional about creating a local, personal atmosphere through stage time, friendly greeters and ushers and volunteers on our host teams and operations teams, local imagery in the lobby, and more. When a campus feels recognizable and personable, people will feel at home there.[31]

This shows Life Church is placing a significant amount of their growth strategy on the ability to provide a consistent brand identity across all of their locations. The positivity of brand identity is mentioned early in *MCR* when the authors write, "The prediction of this book is that multi-site extension of trusted-name churches are something that connect well with today's times. . . . Chances are that one or more multi-site churches will soon form in *your* city, and perhaps your own church will join or create one of these multiple-location clusters."[32]

MCR's argument is that the benefits of brand identity that help a business like "Holiday Inn, Marriott, Hilton, and Omni . . . McDonald's, Burger King, and Shoney's Big Boy" will also help a church grow and reach more people.[33] This premise is exactly what Leeman warns against: churches built on a brand rather than the gospel. He warns that a church built on a brand can also crumble when that brand crumbles.[34] The collapse of Mars Hill Church, previously mentioned, is an example of just such an event.[35]

This issue, however, is attached to a particular model of multisite churches and is not an inherent flaw in the whole multisite movement.

31   "Multisite," *Life Church Open Network*; "One Church in Multiple Locations," *Life Church*. Life Church has a website where you can show your desire to "Bring Life Church to Your City." It encourages someone to "Take a moment to share a city you think we should consider in the future" ("Where Should We Explore?" *Life Church*).

32   Surratt, Ligon, and Bird, *Multi-Site Church Revolution*, 10, emphasis original.

33   Surratt, Ligon, and Bird, *Multi-Site Church Revolution*, 9–10.

34   Leeman, "Twenty-Two Problems with Multi-Site Churches."

35   Cosper, "The Brand"; "Local Churches Update," *Mars Hill Church Archive*; Wax, "The Mars Hill Postmortem"; Welch, "The Rise and Fall of Mars Hill Church"; Zylstra, "Seattle Reboot: Life After Mars Hill."

Scroggins and his executive pastor Steve Wright say their campuses share a "common DNA" which means "they share a strong family resemblance, but they are very, very different."[36] They are concerned with a shared vision, not a replicated brand identity. Chris Surratt, brother of *MCR* coauthor Geoff Surratt and former co-staff member at Seacoast Church, says Seacoast Church's model, even though it utilizes video-based teaching, decentralizes the control of its thirteen campuses. He says, "If you've been to one Seacoast campus, you've been to one Seacoast campus. . . . Each campus has a lot of autonomy to fit the context of the community."[37] House and Allison identify freedom from the "brand of the franchise" as a strength of their Federation through Collective models, writing,

> The federation model church may develop out of the franchise model in an effort to address some of the weaknesses of the franchise model. This can happen as the managers at the cloned sites mature into strong leaders and seek greater flexibility and freedom to deviate from the brand of the franchise. . . . Each campus pastor must own the overall vision of the church while capably adapting it to their particular context. This model is dependent on church leaders understanding the importance of contextualization and possessing the skills to adapt the gospel and its expression in different places.[38]

---

36 Scroggins and Wright, "How Family Church Does Multisite."
37 Morgan and Surratt, "Centralized vs. De-centralized Multisite Models."
38 House and Allison, *MultiChurch*, 62. This perspective runs counter to Life Church's stated philosophy, which is to create a brand that targets a specific subset of the culture. Rather than contextualizing to meet the location, Life Church selects locations to fit its brand's targeted demographic. Life Church's branding guidelines state, "Our Bullseye: Young, Urban, and Modern. We aim directly at this demographic knowing that doing so will also draw a range of people attracted to those qualities. Young: We appeal to growing families and young professionals. Urban: Cities are the centers of movement and progress, and we want Life Church to feel just as vibrant. Modern: We embrace technology and innovation. We look beyond today to anticipate what is relevant tomorrow" ("Life Church Branding Guidelines," *Life Church Open Network*, 2.1).

They also clarify that some level of branding is inevitable and is not inherently wrong. They simply encourage churches to "evaluate their branding strategy and the motivation behind it," seeking to ensure that brand identity is not the primary factor in making decisions.[39]

Honest evaluation must admit that brand identity and brand expansion are realities in non-multisite churches as well. The 9Marks ministry, of which Leeman is on the leadership team, promotes its brand of church structure and organization, seeking to "inform and influence churches." 9Marks develops "networks of like-minded churches, because this work requires patient and prayerful cooperation."[40] There is even an application process by which a church can apply to "get on the map," a search feature where people can find a 9Marks approved church near them.[41] While this network does not mean these churches are clones of one model, it is as much brand promotion and brand-based church building as the multisite church advocates above have suggested. It is identifying with a "brand" that helps potential guests who recognize the 9Marks ministry to have an advanced understanding of the beliefs of the church they are considering.

Multisite campuses have the opportunity to let their gospel-driven contextualization of ministry and gospel proclamation be the foundation for the church's growth, with or without any brand identity attached to the campus.[42] The Gospel Coalition captures this concept, writing,

> The gospel itself holds the key to appropriate contextualization. If we over-contextualize, it suggests that we want too much the approval of the receiving culture. This betrays lack of confidence in the gospel. If we under-contextualize, it suggests that we want the trappings of our own sub-culture too much. This betrays a lack of gospel humility and a lack of love for our neighbor.[43]

39   House and Allison, *MultiChurch*, 89–90.
40   "About," *9Marks*.
41   "Church Search," *9Marks*.
42   House and Allison, *MultiChurch*, 63.
43   "Foundational Documents," *The Gospel Coalition*, Introduction and chap. 7.

Multisite churches who lean toward contextualization rather than brand reliance show that while organization, leadership, and consistency across campuses are beneficial, their true trust is not in their identity as a brand, but in a contextualized, gospel-focused ministry.

MULTISITE CHURCH EXPANSION IS INCOMPATIBLE WITH INTER-CHURCH COOPERATION

Another critique levied against multisite churches is that the model itself is by nature non-cooperative.[44] The goal of multisite churches, critics say, is to gain more "turf" by adding additional campuses. Leeman provides a lengthy description of this critique, writing,

> The multi-site church model depends upon extending the reach of "my" church rather than partnering with and aiding other congregations. That is, it's built on a competitive model of franchise extension, rather than a partnering model of mutual aid that we see in the New Testament. All this can foment "turfyness" and competition between churches. At the very least, every additional campus is a missed opportunity for helping another ministry.[45]

He also makes the broad reaching statement that multisite churches "plant their own campuses so that they *don't have to work together with other churches in their city but can overlook them.*"[46] Leeman's critique, also expressed by White and Yeats, is that the expansion of a single multisite church is inherently, and possibly intentionally, damaging to other churches, and it limits the opportunity for other churches to develop into healthy churches, experience growth, and make their own impact for the kingdom.[47] White and Yeats suggest multisite churches

---

44   Leeman, *One Assembly*, chap. 3; White and Yeats, *Franchising McChurch*, 170–72, 180–83. The primary message of chapter 3 of *One Assembly* is that multisite churches, by definition, work against the unity of the worldwide church.

45   Leeman, "Twenty-Two Problems with Multisite Churches." This section addresses critique 15 of Leeman's twenty-two.

46   Leeman, *One Assembly*, Loc.: 1607, emphasis original.

47   Leeman, "Twenty-Two Problems with Multisite Churches"; White, "Nine Reasons I Don't Like Multi-Site Churches," 50; White and Yeats, *Franchising McChurch*, 168–69, 180–83.

capitalize on weaker local churches by absorbing them as a campus, rebranding them, and creating a replication of the original campus.[48] White even refers to the "cannibalizing of the body of Christ" when a multisite church absorbs the weaker church, closes the campus, sells the assets, and then encourages the members to attend a different campus.[49] This analysis has been fed by some multisite churches that, either in reality or simply by perception, have capitalized on the struggles of smaller churches.[50] These critiques are issues that expanding multisite churches must consider, but despite these authors' claims, there is no inherent capitalist bent in the MCM itself.

While these authors obviously have negative examples in mind, the generalized conclusion that multisite ministry is, by definition, territorial and non-cooperative is careless and unsubstantiated. A 2010 Leadership Network report notes that only one third of all multisite churches added campuses via merger, while Jim Tomberlin says the number is closer to 40 percent.[51] Along with Tomberlin, Warren Bird, one of the co-authors of the report mentioned, also notes that the majority of multisite mergers are initiated by the joining church, dispelling the stereotype that multisite churches view weaker churches as easy prey. Tomberlin and Bird also note that half of all mergers involve both facilities remaining in use by the multisite church as a functioning campus, with one fourth being used for some other purpose, and only one fourth being sold. They say the majority of mergers receive a "yes" vote from 80–100 percent of the members from both merging churches.[52] Many of The Village Church's campuses became a part of the multisite church because they were struggling churches in need of new direction and revitalization. The Village Church provided a redirection that led to healthier models of ministry and greater impact for the kingdom of God. This happened through them coming into The Village Church and, although it was not a part of the original plan for the

48   White and Yeats, *Franchising McChurch*, 168–69.
49   White, "Nine Reasons I Don't Like Multi-Site Churches," 50.
50   Zadrozny, "Controversial Megachurch Pastor Mark Driscoll."
51   Bird and Walters, "Multisite Is Multiplying," 9; Zylstra, "The 'Unintended Consequence.'"
52   Tomberlin and Bird, *Better Together*, 48.

campuses, they have now released them once again as healthy, autonomous churches.[53] This shows that multisite can be a benefit to struggling churches, some of which might otherwise close their doors.

Sam Rainer has coined the terms "church adoption" and "church fostering" to indicate two variations of multisite ministry. He defines them as follows: "Church adoption: a church comes into the family. Church fostering: a church is brought into the family for the short term."[54] Adoption is another name for a merger, whereby two become one. However, a fostering situation is when a healthy church takes some leadership responsibility for the struggling church with the purpose of helping it regain health and then continue on as an autonomous church. Rainer says, "Most fostering will not become adoptions. . . . The goal of fostering is to help them return to a state of independence. . . . Fostering is local churches helping local churches."[55] This example shows some multisite churches are engaged in strengthening and supporting other churches in their community.[56] Other multisite churches seek to be a resource for many churches, even those outside their community. The Family Church Network and The Summit Collaborative not only provide church planting residencies and internships, but also serve as resources for existing churches.[57]

These examples reveal that some multisite churches are interested in supporting and resourcing churches other than their own through a variety of methods. This shows a desire to cooperate with other churches for the sake of the kingdom of God, not their own. The evidence of how the majority of multisite mergers actually comes about, and the model of church fostering presented above, show how multisite ministry, rather than being self-serving, can actually serve as a pathway to serving, supporting, strengthening, and extending the life of other churches. The simplistic suggestion that multisite church models are non-cooperative and predatory is unwarranted and unsupportable.

---

53   Hardin, "A History of Faithfulness"; Hughes, "Preparing and Transitioning a Multi-Site Campus," 3–6; "Multiply," *The Village Church*.
54   Rainer and Rainer, "Church Adoption, Church Fostering, and Church Revitalization."
55   Rainer and Rainer, "Four Things Your Church Should Know about Fostering a Church."
56   Rainer and Rainer, "Church Adoption, Church Fostering, and Church Revitalization."
57   "About Us," *Summit Collaborative*; "Church for the Rest of Us," *Family Church Network*.

CHAPTER 18

CRITIQUES OF THE MULTISITE CHURCH MOVEMENT

THIS CHAPTER WILL NOW TURN to critiques of multisite that do apply to the vast majority of, if not all, multisite churches. These are critiques of the MCM as a whole and are often very broad in their generalizations. The critiques in this category are primarily theological and call into question the biblical validity of the model or of specific practices within the MCM. These are the critiques that are the most important to consider because while the previous chapter dealt primarily with practical issues, the issues discussed here determine if the MCM can be practiced in manner that is faithful to the Scriptures.

Many of these critiques, especially those dealing with historical precedent, are against Baptist churches and come from Baptist voices. The response to these critiques is obviously relevant for Baptist churches but will also be valuable for church leaders faced with the question of whether this model is something new and trendy, or if it has historical validity. These answers will provide historical precedent for multisite churches that can help provide purpose and perspective for the model.

MULTISITE CHURCHES ARE UNBIBLICAL

The strongest critique against the multisite model is that the model is unbiblical. This critique is generally supported by three primary sub-critiques: (1) the New Testament has no example of a multisite church; (2) a church that does not assemble as one body does not meet the criteria of an *ekklesia*; and (3) a church that does not assemble cannot perform the functions of a true church.[1] While these points are interconnected, each one will be addressed individually.

The New Testament Has No Examples of Multisite Churches

Jonathan Leeman writes, "[Multisite churches are] not in the Bible. At all. And that means they work against, not with, Jesus's disciple-making plan."[2] He also says, "There's no clear example of multi-site church in the New Testament, only supposition, 'Well, surely, the Christians in a city could not have all met' (but see Acts 2:46; 5:12; 6:2)."[3] This second critique references the suggestion by some that the church in Jerusalem, and possibly other cities, was so large that it could not possibly gather in a single place.[4] As Leeman correctly notes with the references to passages in Acts, this claim ignores the fact that the Bible

---

1   Anyabwile, "Multi-Site Churches Are from the Devil"; House and Allison, *MultiChurch*, 160–61; Hyatt, "Contribution to 'Multi-Site Churches Are Here.'" Leeman, "Twenty-Two Problems with Multi-Site Churches"; Stetzer, "Multisite Evolution"; White, "Nine Reasons I Don't Like Multi-Site Churches," 49–50; White and Yeats, *Franchising McChurch*, 151–56. Not every one of these authors has called multisite "unbiblical," and each one hasn't made the same critiques. But, they have all contributed to these critiques and the conversation surrounding the biblical validity of multisite churches.

2   Leeman, *One Assembly*, Introduction. This statement shows a glaring problem in Leeman's conclusions in this book, specifically regarding multisite. He often makes dogmatic statements, the implications of which reach further than it seems he would. For example, this statement implies if something is not mentioned in the Bible, then it "works against, not with, Jesus's disciple-making plan." How broad is Leeman willing to apply this dogmatic premise? How many aspects of today's church ministries are "not mentioned in the Bible," yet are present and prominent in biblical churches, even Leeman's? Do things such as student and children's ministries or church-owned facilities "work against . . . Jesus's disciple-making plan" simply because they are not mentioned in the Bible? Others agree that multisite cannot be found in the New Testament (White, "Nine Reasons I Don't Like Multi-Site Churches").

3   Leeman, "Twenty-Two Problems with Multi-Site Churches." This section addresses critique 1 of Leeman's twenty-two.

4   Gehring, *House Church and Mission*, 87.

specifically says the church met together as a whole group, and that the church in Jerusalem is described as gathering together in the temple, a location large enough to hold the thousands added to the church.[5] But the testimony of Acts shows the church met in two types of gatherings: (1) the whole church gathered together in one place and (2) smaller segments of the church gathered in homes.[6] Leeman concedes the church gathered together and also met house to house, although he equates the house to house gatherings to modern day in-home small group meetings.[7] The issue to determine for this section is if the smaller gatherings were considered worship gatherings of the church in which the group functioned as the church.

Brad House and Gregg Allison write, "The church in Jerusalem gathered together in the temple (an assembly of possibly all the members), and the church of Jerusalem gathered together in homes (an assembly of some, but clearly not all, of the members)."[8] Leeman concedes this point but dismisses these house gatherings as irrelevant based on his belief that the evidence of a whole church assembly trumps the house church gatherings.[9] However, these house gatherings warrant further investigation based on a specific action that takes place in these gatherings: the breaking of bread. Acts 2:42 says the Jerusalem church "devoted themselves to the apostles' teaching, to the fellowship, to the breaking of bread, and to prayer." Verse 46 adds, "Every day they devoted themselves to meeting together in the temple, and broke bread from house to house. They ate their food with joyful and sincere hearts." Leeman writes,

---

5   House and Allison, *MultiChurch*, 32; Leeman, *One Assembly,* chap. 2.

6   House and Allison, *MultiChurch*, 32; Leeman, *One Assembly*, 1.9.

7   Leeman, *One Assembly*, chap. 2.

8   House and Allison, *MultiChurch*, 40. They also site the house churches noted in Rome (Rom. 16:5) and Laodicea (Col. 4:15) as evidences of house churches, and conclude that these signify a meeting of small groups of the church in those cities. However, Leeman makes credible arguments against seeing these as portions of the whole church (Leeman, *One Assembly*, chap. 2). I have also previously considered these churches and have concluded that the church in Rome was most likely *not* a single city-wide church. Also, it appears there was a city-wide church in Laodicea, but there is not enough evidence to conclude with certainty that more than one house church existed in the city. It is possible that the whole church of Laodicea met in the home of Nympha (Slaton, "The Citywide Church").

9   Leeman, *One Assembly*, chap. 2.

The questions this passage poses is this: Do the references to "the breaking of bread" in verse 42 and "breaking bread in their homes" in verse 46 suggest the people were receiving the Lord's Supper in their homes, as House and Allison argue? And, if so, doesn't that mean the Jerusalem church (singular) was exercising the church sign and seal of the Supper in its members' homes?[10]

This is a significant question, one which the reader expects Leeman to answer. Leeman says earlier in *One Assembly* that the Lord's Supper is an ordinance of the church to be celebrated only in the gathered body.[11] In a book on the Lord's Supper, which is in a series edited by Leeman, the author, Bobby Jamieson, writes, "What gathering may celebrate the Lord's Supper? . . . In this chapter I will argue that only a local church, gathered as a church, is authorized to celebrate the Lord's Supper. The Lord's Supper effects the unity of the church. It binds many into one. That is why the Lord's Supper belongs to the church and should only be celebrated by the church, as a church."[12]

Leeman, in a different article, confirms Jamieson's statement, writing, "The Supper is a corporate word. It constitutes the church. And therefore I would say that the Supper should *almost* always be served in the gathering of the church. Don't serve it in your wedding ceremonies. Don't serve it around the family table. Don't serve it at summer camp."[13]

Leeman's "*almost*" exception allows for a member who is physically unable to attend worship, such as a homebound church member, to receive the Supper remotely. He calls this an exception because of extraordinary circumstances. Thus, it is obvious that Leeman believes the Lord's Supper should normally only be celebrated by a church in a gathering of that church. In *One Assembly* Leeman writes,

The noun phrase "the breaking of bread" and the verbal phrase "breaking bread" can refer to an ordinary meal or to

---

10   Leeman, *One Assembly*, chap. 2.
11   Leeman, *One Assembly*, chap. 2.
12   Jamieson, *Understanding the Lord's Supper*, chap. 8.
13   Leeman, "Mailbag #10"; emphasis is original.

the consecrated meal that we regard as the Lord's Supper. So
which of the two is in mind in verses 42 and 46? . . . I don't
think we need to nail down answers to those questions. . . .
Whether verse 42, then, is referring to the Lord's Supper or not,
I genuinely don't know but don't think it makes any difference
for my argument.[14]

This dismissal of the question appears to be Leeman's attempt to
avoid a situation that could give credibility to the multisite argument.[15]
If it can be shown that the Jerusalem church was here celebrating the
Lord's Supper in homes, would Leeman be willing to concede a biblical example of one church meeting in multiple locations is evident
in the Bible?

As discussed in the chapter 7 of this book, a majority of scholars take
Acts 2:42 to refer to a celebration of the Lord's Supper. Jamieson, in the
book edited by Leeman, agrees with these conclusions, writing,

Finally, as we've seen in our study of 1 Corinthians 10–11, the
church in Corinth clearly celebrated the Lord's Supper in the
context of a whole meal. Recall that the phrase "the breaking
of bread" may well refer to the Lord's Supper in Acts 20:7. The
use of a similar phrase in Acts 2:46 to describe a normal meal
seems to suggest that "the breaking of bread" was a meal in
which the Lord's Supper was celebrated (cf. Acts 2:42).[16]

Jamieson appears to have come to the same conclusion as F. F.
Bruce, who concluded something significant must be in view in the
phrase "breaking of bread" since a meal is something trivial, but it is

---

14   Leeman, *One Assembly*, chap. 2.
15   Leeman's "argument" that he mentions here is the argument that a church must assem-
     ble together as a whole church. His point is that the conclusion about the Lord's Supper
     in homes is inconsequential because it is apparent that the marks of the church were
     evident in gatherings of the whole church. These whole church gatherings, for Leeman,
     are the foundational reasons why he is able to dismiss the multisite church which "does
     not gather as one church" (Leeman, *One Assembly*, chap. 2).
16   Jamieson, *Understanding the Lord's Supper*, chap. 11.

mentioned with such reverence in the midst of other aspects of corporate gathering and worship.[17]

The conclusion from this analysis is that the burden of proof rests on Leeman to show that the Lord's Supper is not in view in Acts 2:42 and 46. He would prefer to believe the Jerusalem church "presumably . . . partook of the Lord's Supper" in their gatherings of the whole church in the temple complex. Thus, even while chastising multisite advocates for their "assumptions," he rests his argument on an assumed, but not shown, celebration of the Lord's Supper in Jerusalem rather than accepting the consensus of most scholarship that the Lord's Supper is more clearly shown taking place in the homes of believers.[18]

Can it be concluded, then, that evidence for multisite churches does exist in the New Testament church? The church in Jerusalem gives very strong evidence that a multisite church did exist. The church did gather *en masse* in Solomon's Colonnade. Yet the church also gathered in homes and demonstrated the marks of the church in those home gatherings. There is significant evidence that these in-home gatherings of portions of the church included teaching, the Lord's Supper, and a group of people who were "of one mind" demonstrating agreement together.

A Multisite Church Is Not One Church Because It Does Not Assemble Together

The argument that multisite is unbiblical also focuses on the definition of *ekklesia*. *Ekklesia* is the word used in the New Testament to identify the church, and it means "assembly."[19] *Ekklesia*, derived from *ekkaleo*, is formed by *ek*, meaning "out of," and *kaleo*, meaning "to call out."[20] Basing an understanding on the etymology of the word, some interpreters state *ekklesia* shows the church members are "the called out ones."[21] The concept of being "called out" agrees with the usage of the word in the

---

17   Bruce, *The Acts of the Apostles*, 132; Slaton, "Discovering Evidence of Multisite *Ekklesia*."
18   Leeman, *One Assembly*, chap. 1.
19   Goodrick and Kohlenberger, *The NIV Exhaustive Concordance*, 1712. *Ekklesia* occurs 114 times in the New Testament, and is translated by three words: assembly, church(es), and congregation(s).
20   Verbrugge, *The NIV Theological Dictionary of New Testament Words*, 388.
21   Hammett, *Biblical Foundations for Baptist Churches*, 26.

Old Testament and by alternate descriptions of the church in the New Testament.[22] In the Septuagint, *ekklesia* is only used to translate the Hebrew *qahal*.[23] *Qahal* means "a summons to an assembly or the act of assembling," and specifically, it is used to describe the ceremonial summoning of Israel in response to the covenant relationship with Yahweh. In these cases, "*ekklesia* is only used where it is a question of the people as God's assembly, characterized by having answered Yahweh's call." *Ekklesia* is never used to indicate the general population of Israel, but only the specific assembly.[24] In other words, only the people who had heard the call of God and answered by coming together made up the *qahal*. John Hammett believes the New Testament writers used the *ekklesia/qahal* connection to create a specific understanding of the church as the people of God who have gathered in response to his call.[25] In the New Testament, Paul describes the church as the *kletoi*, those called by God (Rom. 1:1–7; 1 Cor. 1:1–2).[26] In these passages, Paul uses *kletoi* as a synonym of the *ekklesia*, tying together the call of the Lord and the reality of the gathered congregation. This is the same idea that is portrayed in *qahal*, as seen above.[27]

The calling out of the church is not the only concept implied in *ekklesia*. The concept of *qahal* also entails an assembling of God's people. The people must be called out and come together for some kind of purpose. As B. H. Carroll says in his lectures on *ekklesia*, "How can there be a *body of Kletoi* if the essential ideas of *ecclesia* are left out? If there be no organization, no assembly, how can there be *a body*? Miscellaneous, scattered, unattached units do not make a body."[28]

Thus, the act of gathering is essential to *ekklesia* and is a key element in many of the multisite critiques. White writes, "The Greek word *ecclesia* most often translated as 'church' means assembly or gathering. The oft

---

22   In the Septuagint, *ekklesia* is only used to translate *qahal* (Gaines, "One Church in One Location," 50).

23   Gaines, "One Church in One Location," 50.

24   Verbrugge, *NIV Theological Dictionary*, 389–90.

25   Hammett, *Biblical Foundations for Baptist Churches*, 27.

26   Verbrugge, *NIV Theological Dictionary*, 392.

27   Hammett, *Biblical Foundations for Baptist Churches*, 27.

28   Carroll, *Ecclesia: The Church*, 48, emphasis original.

heard mantra 'one church many locations' is a contradiction in terms."[29] Similarly, Mark Dever, referencing the multisite church, states, "On one level the question is settled lexically by simply considering the meaning of the word *ekklesia*. The New Testament authors regularly use the word to mean 'assembly'. . . . [Gathering] is essential to their identity as a group."[30] Leeman says a multisite church is fundamentally flawed because it does not assemble together as one body.[31] He writes, "A multi-site church formally removes the concept of 'assembly' from the definition of 'church' since it's a 'church' that never actually assembles. This is what it means to be *multi-site*."[32]

While this critique does pose a significant issue for the majority of multisite churches, in some ways, it belongs in the first section of this chapter, under the category of critiques of a segment of multisite churches. Some multisite churches do periodically gather together as a whole church. House and Allison recommend churches have periodic gatherings of the whole church for "a worship service with the celebration of baptism and the Lord's Supper. This could be a congregational meeting in which the business of the whole church is carried out along with any exercise of church discipline."[33] J. D. Greear says, in a quote Leeman actually includes in *One Assembly*, "At The Summit Church, we're committed to meeting altogether in one place at one time periodically throughout the year—not every week, but on occasion. . . . We think gathering all together, periodically, is an important expression of our assembly."[34] Leeman believes these periodic gatherings do not fit the biblical model, stating, "The trouble is that Scripture presents churches gathering weekly on the Lord's Day."[35] The problem with his

---

29   White, "Nine Reasons I Don't Like Multi-Site Churches," 49–51.
30   Dever, *The Church*, 133.
31   Leeman, *One Assembly*, chap. 1–3; see also Gaines, "One Church in One Location," 47–90.
32   Leeman, "Twenty-Two Problems with Multi-Site Churches," emphasis original. This section answers critique 4, 9, 10, and 21 of Leeman's twenty-two. Others concur: Dever, Leeman, and Chandler, "On Multi-Site Churches"; White, "Nine Reasons I Don't Like Multi-Site Churches"; White and Yeats, *Franchising McChurch*, 154. In the Dever, Leeman, Chandler conversation, Dever and Leeman sees assembly of the whole body as necessary. Chandler does not.
33   House and Allison, *MultiChurch*, 94, 195.
34   Greear, "Is Multi-Site a Biblically Sound Model?"
35   Leeman, *One Assembly*, chap. 2.

analysis, however, is that the passages he cites, 1 Corinthians 16:2 and Revelation 1:10, do not actually include any description that conclusively indicate a gathering of the whole church or that the church gathered weekly.[36] The verses simply mention the first day of the week in certain aspects of church life or an individual member's life.[37] Multisite critics offer no conclusive evidence that multisite churches that gather periodically do not fulfill the biblical expectation of assembling together.[38] Even Dennis Sullivan, whose dissertation questions the Southern Baptist multisite movement, concedes certain parameters exist for a valid multisite model so long as "the church must regularly gather the totality of their membership and campuses in one location."[39] Grant Gaines concedes the same point.[40]

Another aspect of this critique must be considered: Is assembly of the whole church a first-level issue or second-level issue when it comes to the fundamental essence of a church? Some scholars warn against basing the essence of the church on the etymology of original language picture words and Old Testament connections alone. D. A. Carson writes, "One of the most enduring errors, the root fallacy, presupposes that every word actually has a meaning bound up with its shape or its components.... All of this is linguistic nonsense."[41] Allison concurs, describing multiple errors in basing an understanding of the church simply on the etymology of *ekklesia*. One cannot define a concept simply by defining a word. A word often has meaning with depth beyond its mere etymological meaning. A

---

36   Sullivan, "Examining the Ecclesiological Soundness," 235.

37   Gardner, *1 Corinthians*, chap. 35; Thomas and Macchia, *Revelation*, 81–82; see also Leeman, *One Assembly*, chap. 2. Additionally, two paragraphs later, Leeman acknowledges that the early church met daily, as is clearly stated in Acts 2:42–46. Leeman, therefore, enforces his perceived gathering of the whole church, although it is from an unclear passage. Yet, he does not enforce the clear example of the church assembling daily. It makes one wonder to what extent Leeman is willing to let the *regula* of the New Testament rule in his thinking. If he wants to follow the clearest example of the early church's practice, then daily gatherings should be expected (Leeman, *One Assembly*, chap. 2).

38   Frye, "The Multi-Site Church Phenomenon," 229; Gaines, "One Church in One Location," 2; Hammett, "What Makes a Multi-Site Church One Church?," 106.

39   Sullivan, "Examining the Ecclesiological Soundness," 235.

40   Gaines, "One Church in One Location," 2. White and Yeats, while not validating multisite, say multisite churches should at least gather their whole congregation periodically (White and Yeats, *Franchising McChurch*, 161).

41   Carson, *Exegetical Fallacies*, 28.

word may also have multiple meanings, which demonstrates flexibility in its usage. Finally, in the case of multisite critics' use of *ekklesia*, they base their argument on a logically unprovable premise: that the church at some point gathers all its members together. If this is their level of expectancy, then any church not meeting that requirement would not be a truly gathered *ekklesia*.[42]

Greear, Chandler, House, and Allison conclude that the essence of a church is the covenant between the believing members, not in assembling those members together.[43] Greear comments, "The essence of a New Testament local church, however, is not 'assembly' but 'covenant body.' If the local church is essentially an assembly, then it only exists when it assembles and only when all the members are present. 'Assembly' is a much-needed function, but 'covenant' is the essence."[44]

Stanley Grenz notes that congregationalists assert "the church is formed through the covenanting of its members."[45] In his seven characteristics of local churches, Allison does not include "assembly," but he does include "covenantal" as a key element of the gathered church. The members are "gathered as members in new covenant relationship with God and in covenantal relationship with each other."[46] B. H. Carroll lists establishing a church covenant as the second step of establishing a local church, second only to choosing a name.[47]

While assembling signifies the gathering of the church, it does not capture the purpose behind the gathering. Jason Lee notes Baptists have historically viewed covenant as an essential element for forming a local church. He writes, "Through this act of covenant, the people submit to the authority of Christ, becoming a true local church."[48] Interestingly, *qahal*,

---

42   Allison, *Sojourners and Strangers*, 313n47–14n47.
43   Dever, Leeman, and Chandler, "On Multi-Site Churches"; Greear, "A Pastor Defends His Multi-Site Church," 19; Greear, "Is Multisite a Biblically Sound Model?"; House and Allison, *MultiChurch*, 94.
44   Greear, "A Pastor Defends His Multi-Site Church," 19.
45   Grenz, *Theology for the Community of God*, 469.
46   Allison, *Sojourners and Strangers*, 123.
47   Carroll, *Baptist Church Polity and Articles of Faith*, 36–37. Carroll includes choosing a name, establishing a covenant, defining articles of belief, choosing a moderator, and establishing a constitution as the steps to establishing a church.
48   Lee, "Baptism and Covenant," 122.

mentioned above, carries a similar understanding of the assembly being born out of the covenant relationship. Concerning this, Verlyn Verbrugge writes, "*Eda* is the unambiguous and permanent term for the covenant community as a whole, while *qahal* is the ceremonial expression for the assembly that results from the covenant."[49] Essentially, the covenant forms the glue that binds the assembled believers together. Thus, while it is apparent that *ekklesia* as the called-out and gathered community identifies the visible form of the church, the covenant between the gathered members identifies the communal formation of the church. The believers in covenant together form the church, which transcends the assembly because the covenant relationship continues to exist even when the assembly is dismissed. If assembly is the essence of the community, then the community ceases to exist when the assembly dismisses. Without covenant, an assembly of believers is not a church.[50]

A church covenant works together with a statement of beliefs to identify who the church claims to be and what they claim to be about. Dever says covenants define the parameters of membership, working in tandem with a statement of beliefs. He writes, "From the seventeenth to the nineteenth centuries, church covenants, often accompanied by a statement of faith, acted as the most basic document of a Baptist congregation. . . . If a church covenant represents the agenda (things to be done) of a local congregation, statements of faith or confessions represent their credenda (things to be believed)."[51]

Therefore, a covenant works to define the people who constitute a church, not the gathering of that body. The gathering works to give a physical awareness of who constitutes the body. Therefore, it is recommended for multisite churches to gather as one body as frequently as is reasonable.[52] It puts flesh on the covenant community. However, it does not define the community.

49   Verbrugge, *NIV Theological Dictionary*, 390.
50   Grenz, *Theology for the Community of God*, 611–12. In *Ecclesia*, while not arguing for covenantal connection, Carroll does deny that the assembly ceases to exist when the members go their separate ways. This means Carroll saw something outside the act of assembling that created the church (Carroll, *Ecclesia*, 55).
51   Dever, *The Church*, chap. 11.
52   Greear, "Is Multisite a Biblically Sound Model?"

A Multisite Church That Does Not Assemble
Cannot Perform the Functions of a Church

Another multisite critique related to assembly is that a church that does not assemble cannot perform the functions of a church.[53] In these critiques, the "functions" generally refer to aspects such as overseeing membership guidelines, performing church discipline, protecting the administration of the Lord's Supper, and performing the responsibilities of congregational polity. Leeman writes, "Over time, furthermore, people will easily lose sight of their every-member responsibilities and corporate purposes."[54] He also writes, "A multi-site church makes it extremely difficult, if not impossible, for a congregation to fulfill its obligation to exercise the keys over the whole 'church.'"[55] His concern is that a multisite church, which by his definition is a church that does not assemble at one location, cannot functionally exercise its responsibilities.

A solution to this problem has already been provided in the previous section, and by recommendations in chapters 4 and 5 under the sections on church discipline, leadership, and ministry. Therefore, this section will not repeat the same detailed argument, but will only provide the basic conclusion. A multisite church can exercise the functions of a church and can ensure they are handled properly by utilizing certain measures. First, periodic gatherings of the whole church can provide an outlet for exercising and approving church discipline under the oversight of the gathered body. These periodic gatherings also provide an opportunity for the church to perform necessary, non-delegable governing functions of the gathered body.[56] Second, an organizational structure can be set up that helps facilitate decision making in the whole church and campus groups. These delegations can be led and managed by non-staff members of the church and can work in tandem with, rather than in opposition

---

53   Leeman, "Twenty-Two Problems with Multi-Site Churches." This section addresses critiques 2, 11, 12, 17, 18 of Leeman's twenty-two. See also Anyabwile, "Multi-Site Churches Are from the Devil"; White, "Nine Reasons I Don't Like Multi-Site Churches," 49–50; White and Yeats, *Franchising McChurch*, 80–82.
54   Leeman, *One Assembly*, Introduction.
55   Leeman, "Twenty-Two Problems with Multi-Site Churches."
56   House and Allison, *MultiChurch*, 195.

to, congregational polity.[57] Third, a distinction must be made between those aspects of church life that are required to be overseen by the whole church, such as discipline and congregational governance, and those that do not have to be under to oversight of the whole church. Sullivan writes,

> For example, the New Testament also stipulates that churches must carry out the ordinances of baptism, maintain church membership, make disciples, maintain sound doctrine, and live on mission with God. Baptist tradition has also frequently spoken to these ecclesiological functions. However, the New Testament does not explicitly stipulate the assembly of the church for the execution of these ecclesiological functions.[58]

MULTISITE CHURCHES CANNOT FUNCTION AS CONGREGATIONAL CHURCHES

Another critique of multisite churches, one that all multisite churches must intentionally consider and address, is the critique that congregational polity in multisite churches is extremely difficult, if not impossible.[59] Leeman says, "The unity of the church depends on the leaders," and "A multi-site pastor possess[es] all the administrative power that a bishop possesses over churches in his region."[60] White and Yeats describe the general consensus of multisite critics when they write,

> In these multicampus churches, the pastor as CEO becomes like a bishop in an Episcopal structure. . . . In most multicampus structures, the campus is simply a branch of the main congregation, so all decisions are ratified and maintained by the pastor and the leadership team. Instead of being an autonomous church that owns its own facilities and practices

---

57   House and Allison, *MultiChurch*, 146–59.
58   Sullivan, "Examining the Ecclesiological Soundness," 236.
59   White and Yeats, *Franchising McChurch*, 79–82.
60   Leeman, "Twenty-Two Problems with Multi-Site Churches." This section answers critique 5 and 14 of Leeman's twenty-two.

the New Testament model of submitting to one another in Christ, they are subjected to the external control of a centralized business structure. Offerings taken at the satellite campus are deposited into the main campus's accounts, and the bean counters there determine how much goes back out to meet the needs of the satellite. While this is efficient and provides for cost sharing, the ramifications are huge. Your local congregation has zero control. In function, the multicampus church is like a hierarchical McDenomination that dictates what each franchise must do.[61]

The conclusion by these critics is that multisite churches inherently drift toward something other than congregationalism.[62] Heath Kahlbau's dissertation on multisite churches is by far the most in-depth analysis of multisite polity, and he concludes,

Are all multi-site churches episcopal in structure? No. Are the overwhelming majority of multi-site churches episcopal in structure? Absolutely. The episcopal tendencies of multi-site churches are evident in their parallels to the ancient diocese and acknowledged by a majority of multi-site leaders interviewed— whether advocates or opponents of the multi-site model. However, as has been noted numerous times in this study, there are exceptions to almost all rules pertaining to multi-site churches. In this regard, churches such as Sojourn Church in Louisville, Kentucky disprove the assertion that episcopal leadership in multi-site churches in unavoidable and inescapable.[63]

Kahlbau concludes the only thing that distinguishes a collection of campuses from a group of churches is a shared governance. Kahlbau's

---

61 White and Yeats, *Franchising McChurch*, 81–82.
62 Gilbert, "What Is This Thing, Anyway?," 27; Kahlbau, "Is Anything New Under the Sun?," 166–263; Leeman, *One Assembly*, Introduction. Kahlbau's analysis of multisite polity is by far the most in-depth analysis.
63 Kahlbau, "Is Anything New Under the Sun?," 282.

problem with that conclusion is that governance has never been a mark of a church. Thus, in his understanding, a multisite church is really made up of multiple congregations, each separately performing all the functions of a church, yet not referring to themselves as individual churches. He concludes that most of these show episcopal polity, and at best, some multisite churches are a collegial presbytery. Kahlbau believes true congregational polity is near impossible. He says, "If multi-site churches are actually multi-church churches, then Baptists who claim to agree with the Baptist Faith and Message of 2000 regarding 'local autonomous congregations' do seem to face a clear conflict between profession and practice if they embrace a multi-site model."[64]

Kahlbau gives credibility to the critique posed by Leeman and others. Can a church be multisite and truly congregational? House and Allison argue it is possible. In his article for *9Marks Journal*, Allison proposes two forms of congregational polity that he has witnessed functioning in a biblical manner. The first could be considered single-elder congregationalism, and the second represents plural-elder congregationalism. With the first, which Allison describes as the "Traditional Southern Baptist Multi-Site Church," there is a senior pastor, multiple campus pastors representing each campus, deacons representing each campus, ministry staff representing each campus, and administrative committees comprised of members from each location. The pastors and ministry leaders meet weekly for collaboration in ongoing ministry. The congregation meets quarterly for worship, communion, and to vote on decisions that need the gathered congregation's approval.[65] This scenario mirrors the structure of many multi-staff, single-site, single-elder-led churches, which function within acceptable biblical parameters of congregational leadership.[66]

In Allison's second example, which he calls "elder-led, deacon-served, congregational multi-site church for city reaching," a plural-elder polity is

---

64   Kahlbau, "Is Anything New Under the Sun?," 246–62. Kahlbau considers Sojourn Church to resemble a collegial presbytery more than a congregational church led by elders.

65   Allison, "Theological Defense of Multi-Site," 16. This model assumes a church is confined to a region in which the church can reasonably gather for these periodic gatherings.

66   For an example, see Akin, "The Single-Elder-Led Church," or Patterson, "Single-Elder Congregationalism."

revealed. Allison's language makes it quite clear that this is his preferred style of multisite polity, and these few paragraphs in the article are the basis for the content he eventually develops with House in *MultiChurch*.[67] Allison and House propose multiple levels of elder-led councils and teams made up of elders from each location (both paid and nonpaid), deacons, and congregational representatives who are neither elders nor deacons. These various levels of leadership exist to perform the leadership function of the church under the guidance of the whole church.[68]

A structure with elder(s) and staff working with non-staff leadership and deacons, all under the authority of the congregation, provides everything the multisite church needs in the nature of leadership, accountability, and congregational ownership. Brian Frye encourages multisite churches to make a concerted effort to locate the authority of the church with the congregation, writing, "Every effort should be made to include all right standing members of the multi-site congregation in primary decision-making processes, such as matters of church membership, church discipline, budgeting, building programs, and staff leadership selection, for example."[69] The nature of larger churches is that staff inevitably take a more prominent role in the leading the church in carrying out the church's mission. Chandler, a multisite pastor who is keenly aware of the potential problems with the multisite concept, recognizes the challenges of maintaining a functional leadership format that includes accountability, forward mobility, and congregational authority.[70] Regarding this, he comments in an interview for Southern Seminary,

> What I have found is where you have all three pieces you tend to have a really healthy church: where you have an elder body, an elder-governing body, like we see in the Scriptures, that sets philosophy, theology and direction; where you have a staff team that handles the outworkings of that philosophy

67   Allison, "Theological Defense of Multi-Site," 16; House and Allison, *MultiChurch*, 150–58.
68   House and Allison, *MultiChurch*, 150–58.
69   Frye, "The Multi-Site Church Phenomenon," 215–16.
70   Chandler, "Clouds on the Horizon," 32.

and theology, and where you continue to come to the body and inform, get pushback and create feedback loops. When you have those three heads, you tend to have a very healthy place.[71]

This description is functionally possible in any of the forms of congregational church polity, except perhaps a pure democracy.[72]

The above description shows a model of congregational polity is possible in multisite churches, but it does not address Kahlbau's critique that campuses are united under a non-mark of the church: governance. The answer to this critique goes once again to essence of a church, as discussed above in the critique on multisite assembly. A church is created no more because of its governance structure than it is created by the fact that it assembles in one place. Assembly and governance are a functional activity or structure of a church, but the church itself is created by the covenanting of its people together.[73] This is why a church can undergo a change in governing structure without having to close a church and begin a new one. What holds a group of campuses together as one church is not their assembly, their government, their budget, or their leaders, but their covenanting together as a body.[74] If, as in Kahlbau's critique, a local church becomes a campus, its members will join the new church and agree to their covenant, which is the glue that binds them to the body. And if, as in Kahlbau's critique, a campus becomes a local church, the members will remove themselves from under the covenant obligations of the sending church and create for themselves a new covenant, by which they will become an autonomous church.[75]

This analysis shows that a multisite church can function with congregational church polity. It also shows that the essential aspect of the church that binds the campuses together as one is its covenant. This gives the church its identity, unlike aspects such as budget, leaders, and governance, which are simply functional and organizational aspects of the church.

---

71   Wishall, "Matt Chandler," 6.

72   See "The Single-Elder Led Church," "The Congregation-Led Church," and "The Plural-Elder-Led Church," in Brand and Norman, *Perspectives on Church Government*.

73   Grenz, *Theology for the Community of God*, 611–12; Lee, "Baptism and Covenant," 122.

74   Greear, "A Pastor Defends His Multi-Site Church," 19–20.

75   Kahlbau, "Is Anything New Under the Sun?," 260–63.

MULTISITE CHURCH PASTORS CANNOT
SHEPHERD THEIR FLOCKS

Another critique levied against multisite churches is that pastors are unable to shepherd their flocks as they are supposed to. Leeman writes, "The pastor of a large church has difficulty knowing all his members, but he can at least have some sense of the room in which he's preaching. Both of these are impossible by definition in a multi-site church that employs video preaching."[76] White states in his *9Marks* article, "Hebrews 13:17 says that leaders will give account for their actions and those under their charge. I wonder if video ministers will give account for those multi-site members—people who have never prayed with their pastor at the steps of an altar, shaken his hand on the way out the door, or ever seen him in person."[77]

White's conclusion is clear: multisite lead pastors cannot provide pastoral care to members of his church who attend satellite campuses. Unfortunately, in this statement, White betrays the personal bias against multisite churches that drives his article. There is nothing in Hebrews 13:17 to imply that a single person is responsible for the care of the flock. In fact, as noted previously in chapter 8, pastoral care is the responsibility of the elders. In a single-elder-led church, the burden would fall on the senior pastor to develop a plan for pastoral care. In the case of multiple staff at the church, which would be the case in multisite churches, the staff would share their portion of the delegated responsibility under the guidance of the pastor, just as a pastor would delegate responsibility in a single-site church.[78] In a plural-elder church, the responsibility would be shared among the elders. Nothing in the text implies all of the accounting will fall back on a single leader. As a church grows, just as with the New Testament church, leadership and responsibility for caring for the flock must be disseminated among elders and staff, all of whom will give an account for their charge.[79] About this very topic and this Scripture,

76   Leeman, "Twenty-Two Problems with Multi-Site Churches." This section addresses critique 16 of Leeman's twenty-two.
77   White, "Nine Reasons I Don't Like Multi-Site Churches," 50.
78   Montoya, "Leading," 243–45.
79   Bryant and Brunson, *The New Guidebook for Pastors*, 86–87; Criswell, *Criswell's Guidebook for Pastors*, 82–83.

Andrew Davis, himself a pastor, says, "It is biblical for a pastor to be shepherding the flock in co-labor with other elders who are called by the congregation for the same purpose. Therefore, it is not necessary for any one elder to know everything about every individual member but rather simply to ensure that every member is being shepherded and cared for by the ministry of the church."[80] Therefore, it is up to the body of elders, or ministerial staff, and deacons to know the people in their flock and to know their condition, both physical and spiritual.[81] This is the same for churches large and small, single-site or multisite.

Multisite advocates believe pastoral ministry does not suffer in a multisite church. Greear says the problem of pastors having a connection to each of his members is not an issue that only faces multisite churches. He says, "It happens at any church above two hundred!"[82] Even Leeman's statement above notes the problems large church pastors face in having a connection with their members.[83] Multisite churches allow for the church members to be identified with a set group of people, much like they would in a small group, and also allows them to have a better opportunity to have a personal connection to the pastoral staff and elders of their campus.[84] For churches that provide live, in-person preaching at each campus, this means the pastor sharing the Word with them is also the pastor they have a good opportunity to shake hands with on their way out of the church. Frye says this personal connection has to be intentionally sought by the pastors, encouraging "intentional efforts of multi-site pastoral leaders to remain intimately involved in the life and ministry of the congregation wherever the various pastors and sites locate."[85] If multisite pastors, campus pastors, associate staff, and non-staff elders will work together with these intentional processes, pastoral ministry will not lack.

---

80   Davis, "Those Who Must Give an Account, 211.
81   Davis, "Those Who Must Give an Account," 211–15.
82   Greear, "A Pastor Defends His Multi-Site Church," 22.
83   Leeman, "Twenty-Two Problems with Multi-Site Churches."
84   Greear, "A Pastor Defends His Multi-Site Church," 22; House and Allison, *MultiChurch*, 155.
85   Frye, "The Multi-Site Church Phenomenon," 216.

MULTISITE CHURCHES ARE NOT SUPPORTED BY HISTORICAL PRACTICE

Multisite critics have been most vocal in Baptist circles and have said multisite has no true precedent, specifically in Baptist church history.[86] The evidence to the contrary is minimal, but enough evidence exists to suggest historical Baptists were flexible enough to put multisite type models into practice. One authority on the matter that both multisite advocates and critics point to is G. Hugh Wamble, who wrote a dissertation on connectionalism in early English Baptist churches.[87] In his findings, he describes churches that were connected through associationalism, mild connectionalism, and strong connectionalism. The first two do not characterize multisite churches. However, the last group does. These strong-connectionalism churches, primarily in Wales in the seventeenth century, considered themselves to be one church but met in multiple locations. The churches held weekly worship services at all their locations, and they also held monthly gatherings of the whole church in a single location. They initially celebrated the Lord's Supper only at the whole church gathering but eventually began serving the ordinance in some of the scattered meetings as well. All members were expected to attend once a quarter in the whole church gatherings.[88] Leon McBeth describes this as a practice of the early General Baptists in England, concluding, "The General Baptists regarded local congregations as in some sense branches, or local units, of the larger church."[89] Allison cites Wamble's work as evidence of multisite precedent, writing, "Consideration of these historical precedents may help to dispel the notion that the contemporary multi-site church phenomenon is merely the latest . . . fad fueled by business models of franchising and branding, lust for notoriety, or other insidious reasons."[90] Hammett and Gaines,

---

86   Gaines, "One Church in One Location," 127–46. Gaines provides an excellent analysis of the history of "possible" multisite precedents in Baptist history, albeit from the position of denying the multisite precedent.
87   Wamble, "The Concept and Practice of Christian Fellowship."
88   Wamble, "The Concept and Practice of Christian Fellowship," 256–59. Wamble, while acknowledging the forms of the church, does conclude that this was unusual for Baptist congregational polity and that the practice does not fit the usual Baptist practice.
89   McBeth, *The Baptist Heritage*, 76.
90   Allison, "Theological Defense of Multi-Site," 13.

however, use Wamble's descriptions as evidence that the multisite claims of precedent are still lacking.[91] Gaines concludes that "some early English Baptist churches met in multiple locations and still considered themselves one church, [however] this structure was short-lived in Baptist history . . . this can by no means be considered a Baptist distinctive."[92] Gaines demonstrates how each of the early English Baptist churches eventually moved towards autonomy for multiple reasons.[93]

Sullivan and Willis make similar statements regarding certain early Baptist churches in the United States, providing examples of churches in the Philadelphia, Charleston, and Sandy Creek Baptist associations.[94] Sullivan writes, "The Philadelphia Baptist Association . . . formed because various congregations wanted to belong to the same church."[95] The Charleston church developed in the late 1600s and early 1700s, and "by 1740, there were five churches in South Carolina, most of them being branches of the Charleston church."[96] The Sandy Creek Association's "inaugural meeting of the association included nine churches in addition to several branches."[97] The branches in each of these locations were considered parts of their mother church. McBeth writes concerning the Charleston church, "Members were still related to the central church."[98] Willis states there is similarity between these early associations and modern multisite churches, but he limits that similarity to their goal of reaching as many as possible with the gospel.[99]

These authors provide many reasons why these early churches, though functionally similar to multisite churches, should not be considered precursors of the multisite movement. One reason is that the churches sought to transition the branches into autonomous churches

---

91 Gaines, "One Church in One Location," 127–46; Hammett, "Have We Ever Seen This Before?," 29–30.

92 Gaines, "One Church in One Location," 146.

93 Gaines, "One Church in One Location," 127–46.

94 Sullivan, "Examining the Ecclesiological Soundness," 50–64; Willis, "Multi-Site Churches and Their Undergirding Ecclesiology," 18–90.

95 Sullivan, "Examining the Ecclesiological Soundness," 55.

96 Sullivan, "Examining the Ecclesiological Soundness," 58.

97 Sullivan, "Examining the Ecclesiological Soundness," 60.

98 McBeth, The Baptist Heritage, 217.

99 Willis, "Multi-Site Churches and Their Undergirding Ecclesiology," 37, 62, 83.

as soon as they could.[100] The claim is that today's multisite churches have no desire or intention to eventually plant their campuses as autonomous churches. However, this reasoning fails to draw a true distinction between the early practices and today's because this reason is based on the intention of the church rather than the form of the church. The form of these early churches parallels multisite attributes, even if the supposed intention is not consistent with the intentions of multisite churches of today. Even so, Sullivan's and Willis's conclusion also fails because some multisite churches do use the multisite model as a church planting process.[101]

Second, Sullivan notes a difference between the associations' use of the terms "churches" and "congregations" compared to the multisite movement's use of the terms. He notes the associations used the terms interchangeably to refer to the same entity, whereas multisite advocates make a distinction between a church and a congregation, citing House and Allison as examples.[102] However, the problem with his citation is that House and Allison actually do just the opposite: they use the two terms interchangeably as well.[103] In addition, the landscape of multisite authors and practitioners do not all use a single, consistent terminology.[104]

The third distinction that Sullivan and Willis draw between these early examples and the modern multisite churches is that these early churches used branches because they lacked qualified ministers to lead the churches. Once qualified ministers were found, they say, the churches

100 Sullivan, "Examining the Ecclesiological Soundness," 56, 59–60, 63; Willis, "Multi-Site Churches and Their Undergirding Ecclesiology," 62–64, 86.
101 Dever, Leeman, and Chandler, "On Multi-Site Churches"; Rainer and Rainer, "Church Adoption, Church Fostering, and Church Revitalization"; Surratt, Ligon, and Bird, *Multi-Site Church Revolution*, 18, 51.
102 Sullivan, "Examining the Ecclesiological Soundness," 57–58.
103 House and Allison, *MultiChurch*, 16. Examples from this one page: "multichurch is a local community of Christians that matures and multiplies its influence through launching, developing, and resourcing *multiple congregations to reach its city* with the gospel of Jesus Christ" (emphasis original). "This is one church with multiple congregations or 'churches' in a set geographic area . . ." "A multichurch is one church expressed in multiple *churches*" (emphasis original).
104 House and Allison, *MultiChurch*, 16; Murashko, "Mars Hill Church"; Surratt, Ligon, and Bird, *Multi-Site Church Revolution*, 28.

became autonomous.[105] Even if this is the case, the authors err if they consider pastoral leadership as an essential requirement before a church can exist autonomously, because a church exists based on the covenanting and functioning of the congregation, not the leaders.[106] Even granting their premise, the reasoning sounds very similar to Rainer's purpose in church fostering: to help a church to develop new leadership and healthy structures before being released again as an autonomous church.[107] Like the first "difference," this third "difference" reveals another conclusion based on these early churches' intentions and preferences. They preferred to develop leadership before launching their churches into autonomy. This is a model of ministry. One church met in multiple locations, performing the functions of a church, until such a time as they could divide into multiple autonomous churches.[108] It was a multisite model used for the purpose of church planting.

Sullivan's and Willis's conclusions are understandable because they are critiquing the mainstream MCM. However, while their critiques may be accurate in many areas of the MCM, they do not reflect all multisite churches. Additionally, their primary arguments that make a distinction between the early examples and modern-day multisite churches fail. While they do find some differences in the purpose and intention of the early churches compared to today, they do not demonstrate enough difference in the form of the churches. The early Baptist church examples used a multisite form to accomplish the purposes, preferences, and intentions they considered important. Multisite churches today use a similar form for different, albeit similar, purposes. While Sullivan and Willis claim the purpose behind using the model creates enough distinction to contrast the early examples and today's multisite

---

105 Sullivan, "Examining the Ecclesiological Soundness," 58, 63; Willis, "Multi-Site Churches and Their Undergirding Ecclesiology," 62.

106 Carroll, *Baptist Church Polity and Articles of Faith*, 36–37; Dever, *The Church*, Introduction. This is not to say leaders are not an important aspect of a biblical church. A church does not cease to exist if a pastoral elder is not present in the church. Otherwise, a single-elder-led church would cease to exist in the resignation, retirement, or removal of their single elder.

107 Rainer and Rainer, "Church Adoption, Church Fostering, and Church Revitalization."

108 Gillette, *Minutes of the Philadelphia Baptist Association*, 60–61.

churches, multisite advocates have long said that various purposes lead churches to use multisite ministry, and various multisite models result because of those purposes.[109] For these early churches, the branch was the model that served their purpose. Willis even includes a quote in his dissertation that says this very thing: "Their scriptural orientation and desire for denominational continuity gave the first Baptists of the Philadelphia Association the theological and emotional motivation for extension. Satellite congregations gave them their means."[110] Sullivan's and Willis's conclusions do not provide sufficient evidence to completely sever the branch churches of the past from some multisite models of the present. Therefore, the evidence provided does in fact show that primitive multisite models exist in Baptist history.[111] This is, of course, in addition to the examples of First Baptist Church of Dallas and Highland Park Baptist Church of Chattanooga described in chapter 2.

MULTISITE CHURCHES ARE NOT SUPPORTED BY HISTORICAL SCHOLARSHIP

Baptist critics have also argued that Baptist scholarship has historically disallowed the premises of multisite ecclesiology. Sullivan writes, "The pervasive presence of the MCM in the SBC would be shocking to previous generations of Baptists."[112] It is true that Baptist scholarship has upheld the autonomy of local churches and has consistently denied that any ecclesiastical authority exists above a local congregation.[113] It is also

---

109   Easum and Travis, *Beyond the Box*, 86–96; Ferguson, "The Multi-Site Church and Disciplemaking," 19–27; Schaller, *Innovations in Ministry*, 71–72, 121; Sullivan, "Examining the Ecclesiological Soundness," 56–64; Willis, "Multi-Site Churches and Their Undergirding Ecclesiology," 64.

110   Willis, "Multi-Site Churches and Their Undergirding Ecclesiology," 32–33; see also Smith, *The Advance of Baptist Associations Across America*, 29.

111   Willis also suggests that "multi-site is actually a rejection of associationalism." This is an accusation that a fundamental tenet of multisite models is a lack of cooperation with other churches. This will be shown to be false in the next section. He notes most multisite churches do not assemble as one body, whereas the early churches sought to at times. He says this is an issue for congregational polity. However, he also acknowledges some multisite churches do have occasionally whole church gatherings (Willis, "Multi-Site Churches and Their Undergirding Ecclesiology," 40, 63).

112   Sullivan, "Examining the Ecclesiological Soundness," 104.

113   Examples: Dagg, *A Treatise on Church Order*, 83; Johnson, *The Gospel Developed*, 172–76.

true that Baptists have historically considered a local church's ability to assemble together as an essential aspect of a local church.[114] However, while affirming autonomy and assembly, some Baptist forefathers also allowed for a single church to meet in multiple locations separate of one another. John Broadus wrote concerning the word *ekklesia* in Acts 9:31,

> In [Acts 9:31] the word probably denotes the original church at Jerusalem, whose members were by the persecution widely scattered throughout Judea and Galilee and Samaria, and *held meetings wherever they were, but still belonged to the one original organization.* When Paul wrote to the Galatians, nearly twenty years later, these separate meetings had been organized into distinct churches.[115]

This shows that Broadus believed the scattered church, as it met in many locations throughout the region, still belonged to the Jerusalem church for a period of time less than twenty years. B. H. Carroll concedes the same possibility when, after quoting Broadus, he writes, "So when in the paragraph just preceding our Scripture, there is an account of Saul, as a convert, worshipping and preaching with the church he had formerly persecuted, we may not be surprised at the statement 'So the church throughout all Judea and Galilee and Samaria had peace.'"[116]

He had stated previously,

> Nor does [*ecclesia*] require that all its *Kletoi* or members shall be present at every session. . . . Some are sick, some travel, some backslide. Conditions of weather, politics or war affect the attendance. Yea, more, storms, plagues, or persecution may for the time being scatter the members of a particular church over a wide area of territory. None of these things in the slightest degree affect the meaning of the word.[117]

---

114 Examples: Carroll, *Ecclesia*, 42; Keach, *The Glory of a True Church*, 64–65.
115 Broadus, *Commentary on the Gospel of Matthew*, 359, emphasis added.
116 Carroll, *Ecclesia*, Loc.: 470.
117 Carroll, *Ecclesia*, Loc.: 413.

Carroll makes clear that he believes the existence of a particular church is not dependent upon its ability to assemble weekly. Carroll makes a distinction between members being absent from an occasional meeting (sick, travel, weather) and those who miss many gatherings, having been scattered "over a wide territory" for an extended period of time. Neither, according to Carroll, change the meaning of the *ekklesia*. Therefore, even as it has been shown previously that Carroll considers assembly of the members as an essential function of a local church, he apparently does not believe the non-assembly of those members inherently changes the existence of the assembly.[118] For multisite churches, therefore, this opens the door for the allowance of multiple locations, while it must be acknowledged that Carroll would likely see this as an impermanent situation.

William Williams provides even more potential support for multisite views.[119] He writes,

> It is doubtless true, that, in a large city like Jerusalem, and it may be Antioch, Ephesus, and Corinth, the number of Christians was too large to meet as one body ordinarily. Prudential reasons would cause them most probably to meet in several assemblies in different places. The fallacy, however, in the above theory lies in supposing that these several congregations were several distinct churches, and not sections of the same church meeting in different places for ordinary worship, but the "whole multitude" coming together when anything of special importance required.[120]

With this statement, Williams shows he believes the practice of the early Christian church was to "ordinarily . . . meet in several assemblies in different places." These "several congregations" were parts of "the same church meeting in different places for ordinary worship." Thus, for Williams, the practice among the early church was to meet separately on most occasions and as a whole group only "when something of special

---

118   Carroll, *Ecclesia*, Loc.: 395.
119   Dever, *Polity*, 526.
120   Williams, *Apostolic Church Polity*, 43–44.

importance required" the whole church to gather.[121] This parallels the multisite model recommended by House and Allison and by this book.[122]

J. L. Reynolds is another Baptist writer who clearly held firm to church autonomy and the importance of church assembly, yet who allowed that the church does not have to always meet together in order to be a single church.[123] Citing Rev. Heneage Elsley, Reynolds acknowledges some churches met in multiple locations in the New Testament, writing, "Perhaps the explanation given by Elsley and others is the most satisfactory. 'In that age,' he remarks, 'Christians had no public edifices, but held their meetings in private houses. When they were numerous, these meetings, and the inspectors or bishops who presided over them, were multiplied in proportion.'"[124]

This shows Reynolds accepted the fact that multiple house gatherings existed, each of which required its own elders. He writes earlier, in the same book,

> In other [New Testament] cities, where the number of members was very large, local convenience may have been consulted; and there may have been portions of the Church . . . that held their religious meetings in different places, but still constituting, as in some of our large cities, branches or arms of the Church . . . located in those cities. This is rendered possible, by the existence of a plurality of bishops. It is sufficient to show that the Churches . . . of the New Testament were single societies, that the members of a certain locality constituted a Church . . . not Churches . . . and that they were addressed by the Apostles, as a unit and not a plurality. Even if it be conceded, therefore, that the number of elders, found in the primitive Churches . . . was rendered necessary by their habit of assembling in different places of worship, this does not affect the

---

121 Williams *Apostolic Church Polity*, 43–44.
122 House and Allison, *MultiChurch*, 94, 195.
123 Reynolds, *Church Polity*, 51–53.
124 Reynolds, *Church Polity*, 113; see also Elsley, *Annotations on the Four Gospels and the Acts*, 351.

congregational character of these Churches . . . since each body
of elders was addressed as officers of "the Church" . . . plainly
evincing that the community to which they were attached,
constituted a single society.[125]

Again, Reynolds mentions a plurality of church leaders. These elders
allowed the single church in a city to meet in multiple locations, while
still constituting "a Church . . . not Churches . . . as a unit and not a plurality." He clearly states this plurality of elders and plurality of locations
did "not affect the congregational character of these Churches," and that
the plurality of elders and plurality of locations were attached to a church
community that "constituted a single society."[126] Reynolds, therefore,
acknowledges a single church can, and he believes did, meet in multiple
locations with elders presiding over each location, and still be considered
a single congregation. Having multiple locations does not, by default,
change the congregational nature of the church.

These examples show that some in historic Baptist scholarship have left
the door open for a particular form of multisite ministry. While Sullivan's
statement that Baptists of the past would be shocked at the pervasiveness
of many multisite movement practices in the SBC might be partially true,
it seems they would not be shocked at all of the multisite practices in the
SBC.[127] This is not to suggest that multisite churches are a Baptist distinctive,
as Gaines makes clear.[128] However, if Baptist multisite churches employ a
unified model of leadership across campuses while retaining a congregational authority and polity, and have a practice of meeting together as a
whole church on occasion, they would fit within the parameters expressed
by the Baptist scholars cited above.

125 Reynolds, *Church Polity*, 53–54. Note Reynolds's reference to "branches or arms of the
     Church" in "our large cities." He is comparing the early church's practice of meeting in
     multiple places with multiple elders to the same practice in the church of his own time
     period, the mid-nineteenth century.
126 Reynolds, *Church Polity*, 53–54.
127 Sullivan, "Examining the Ecclesiological Soundness," 104.
128 Gaines, "One Church in One Location," 146.

MULTISITE CHURCHES ARE IN CONFLICT WITH CHURCH PLANTING

Critics of multisite churches have also claimed that multisite churches hinder church planting efforts or that multisite churches should exchange their multiple campus model for a more "biblical" model of church planting.[129] Leeman goes so far as to say that if a church chooses to add campuses rather than to plant autonomous churches, the church is deficient in one of two ways. He writes, "The only reason [to add campuses and] not to plant churches stems from one of two failures: either the church has failed to do the discipling work of raising up more elders and pastors; or the church has decided to accommodate celebrity and consumeristic culture."[130] Similarly, White and Yeats suggest that multisite models should be dismissed in favor of church planting because church plants "avoid consumerism of entertaining speakers . . . avoid compromising congregational polity . . . avoid sacrificing local church autonomy . . . allow other leaders to develop and excel . . . allow us to multiply disciples."[131] White even criticizes multisite churches who also have church planting efforts because he says they are dividing their resources, which could otherwise be focused solely on planting.[132]

These critiques may have been birthed out of valid examples in the multisite world, although the authors' sweeping generalizations include no examples. Even if the negative examples exist, research shows that multisite church models are not at all incompatible with church planting, or even that multisite models hinder church planting. Research on multisite churches shows that 48 percent of multisite churches directly sponsor church plants. Multisite churches also support denominational church

---

129 Leeman, "The Alternative Case," 54; White, "Nine Reasons I Don't Like Multi-Site Churches," 50; White and Yeats, *Franchising McChurch*, 169, 178–80.

130 Leeman, "The Alternative Case," 52. This critique demonstrates a false dilemma fallacy, a fallacy that is common in Leeman's critiques.

131 White and Yeats, *Franchising McChurch*, 180. Of course, church plants do not guarantee any of these desired effects any more than multisite campuses guarantee their negative counterparts. These claims employ the same false dilemma fallacy as Leeman's statement above.

132 White, "Nine Reasons I Don't Like Multi-Site Churches," 50.

planting efforts (47 percent) and/or are part of church planting networks (36 percent). Only 19 percent of surveyed multisite churches say they are not involved in any type of church planting. Twenty-nine percent of the multisite churches that support church planting say their multisite model actually has been a catalyst that increased their involvement in church planting.[133] Compare this to research among all types of churches that shows only 28 percent of churches in the US participate in any form of church planting efforts, and only 12 percent of that 28 percent are churches that function as a mother church, accepting primary responsibility for a church plant.[134] Multisite churches, as a distinct subset, are more involved in church planting than the general population of churches.

Multisite church leaders would disagree with the belief that church planting and multisite are incompatible. Greear acknowledges that church planting is the "New Testament's most effective evangelistic strategy," but he disagrees that church planting and multisite are opposed to each other. His church has a commitment to plant one thousand churches in forty years. He believes that whereas church planting answers the question of multiplication, multisite ministry provides a solution to space problems due to growth in a specific church, which planting often cannot solve.[135] Even Leeman acknowledges church planting cannot sufficiently solve the space demands in a rapidly growing church.[136] Matt Chandler not only pastors a church but was also the executive chairman of the Acts 29 Network in 2023, an interdenominational church planting group.[137] His church, The Village Church, actively supports church planting and lists sixteen church planters who they are currently supporting and/or training.[138] The Village Church is also an example of a church that understands the necessity of adapting a church's model depending on the needs of their congregation, as they have transitioned all of their multisite campuses

---

133 Bird, "Multisite Church Scorecard," 23.
134 Stetzer and Bird, *Viral Churches*, 149.
135 Greear, "A Pastor Defends His Multi-Site Church," 19, 21; Greear, "Why Is the Summit Multi-Site?"
136 Leeman, *One Assembly*, Loc.:1848.
137 "Acts 29," *Acts 29*.
138 "Church Planting," *The Village Church*.

to autonomous churches.[139] Family Church, The Summit Church, and Sojourn Church have either their own church planting residencies or are part of church planting networks that train, resource, support, and send church planters to plant autonomous churches.[140] These are only a few examples of multisite churches that are actively planting churches outside of their own multisite congregation. To suggest that multisite ministry is inherently at odds with church planting is, at best, a statement of ignorance or, at worst, a statement of dishonesty.

---

139 "Campus Transitions," *TVC Resources.*
140 "Church Planting Residency," *Family Church Network*; "Our Mission," *Harbor Network*;
      "Plant: We Equip Leaders to Plant Churches," *Summit Collaborative.*

CHAPTER 19

CONCLUSION

THIS BOOK HAS SHOWN A BIBLICAL and historical foundation for multisite churches does indeed exist. It has done so by evaluating the validity of the multisite church model through an investigation of Scripture and historical precedent, and by providing solutions to the critiques levied against the model. The goal of the book has been to discover a biblical ecclesiology for multisite churches and to determine how churches can employ a multisite model that is consistent with congregational polity. What is now needed is a better definition for multisite churches.

A NEW DEFINITION FOR MULTISITE CHURCHES

Chapter 1 provided a definition typical of the multisite church movement. It states, "A multisite church is one church meeting in multiple separate physical campuses. These locations may be in the same city or region, or they may be in different cities, states, or nations. A multisite church shares a common vision, budget, and leadership."[1] This definition

---

1   As described in chapter 1, this definition only considers churches to be "multisite" if they have two or more separate physical campuses. Churches with multiple venues on the same campus, internet campuses, or multiple services but no physical campus were not the focus of this book and were not included in the definition.

is based on various definitions and models presented by multisite advocates, most heavily relying on the definition provided by *The Multi-Site Church Revolution*.[2] The definition in *MCR* has been shown to be lacking for congregational churches, as it does not provide strong enough parameters to fit within their polity.

A multisite definition must supplement a church or denomination's statement on what a church is. For example, the BFM defines a church:

> A New Testament church of the Lord Jesus Christ is an autonomous local congregation of baptized believers, associated by covenant in the faith and fellowship of the gospel; observing the two ordinances of Christ, governed by His laws, exercising the gifts, rights, and privileges invested in them by His Word, and seeking to extend the gospel to the ends of the earth.[3]

Since the BFM, or a church or denomination's own definition defines what a church is and does, the multisite church definition does not have to include everything this includes. It should be seen as supplemental, not as a replacement or alternative.

The multisite definition above, as has been shown in the preceding chapters, is not an adequate supplement to the definition of a true biblical church. The multisite definition only has "vision, budget, and leadership" as the uniting aspects of the church. While these are important, especially for defining how multisite churches function, they are not fully sufficient to describe how a biblically faithful multisite church should function and what holds it together as one church. Specifically, since a multisite church gathers its membership in separate gatherings for weekly worship, something needs to be included in the definition to show that the church is actually united by something other than a vision, a budget, and its leaders. Therefore, the following definition is recommended as an alternative, more complete, definition for a multisite church:

---

2   Surratt, Ligon, and Bird, *Multi-Site Church Revolution*, 18.
3   "The 2000 Baptist Faith and Message," *Southern Baptist Convention*.

A multisite church is one church whose members ordinarily gather at multiple campuses and ideally gather together as a whole church occasionally. The campuses of a multisite church function under the authority of the whole membership who are united together by covenant to carry out the biblical responsibilities, functions, and ministries of a church. Multisite churches share a common vision, budget, and leadership.

This definition provides guidance for multisite churches to function in a manner that is faithful to the definition of a church, yet it remains general enough to allow for flexibility in areas such as the type of congregational polity, the frequency of gathering, and ministry emphasis.

This definition first demonstrates the obvious fact that a multisite church is one in which the members of the church gather at campuses that are separated by distance, and that this pattern is the normal mode of gathering for most weeks of worship. The definition then specifies that a multisite church will ideally also gather periodically as a whole church. There is flexibility in the frequency of these gatherings and the purpose of the gatherings.

Second, the definition specifies that the authority of the church rests with the members of the church. This helps remind multisite churches that leaders are responsible for leading, but members retain authority and final responsibility for the church under the lordship of Christ. The covenant of the church is that which binds these multisite churches together, as it helps to define the mission of the church and the responsibilities the members have to one another. The definition also mentions the purpose of their covenanting together, which is to ensure the biblical responsibilities, functions, and ministries of the church are taking place.

Finally, as with the original multisite definition, the new definition states that a multisite church shares a common vision, budget, and leadership. This shows that while a multisite church is primarily united by covenant, it is also united organizationally. This new definition can function as a starting point for churches seeking to move toward a multisite model and will help steer the multisite movement into a more biblically faithful direction.

THE GOAL OF MULTISITE CHURCHES

I have read numerous articles in the past few years that said multisite church models were a fad. Fads have the tendency to fade away after a short period of time. However, the multisite church movement does not appear to be going away. In fact, the models only seem to be expanding and the processes maturing as the movement goes forward.

My hope is that multisite churches will seek to be practical and biblical in their multisite strategy, just as I hope they will be in their other ministry strategies. There is no room for pragmatism at the expense of biblical fidelity. At the same time, there is no reason to call something unbiblical simply because it does not fit into our self-selected paradigms. The multisite church model provides a way forward for many churches and an opportunity to see many churches across our nation thrive rather than die. Multisite churches exist to expand the ministry of churches to more people so those people can experience new life in Jesus Christ.

My hope is that God will be honored as his church expands and as people come to faith. May we move forward in step with him, in every church, at every campus, until the day he calls us all home, at which time we will finally and truly be one church assembled together.

BIBLIOGRAPHY

BOOKS

Ahlen, J. Timothy, and J. V. Thomas. *One Church, Many Congregations: The Key Church Strategy*. Nashville, TN: Abingdon, 1999.

Akin, Danny. "The Meaning of Baptism." In *Restoring Integrity in Baptist Churches*, edited by Thomas White, Jason G. Duesing, and Malcolm B. Yarnell III, 63–80. Grand Rapids, MI: Kregel, 2008.

_____. "The Person of Christ." In *A Theology for the Church*, edited by Danny Akin, 480–544. Nashville, TN: Broadman & Holman, 2007.

_____. "The Single-Elder-Led Church: The Bible's Witness to a Congregational/Single-Elder-Led Polity." In *Perspectives on Church Government: 5 Views*, edited by Chad Owen Brand and R. Stanton Norman, 25–74. Nashville, TN: Broadman & Holman, 2004.

_____, ed. *A Theology for the Church*. Nashville: Broadman & Holman, 2007.

Alcorn, Randy. *Managing God's Money: A Biblical Guide*. Carol Stream, IL: Tyndale House, 2011.

Allison, Gregg. *Sojourners and Strangers: The Doctrine of the Church*. Wheaton, IL: Crossway, 2012.

Armstrong, John H. "Introduction." In *Understanding Four Views on Baptism*, edited by John H. Armstrong, 11–22. Grand Rapids, MI: Zondervan, 2007.

_____. "Introduction." In *Understanding Four Views on the Lord's Supper*, edited by John H. Armstrong, 11–25. Grand Rapids, MI: Zondervan, 2007.

_____, ed. *Understanding Four Views on Baptism*. Grand Rapids, MI: Zondervan, 2007.

_____, ed. *Understanding Four Views on the Lord's Supper.* Grand Rapids, MI: Zondervan, 2007.

Aune, David E. *Revelation 1–5.* Word Biblical Commentary. Vol. 52. Dallas, TX: Word, 1997.

Banks, Robert, and Julia Banks. *The Church Comes Home: Building Community and Mission through Home Churches.* Peabody, MA: Hendrickson, 1998.

Beck, James. *Two Views on Women in Ministry.* Revised edition. Grand Rapids, MI: Zondervan, 2005.

The Belgic Confession. 1561. In *The Creeds of Christendom,* edited by Philip Schaff. Vol. 3. 4th ed. New York, NY: Harper & Brothers, 1877.

Block, Daniel I. *For the Glory of God: Recovering a Biblical Theology of Worship.* Grand Rapids, MI: Baker, 2014.

Blum, Edwin A. "1 Peter." In *Hebrews–Revelation,* edited by Frank E. Gaebelein. The Expositor's Bible Commentary. Vol. 12. 209–56. Grand Rapids, MI: Zondervan, 1981.

Bock, Darrell L. *Acts.* Baker Exegetical Commentary on the New Testament. Grand Rapids, MI: Baker, 2007.

Boice, James Montgomery. *Foundations of the Christian Faith: A Comprehensive and Readable Theology.* Downers Grove, IL: InterVarsity, 1986.

Booth, Steve. "The Place of Prayer in the Early Church." In *Giving Ourselves to Prayer: An Acts 6:4 Primer on Ministry,* edited by Daniel R. Crawford, 283–88. Terre Haute, IN: Prayer Shop Publishing, 2008.

Bounds, E. M. *The Necessity of Prayer.* Grand Rapids, MI: Baker, 1976.

Boyce, James P. *Abstract of Systematic Theology.* 1887.

Brand, Chad Owen, and R. Stanton Norman, eds. *Perspectives on Church Government: 5 Views.* Nashville, TN: Broadman & Holman, 2004.

Broadus, John A. "A Catechism of Bible Teaching." In *Saved to Serve: Comprising Appealing and Vital Messages on the Duties of Christians to Give of Their Time, Thought and Means to God,* edited by J. W. Crowder and J. B. Cranfill, 221–38. Dallas, TX: Helms, 1941.

_____. *Commentary on the Gospel of Matthew.* An American Commentary on the New Testament. Philadelphia, PA: American Baptist Publication Society, 1886.

_____. "The Duty of Baptists to Teach Their Distinctive Views." In *A Baptist Treasury,* edited by Sydnor L. Stealey. New York, NY: Thomas Y. Crowell, 1958.

_____. *Lectures on the History of Preaching.* New York, NY: A. C. Armstrong & Son, 1889.

_____. *Sermons and Addresses.* Richmond, VA: B. F. Johnson and Co., 1887.

_____. *A Treatise on the Preparation and Delivery of Sermons,* edited by Edwin Charles Dargan. 26th ed. New York, NY: A. C. Armstrong & Son, 1903.

_____. "Worship." In *Classic Sermons on Worship*, edited by Warren W. Wiersbe, 11–29. Peabody, MA: Hendrickson, 1988.

Bruce, F. F. *The Acts of the Apostles: The Greek Text with Introduction and Commentary*. 3rd ed. Grand Rapids, MI: Eerdmans, 1990.

_____. *The Epistle to the Colossians, to Philemon, and to the Ephesians*. The New International Commentary on the New Testament. Grand Rapids, MI: Eerdmans, 1984.

_____. *The Epistle to the Hebrews*. The New International Commentary on the New Testament. Rev. ed. Grand Rapids, MI: Eerdmans, 1990.

Bryant, James W., and Mac Brunson. *The New Guidebook for Pastors*. Nashville, TN: Broadman & Holman, 2007.

Cairns, Earle E. *An Endless Line of Splendor: Revivals and Their Leaders from the Great Awakening to the Present*. Wheaton, IL: Tyndale House, 1986.

Calvin, John. *Institutes of Christian Religion*. Translated by John Allen. Vol. 3. New Haven, CT: Hezekiah Howe, 1816.

Caner, Emir, and Ergun Caner. *The Sacred Trust: Sketches of the Southern Baptist Convention Presidents*. Nashville, TN: Broadman & Holman, 2003.

Carey, William. "An Enquiry into the Obligations of Christians to Use Means for the Conversions of the Heathens, in which the Religious State of the Different Nations of the World, the Success of Former Undertakings, and the Practicability of Further Undertakings are Considered." In *A Baptist Treasury*, edited by Sydnor L. Stealey, 23–47. New York, NY: Thomas Y. Crowell, 1958.

_____. "An Enquiry into the Obligations of Christians to Use Means for the Conversions of the Heathens, in which the Religious State of the Different Nations of the World, the Success of Former Undertakings, and the Practicability of Further Undertakings are Considered." In *Treasuries from the Baptist Heritage*, edited by Timothy George and Denise George, 9–56. Nashville, TN: Broadman and Holman, 1996.

Carroll, B. H. *Baptist Church Polity and Articles of Faith*, edited by J. W. Crowder. Ft. Worth, TX: J. W. Crowder, 1957.

_____. *Baptists and Their Doctrines: Sermons on Distinctive Baptist Principles*, edited by J. B. Cranfill. New York, NY: Fleming H. Revell, 1913.

_____. *Ecclesia: The Church*. Louisville, KY: Baptist Book Concern, 1903.

_____. *Saved to Serve: Comprising Appealing and Vital Messages on the Duties of Christians to Give of Their Time, Thought and Means to God*, edited by J. W. Crowder and J. B. Cranfill. Dallas, TX: Helms, 1941.

_____. *The Supper and Suffering of our Lord: Sermons by B. H. Carroll*, edited by J. W. Crowder. Ft. Worth, TX: J. W. Crowder, 1947.

Carson, D. A. *Exegetical Fallacies*. 2nd ed. Grand Rapids, MI: Baker, 1996.

_____. "Matthew." In *Matthew, Mark, Luke*, edited by Frank E. Gaebelein. The Expositor's Bible Commentary. Vol. 8. Grand Rapids, MI: Zondervan, 1984.

"Catechism of the Catholic Church, 1.2.3.9.3: The Church is One, Holy, Catholic, and Apostolic." *The Holy See*. Accessed October 2, 2020. https://www.vatican.va/archive/ENG0015/__P29.HTM.

Cathcart, William. *Baptist Encyclopedia*. 1881. In *Polity: Biblical Arguments on How to Conduct Church Life*, edited by Mark Dever, 406–7. Washington, DC: Center for Church Reform, 2001.

Chandler, Russell. *Racing Toward 2001: The Forces Shaping America's Religious Future*. Grand Rapids, MI: Zondervan, 1992.

Cheong, Robert. *God Redeeming His Bride: A Handbook for Church Discipline*. Greanies House, Scotland: Christian Focus Publications, 2012.

Cockerill, Gareth Lee. *The Epistle to the Hebrews*. The New International Commentary on the New Testament. Grand Rapids, MI: Eerdmans, 2012.

Confession of Faith. 1677. In *Baptist Confessions of Faith*, edited by William Lumpkin, 241–95. Rev. ed. Valley Forge, PA: Judson, 1969.

Cowan, Steven B., ed. *Who Runs the Church?: 4 Views on Church Government*. Grand Rapids, MI: Zondervan, 2004.

Cowen, Gerald P. *Who Rules the Church?: Examining Congregational Leadership and Church Government*. Nashville, TN: Broadman & Holman, 2003.

Cranmer, Thomas. *The Articles of Religion*. In *A History of the Articles of Religion*, edited by Charles Hardwick, 289–353. London: George Bell & Sons, 1890.

Criswell, W. A. *Criswell's Guidebook for Pastors* Nashville, TN: Broadman, 1990.

_____. *Prayer / Angelology*. Great Doctrines of the Bible. Vol. 7. Grand Rapids, MI: Zondervan, 1987.

Croteau, David, ed. *Perspectives on Tithing: 4 Views*. Nashville, TN: Broadman & Holman, 2011.

Dagg, John L. "The Duty of Baptists." In *Baptist Roots: A Reader in the Theology of a Christian People*, edited by Curtis W. Freeman, James Wm. McClendon Jr., and C. Rosalee Velloso Ewell, 196–200. Valley Forge, PA: Judson, 1999.

_____. *A Treatise on Church Order*. 1858. Paris, AR: The Baptist Standard Bearer, 2006.

Dargan, Edwin Charles. *The Art of Preaching in the Light of Its History*. Nashville, TN: Sunday School Board, 1922.

Davis, Andrew M. "Practical Issues of Church Discipline." In *Those Who Must Give an Account: A Study in Church Membership and Church Discipline*, edited by John S. Hammett and Benjamin L. Merkle, 157–85. Nashville, TN: Broadman & Holman, 2012.

de Rys, John, and Lubbert Gerrits. *A Brief Confession of the Principal Articles of the Christian Faith*. 1580. In *Baptist Confessions of Faith*, edited by William Lumpkin, 44–46. Rev. ed. Valley Forge, PA: Judson, 1969.

Delitzsch, Franz, and Carl Friedrich Keil. *Genesis to Judges 6:32*. Keil and Delitzsch Old Testament Commentaries. Vol. 1. Grand Rapids, MI: Associated Publishers & Authors, 1864.

Dever, Mark. *The Church: The Gospel Made Visible*. Nashville, TN: Broadman & Holman, 2012.

———. "John L. Dagg." In *Theologians of the Baptist Tradition*, edited by Timothy George and David S. Dockery, 52–72. Nashville, TN: Broadman & Holman, 2001.

———. *Nine Marks of a Healthy Church*. Washington, DC: Center for Church Reform, 1998.

———. *Nine Marks of a Healthy Church*. 3rd ed. Wheaton, IL: Crossway, 2013.

———, ed. *Polity: Biblical Arguments on How to Conduct Church Life*. Washington, DC: Center for Church Reform, 2000.

———. "The Practical Issues of Church Membership." In *Those Who Must Give an Account: A Study of Church Membership and Church Discipline*, edited by John S. Hammett and Benjamin L. Merkle, 81–101. Nashville, TN: Broadman & Holman, 2012.

———. "Regaining Meaningful Church Membership." In *Restoring Integrity in Baptist Churches*, edited by Thomas White, Jason G. Duesing, and Malcolm B. Yarnell, 45–62. Grand Rapids, MI: Kregel, 2007.

Dever, Mark, and Jonathan Leeman, eds. *Baptist Foundations: Church Government for an Anti-Institutional Age*. Nashville, TN: Broadman & Holman, 2015.

Devine, Mark. *Replant: How a Dying Church Can Grow Again*. Colorado Springs, CO: David C. Cook, 2014.

Dockery, David S. "Herschel H. Hobbs." *Theologians of the Baptist Tradition*, edited by Timothy George and David S. Dockery, 216–32. Nashville, TN: Broadman & Holman, 2001.

Draper, James T. *Authority: The Critical Issue for Southern Baptists*. Old Tappan, NJ: Fleming H. Revell, 1984.

Driscoll, Mark, and Gerry Breshears. *Doctrine: What Christians Should Believe*. Wheaton, IL: Crossway, 2010.

———. *Vintage Church: Timeless Truths and Timely Methods*. Wheaton, IL: Crossway, 2008.

Drummond, Lewis. *The Word of the Cross: A Contemporary Theology of Evangelism*. Nashville, TN: Broadman & Holman, 1992.

Dunn, James D. G. *Romans 9–16*. Word Biblical Commentary. Vol. 38B. Dallas, TX: Word, 1988.

Easum, Bill. *Dancing with Dinosaurs: Ministry in a Hostile and Hurting World.*
Nashville, TN: Abingdon, 1993.

Easum, Bill, and Dave Travis. *Beyond the Box: Innovative Churches That Work.*
Loveland, CO: Group, 2003.

Edwards, James R. *The Gospel According to Luke.* The Pillar New Testament
Commentary. Grand Rapids, MI: Eerdmans, 2015.

Ferguson, Dave, Jon Ferguson, and Eric Bramlett. *The Big Idea: Focus the Message—Multiply the Impact.* Grand Rapids, MI: Zondervan, 2006.

Ferguson, Everett. *The Church of Christ: A Biblical Ecclesiology for Today.* Grand
Rapids, MI: Eerdmans, 1996.

Fergusson, James. *A Brief Refutation of the Doctrine of Erastianism.* Glasgow:
The Fife Sentinel Office, 1843.

Finn, Nathan A. "A Historical Analysis of Church Membership." In *Those Who
Must Give an Account: A Study of Church Membership and Church Discipline,* eds. John S. Hammett and Benjamin L. Merkle, 53–79. Nashville, TN:
Broadman & Holman, 2012.

Floyd, Ronnie. *How to Pray: Developing an Intimate Relationship with God.* Rev.
ed. Nashville, TN: W Publishing, 2019.

Frazee, Randy. *The Connecting Church 2.0: Beyond Small Groups to Authentic
Community.* Grand Rapids, MI: Zondervan, 2013.

Friedberger, Balthasar, et al. *Eighteen Dissertations Concerning the Entire Christian
Life and of What It Consists.* 1524. In *Baptist Confessions of Faith,* edited by
William H. Lumpkin, 19–21. Rev. ed. Valley Forge, PA: Judson, 1969.

Fuller, Andrew. "The Admission of Unbaptized Persons to the Lord's Supper
Inconsistent with the New Testament." In *The Complete Works of the Rev.
Andrew Fuller: With a Memoir of his Life by Andrew Gunton Fuller,* edited
by Joseph Belcher, 3:508–515. Harrisonburg, VA: Sprinkle, 1988.

———. "Alms-Giving and Prayer." In *The Complete Works of the Rev. Andrew
Fuller: With a Memoir of His Life by Andrew Gunton Fuller,* edited by Joseph
Belcher, 1:575–79. Harrisonburg, VA: Sprinkle, 1988.

———. *The Diary of Andrew Fuller, 1780–1801.* Edited by Michael D. McMullen
and Timothy D. Whelan. The Complete Works of Andrew Fuller. Vol. 1.
Boston, MA: De Gruyter, 2016.

———. "The Fellowship of God's People in Evil Times." In *The Complete Works
of the Rev. Andrew Fuller: With a Memoir of His Life by Andrew Gunton Fuller,* edited by Joseph Belcher, 1:442–43. Harrisonburg, VA: Sprinkle, 1988.

———. "God's Approbation of Our Labors Necessary to the Hope of Success."
In *The Complete Works of the Rev. Andrew Fuller: With a Memoir of His Life
by Andrew Gunton Fuller,* edited by Joseph Belcher, 1:183–96. Harrisonburg,
VA: Sprinkle, 1988.

_____. "Instances, Evil, and Tendency of Delay, in the Concerns of Religion." In *The Complete Works of the Rev. Andrew Fuller: With a Memoir of His Life by Andrew Gunton Fuller*, edited by Joseph Belcher, 1:145–51. Harrisonburg, VA: Sprinkle, 1988.

_____. "Practical Uses of Christian Baptism." In *The Complete Works of the Rev. Andrew Fuller: With a Memoir of His Life by Andrew Gunton Fuller*, edited by Joseph Belcher, 3:339–45. Harrisonburg, VA: Sprinkle, 1988.

Gallaty, Robby. *Rediscovering Discipleship: Making Jesus' Final Words Our First Work*. Grand Rapids, MI: Zondervan, 2015.

Gardner, Paul D. *1 Corinthians*. Zondervan Exegetical Commentary on the New Testament. Grand Rapids, MI: Zondervan, 2018.

Garrett, Bob. "The Next Frontier: The Implications for Missions of Global Urbanization in the Twenty-first Century." In *Reaching the City: Reflections on Urban Mission for the Twenty-first Century*, edited by Gary Fujino, Timothy R. Sisk, and Tereso C. Casino, 19–33. Pasadena, CA: William Carey Library, 2012.

Garrett, James Leo, Jr. "The Congregation-Led Church: Congregational Polity." In *Perspectives on Church Government: 5 Views*, edited by Chad Owen Brand and R. Stanton Norman, 157–94. Nashville, TN: Broadman & Holman, 2004.

Gehring, Roger. *House Church and Mission: The Importance of Household Structures in Early Christianity*. Peabody, MA: Hendrickson, 2004.

Geisler, Norman. *Systematic Theology*. Vol. 4. Minneapolis, MN: Bethany House, 2005.

George, Timothy, and David S. Dockery, eds. *Theologians of the Baptist Tradition*. Rev. ed. Nashville, TN: Broadman & Holman, 2001.

Giboney, Ezra P., and Agnes M. Potter. *The Life of Mark A. Matthews: "Tall Pines of the Sierras."* Grand Rapids: Eerdmans, 1948.

Gill, Ben. *Stewardship: The Biblical Basis for Living*. Arlington, TX: The Summit Group, 1996.

Gill, John. *A Complete Body of Doctrinal and Practical Divinity: Or a System of Evangelical Truths Deduced from the Sacred Scriptures*. Vol. 2. London: Thomas Tegg, 1839.

_____. "A Defence . . . of a Book, Entitled, *The Ancient Mode of Baptizing by Immersion, Plunging, or Dipping, in Water, etc.*" In *Gospel Baptism: A Collection of Sermons, Tracts, Etc. About Scriptural Authority, the New Testament Church, and the Ordinance of Baptism*. Paris, AR: The Baptist Standard Bearer, 2006.

Gillette, A. D., ed. *Minutes of the Philadelphia Baptist Association, 1707 to 1807: Being the First One Hundred Years of Its Existence*. Atlas, MI: Baptist Book Trust, 1851.

Goodrick, Edward W., and John R. Kohlenberger III. *The NIV Exhaustive Concordance*. Grand Rapids, MI: Zondervan, 1990.

Gow, Murray D. "Fall." In *Dictionary of the Old Testament Pentateuch: A Compendium of Contemporary Scholarship*, edited by T. Desmond Alexander and David W. Baker. Downers Grove, IL: InterVarsity, 2003.

Grantham, Thomas. Quoted in *The Baptist Heritage: Four Centuries of Baptist Witness*, by Leon McBeth, 78–79. Nashville, TN: Broadman, 1987.

Graves, J. R. *The Acts of Christian Baptism*. Memphis, TN: The Baptist Book House, 1881.

———. *Gaining by Losing: Why the Future Belongs to Churches That Send*. Grand Rapids, MI: Zondervan, 2015.

Grenz, Stanley J. *Prayer: The Cry for the Kingdom*. Rev. ed. Grand Rapids, MI: Eerdmans, 2005.

———. *Theology for the Community of God*. Nashville, TN: Broadman & Holman, 1994.

Grenz, Stanley J., David Guretzki, and Cherith Fee Nordling. *Pocket Dictionary of Theological Terms*. Downers Grove, IL: InterVarsity, 1999.

Grudem, Wayne. *Systematic Theology: An Introduction to Christian Doctrine*. Grand Rapids, MI: Zondervan, 1994.

Guthrie, George H. *2 Corinthians*. Baker Exegetical Commentary on the New Testament. Grand Rapids, MI: Baker, 2015.

Hammett, John S. ed. *Biblical Foundations for Baptist Churches*. Grand Rapids, MI: Kregel, 2005.

———. "Membership, Discipline and the Nature of the Church." In *Those Who Must Give an Account: A Study of Church Membership and Church Discipline*, edited by John S. Hammett and Benjamin L. Merkle, 7–28. Nashville, TN: Broadman & Holman, 2012.

———. "Regenerate Church Membership." In *Restoring Integrity in Baptist Churches*, edited by Thomas White, Jason G. Duesing, and Malcolm B. Yarnell III, 21–44. Grand Rapids, MI: Kregel, 2008.

———. "The Why and Who of Church Membership." In *Baptist Foundations: Church Government for an Anti-Institutional Age*, eds. Mark Dever and Jonathan Leeman, 167–79. Nashville, TN: Broadman & Holman, 2015.

Hammett, John S., and Benjamin L. Merkle, eds. *Those Who Must Give an Account: A Study of Church Membership and Church Discipline*. Nashville, TN: Broadman & Holman, 2012.

Harrison, Everett F., and Donald A. Hagner. "Romans." In *Romans–Galatians*. Edited by Tremper Longman III and David E. Gardner. The Expositor's Bible Commentary. Vol. 11. Rev. ed. Grand Rapids, MI: Zondervan, 2008.

Harrison, Rodney, Tom Cheyney, and Don Overstreet. *Spin-Off Churches: How One Church Successfully Plants Another*. Nashville, TN: Broadman & Holman, 2008.

Hawkins, O. S. *Money Talks: But What Is It Really Saying?* Dallas, TX: Guidestone, 1999.

Haykins, Michael A. G. "Some Historical Roots of Congregationalism." In *Baptist Foundations: Church Government for an Anti-Institutional Age*, edited by Mark Dever and Jonathan Leeman, 27–45. Nashville, TN: Broadman & Holman, 2015.

Hellerman, Joseph H. *When the Church Was a Family: Recapturing Jesus' Vision for Authentic Christian Community*. Nashville, TN: Broadman & Holman, 2009.

Helms, Elaine. "Church Prayer Ministries and Prayer Rooms." In *Giving Ourselves to Prayer: An Acts 6:4 Primer for Ministry*, edited by Daniel R. Crawford, 342–46. Terre Haute, IN: Prayer Shop Publishing, 2008.

Helwys, Thomas. "Confession of Faith of the True English Church." In *The Life and Writings of Thomas Helyws*, edited by Joe Early Jr., 60–63. Early English Baptist Texts. Macon, GA: Mercer University Press, 2009.

————. *A Declaration of Faith of English People Remaining at Amsterdam in Holland*. 1611. In *Baptist Confessions of Faith*, edited by William Lumpkin, 116–23. Rev. ed. Valley Forge, PA: Judson, 1969.

Hiscox, Edward T. *The New Directory for Baptist Churches*. Philadelphia, PA: American Baptist Publication Society, 1894.

Hobbs, Herschel H. *What Baptists Believe*. Nashville, TN: Broadman, 1964.

Hobbs. T. R. *1, 2 Kings*. Word Biblical Themes. Dallas, TX: Word, 1989.

House, Brad. *Community: Taking Your Small Group Off Life Support*. Wheaton, IL: Crossway, 2011.

House, Brad, and Gregg Allison. *MultiChurch: Exploring the Future of Multisite*. Grand Rapids, MI: Zondervan, 2017.

Howerton, Rick. *A Different Kind of Tribe: Embracing the New Small-Group Dynamic*. Colorado Springs, CO: NavPress, 2012.

Jamieson, Bobby. *Understanding the Lord's Supper*. Church Basics. Nashville, TN: Broadman & Holman, 2016.

Johns, Timothy. *Micro Church: Families on Mission*. Ft. Collins, CO: Jesus Tribes, 2017.

Johnson, William B. *The Gospel Developed Through the Government and Order of the Churches of Jesus Christ*. Richmond, VA: H. K. Ellyson, 1846. In *Polity: Biblical Arguments on How to Conduct Church Life*, edited by Mark Dever, 161–245. Washington, DC: Center for Church Reform, 2001.

Keach, Benjamin. *The Glory of a True Church, and Its Discipline Display'd*. London: John Robinson, 1697. In *Polity: Biblical Arguments on How to Conduct Church Life*, edited by Mark Dever, 63–91. Washington, DC: Center for Church Reform, 2001.

Keller, Timothy. *Center Church*. Grand Rapids, MI: Zondervan, 2012.

Kimble, Jeremy M. *That His Spirit May Be Saved: Church Discipline as a Means of Repentance and Perseverance*. Eugene, OR: Wipf & Stock, 2013.

Kruse, Colin G. *Paul's Letter to the Romans*. The Pillar New Testament Commentary. Grand Rapids, MI: Eerdmans, 2012.

Ladd, George Eldon. *A Theology of the New Testament*. Rev. ed. Grand Rapids, MI: Eerdmans, 1995.

Leavell, Frank H. *Training in Stewardship*. Nashville, TN: Sunday School Board, 1920.

Lee, Jason K. "Baptism and Covenant." In *Restoring Integrity in Baptist Churches*, edited by Thomas White, Jason G. Duesing, and Malcolm B. Yarnell, 119–36. Grand Rapids, MI: Kregel, 2008.

Leeman, Jonathan. *Church Discipline: How the Church Protects the Name of Jesus*. Wheaton, IL: Crossway, 2012.

———. *One Assembly: Rethinking the Multisite and Multiservice Models*. Wheaton, IL: Crossway, 2020.

Leith, John H., ed. *Creeds of the Churches: A Reader in Christian Doctrine from the Bible to the Present*. 3rd ed. Louisville, KY: Westminster John Knox, 1982.

Lumpkin, William. *Baptist Confessions of Faith*. Rev. ed. Valley Forge, PA: Judson, 1969.

Luther, Martin. "On the Councils and the Church." 1539. In *Church and Sacraments*, The Annotated Luther. Vol. 3. Edited by Paul W. Robinson. Minneapolis, MN: Fortress, 2016.

Malphurs, Aubrey. *Advanced Strategic Planning: A 21st-Century Model for Church and Ministry Leaders*. 3rd ed. Grand Rapids, MI: Baker, 2013.

———. *Being Leaders: The Nature of Authentic Christian Leadership*. Grand Rapids, MI: Baker, 2003.

Manser, Martin. *Dictionary of Bible Themes*. Pennsauken, NJ: Book Baby, 2009.

McBeth, Leon. *The Baptist Heritage: Four Centuries of Baptist Witness*. Nashville, TN: Broadman, 1987.

McConnell, Scott. *Multi-Site Churches: Guidance for the Movement's Next Generation*. Nashville, TN: Broadman & Holman, 2009.

McGavran, Donald. *The Bridges of God: A Study in the Strategy of Missions*. Rev. ed. New York, NY: Friendship Press, 1955.

———. *Understanding Church Growth*. 3rd ed. Grand Rapids, MI: Eerdmans, 1990.

McGowan, Andrew B. *Ancient Christian Worship: Early Church Practices in Social, Historical, and Theological Perspective*. Grand Rapids, MI: Baker, 2014.

McIntosh, Gary L. *Make Room for the Boom . . . or Bust: Six Church Models for Reaching Three Generations*. Grand Rapids, MI: Revell, 1997.

Meadows, Gary T. "The Bible and Prayer." In *Giving Ourselves to Prayer: An Acts 6:4 Primer for Ministry*, edited by Dan R. Crawford, 10–16. Terre Haute, IN: Prayer Shop Publishing, 2008.

Melancthon, Philip. *The Augsburg Confession*. 1530. In *Creeds of the Churches: A Reader in Christian Doctrine from the Bible to the Present*, edited by John H. Leith, 63–107. 3rd ed. Louisville, KY: Westminter John Knox, 1982.

Mell, P. H. *Corrective Church Discipline with a Development of the Scriptural Principles upon which It Is Based*. Charleston, SC: Southern Baptist Publication Society, 1860. In *Polity: Biblical Arguments on How to Conduct Church Life*, edited by Mark Dever, 409–76. Washington, DC: Center for Church Reform, 2001.

Melton, J. Gordon. *Nelson's Guide to Denominations: The Primary Resource for Understanding and Navigating America's Christian Organizations*. Nashville, TN: Thomas Nelson, 2007.

Merkle, Benjamin L. "The Biblical Basis for Church Membership." In *Those Who Must Give an Account: A Study of Church Membership and Church Discipline*, edited by John S. Hammett and Benjamin L. Merkle, 31–52. Nashville, TN: Broadman & Holman, 2012.

———. "The Biblical Role of Elders." In *Baptist Foundations: Church Government in an Anti-Institutional Age*, edited by Mark Dever and Jonathan Leeman, 271–89. Nashville, TN: Broadman & Holman, 2015.

———. "The Office of Deacon." In *Baptist Foundations: Church Government in an Anti-Institutional Age*, edited by Mark Dever and Jonathan Leeman, 311–24. Nashville, TN: Broadman & Holman, 2015.

———. "The Scriptural Basis for Elders." In *Baptist Foundations: Church Government for an Anti-Institutional Age*, edited by Mark Dever and Jonathan Leeman, 243–52. Nashville, TN: Broadman & Holman, 2015.

Mohler, Albert. "Church Discipline: The Missing Mark." In *Polity: Biblical Arguments on How to Conduct Church Life*, edited by Mark Dever, 43–56. Washington, DC: Center for Church Reform, 2001.

Monck, Thomas. *An Orthodox Creed*. London, 1679. In *Baptist Confessions of Faith*, edited by William Lumpkin, 297–334. Rev. ed. Valley Forge, PA: Judson, 1969.

Montoya, Alex D. "Leading." In *Pastoral Ministry: How to Shepherd Biblically*, edited by John MacArthur, 228–46. The John MacArthur Pastor's Library. Nashville, TN: Thomas Nelson, 2005.

Mosley, Eddie. *Connecting in Communities: Understanding the Dynamics of Small Groups*. Colorado Springs, CO: NavPress, 2011.

Mullins, E. Y. *The Christian Religion in Its Doctrinal Expression*. Philadelphia, PA: Judson, 1917.

_____. *Talks on Soul Winning*. Nashville, TN: Sunday School Board, 1920.

Murray, Andrew. *With Christ in the School of Prayer: Thoughts on Our Training for the Ministry of Intercession*. Westwood, NJ: Fleming H. Revell, 1953.

Murray, John. *The Epistle to the Romans*. The New International Commentary on the New Testament. Grand Rapids, MI: Eerdmans, 1968.

Neighbor, Ralph W., Jr. *Where Do We Go from Here? A Guidebook for the Cell Group Church*. Rev. ed. Houston, TX: Touch Publications, 2000.

Nettles, Thomas J. "Baptist View: Baptism as a Symbol of Christ's Saving Work." In *Understanding Four Views on Baptism*, edited by John H. Armstrong, 25–41. Grand Rapids, MI: Zondervan, 2007.

Newton, Phil. "Your Church Can Reach the Nations Without Leaving the Neighborhood." In *Essential Reading on Evangelism*, edited by Jeff Robinson, 19–22. Louisville, KY: Southern Equip, 2019.

Norman, R. Stanton. *The Baptist Way: Distinctives of a Baptist Church*. Nashville, TN: Broadman & Holman, 2005.

_____. "The Reestablishment of Proper Church Discipline." In *Restoring Integrity in Baptist Churches*, edited by Thomas White, Jason G. Duesing, and Malcolm B. Yarnell III, 199–219. Grand Rapids, MI: Kregel, 2008.

Norris, J. Frank. "How Dual Pastorate Was Brought About." In *Inside History of First Baptist Church, Fort Worth, and Temple Baptist Church, Detroit: Life Story of Dr. J. Frank Norris*, edited by Joel A. Carpenter. New York, NY: Garland, 1988.

O'Brien, Peter T. "Church." In *Dictionary of Paul and His Letters: A Compendium of Contemporary Scholarship*, edited by Gerald F. Hawthorne, Ralph P. Martin, and Daniel G. Reid. Downers Grove, IL: InterVarsity, 1993.

Olsen, Charles M. *The Base Church: Creating Community Through Multiple Forms*. Atlanta, GA: Forum House, 1973.

Orr, J. Edwin. *The Eager Feet: Evangelical Awakenings 1790–1830*. Chicago, IL: Moody, 1975.

Osborne, Grant R. *Colossians & Philemon*. Osborne New Testament Commentaries. Bellingham, WA: Lexham, 2016.

_____. *Matthew*. Zondervan Exegetical Commentary on the New Testament. Grand Rapids, MI: Zondervan, 2010.

_____. *Philippians*. Osborne New Testament Commentaries. Bellingham, WA: Lexham, 2017.

Otto, Rudolf. *The Kingdom of God and the Son of Man: A Study in the History of Religion*. Translated by Floyd V. Flison and Bertram Lee-Woolf. Rev ed. Eugene, OR: Wipf & Stock, 2006.

Pao, David W. *Colossians and Philemon*. Zondervan Exegetical Commentary on the New Testament. Grand Rapids, MI: Zondervan, 2012.

Patterson, Paige. "Single-Elder Congregationalism." In *Who Runs the Church? 4 Views on Church Governance*, edited by Steven B. Cowan, 131–52. Grand Rapids, MI: Zondervan, 2004.

Payne, Ernest A. *The Fellowship of Believers: Baptist Thought and Practice Yesterday and Today*. Rev. ed. London: Carey Kingsgate, 1952.

Pendleton, J. M. *Church Manual: Designed for the Use of Baptist Churches*. Philadelphia, PA: Judson, 1958.

_____. *Distinctive Principles of Baptists*. Philadelphia, PA: American Baptist Publication Society, 1882.

_____. *Ecclesiological*. Edited by Thomas White. Selected Writings of James Madison Pendleton. Vol 2. Paris, AR: The Baptist Standard Bearer, 2006.

_____. *Theological*. Edited by Thomas White. Selected Writings of James Madison Pendleton. Vol 3. Paris, AR: The Baptist Standard Bearer, 2006.

Piper, John. *Let the Nations Be Glad: The Supremacy of God in Missions*. 2nd Edition. Grand Rapids, MI: Baker, 2003.

Platt, David. "Foreword." In *Nine Marks of a Healthy Church*, by Mark Dever. 3rd ed. Wheaton, IL: Crossway, 2013.

Raikes, Robert. "Letter from Robert Raikes Dates June 5, 1784." Quoted in Clay H. Trumbull, *The Sunday-School: Its Origins, Mission, Method, and Auxiliaries: The Lyman Beecher Lectures Before Yale Divinity School for 1888*, 110. Philadelphia, PA: J. D. Wattles, 1893.

Rainer, Thom. *The Book of Church Growth: History, Theology, and Principles*. Nashville, TN: Broadman & Holman, 1993.

_____. *I Am a Church Member: Discovering the Attitude That Makes the Difference*. Nashville, TN: Broadman & Holman, 2013.

Rainer, Thom, and Daniel Akin. *Vibrant Church: Becoming a Healthy Church in the 21st Century*. Nashville, TN: Lifeway, 2008.

Reeves, Stan, ed. *The 1689 Baptist Confession of Faith in Modern English*. Cape Coral, FL: Founders, 2017.

Reid, Alvin. *Introduction to Evangelism*. Nashville, TN: Broadman & Holman, 1998.

Reynolds, J. L. *Church Polity: Or the Kingdom of Christ in Its Internal and External Development*. Richmond, VA: Harrold & Murray, 1849.

_____. "Church Polity or The Kingdom of Christ." In *Polity: Biblical Arguments for How to Conduct Church Life*, edited by Mark Dever, 295–403. Washington, DC: Center for Church Reform, 2000.

Robertson, A. T. *Jesus as a Soul-Winner and Other Sermons*. New York, NY: Fleming H. Revell, 1937.

_____. *Modern Scholarship and the Form of Baptism*. Nashville, TN: Sunday School Board, 1900.

_____. "'Our Baptist Democracy—How It Works,' from *Church Administration*, December 1930." In *The Best of A. T. Robertson*, edited by David S. Dockery, Timothy George, and Denise George, 223–26. Nashville, TN: Broadman & Holman, 1996.

_____. "Preaching and Scholarship: The Inaugural Address to the Faculty, The Southern Baptist Theological Seminary, October 3, 1890." In *The Best of A. T. Robertson*, edited by David S. Dockery, Timothy George, and Denise George, 151–69. Nashville, TN: Broadman & Holman, 1996.

_____. "The Spiritual Interpretations of the Ordinances: Baptist World Alliance Proceedings, June 20, 1911." In *The Best of A. T. Robertson*, edited by David S. Dockery, Timothy George, and Denise George, 209–16. Nashville, TN: Broadman & Holman, 1996.

Robinson, Haddon W. *Biblical Preaching: The Development, and Delivery of Expository Messages*. 2nd ed. Grand Rapids, MI: Baker, 2001.

Sanders, Brian. *Microchurches: A Smaller Way*. Tampa, FL: Underground Network, 2019.

_____. *Underground Church: A Living Example of the Church in Its Most Potent Form*. Grand Rapids, MI: Zondervan, 2018.

Scarborough, L. R. *My Conception of the Gospel Ministry*. Nashville, TN: The Sunday School Board, 1935.

_____. *With Christ After the Lost: A Search for Souls*. Nashville, TN: Broadman, 1952.

Schaller, Lyle E. *44 Questions for Church Planters*. Nashville, TN: Abingdon, 1991.

_____. *Discontinuity and Hope: Radical Change and the Path to the Future*. Nashville, TN: Abingdon, 1999.

_____. "Foreword." In *One Church, Many Locations: The Key Church Strategy*, by Timothy Ahlen and J. V. Thomas, 11–15. Nashville, TN: Abingdon, 1999.

_____. *Innovations in Ministry: Models for the 21st Century*. Nashville, TN: Abingdon, 1994.

_____. *A Mainline Turnaround: Strategies for Congregations and Denominations*. Nashville, TN: Abingdon, 2005.

_____. *The Small Church Is Different!* Nashville, TN: Abingdon, 1982.

Schnabel, Eckhard J. *Acts*. Zondervan Exegetical Commentary on the New Testament. Grand Rapids, MI: Zondervan, 2012.

Schofield, J. Chris. "The Bible and Church Prayer." In *Giving Ourselves to Prayer: An Acts 6:4 Primer for Ministry*, edited by Daniel R. Crawford, 274–82. Terre Haute, IN: Prayer Shop Publishing, 2008.

Schreiner, Thomas R. "The Biblical Basis for Church Discipline." In *Those Who Must Give an Account: A Study of Church Membership and Church Discipline*, edited by John S. Hammett and Benjamin L. Merkle, 105–30. Nashville, TN: Broadman & Holman, 2012.

_____. "The Lord's Supper and the Bible." In *Baptist Foundations: Church Government in an Anti-Institutional Age*, edited by Mark Dever and Jonathan Leeman, 131–43. Nashville, TN: Broadman & Holman, 2015.

_____. "Women in Ministry: Another Complementarian Perspective." In *Two Views on Women in Ministry*, edited by James Beck, 265–322. Rev. ed. Grand Rapids, MI: Zondervan, 2005.

Schreiner, Thomas R., and Matthew R. Crawford, eds. *The Lord's Supper: Remembering and Proclaiming Christ Until He Comes*. Nashville, TN: Broadman & Holman, 2010.

Schreiner, Thomas R., and Shawn D. Wright. *Believer's Baptism: Sign of the New Covenant in Christ*. Nashville, TN: Broadman & Holman, 2007.

Smith, Elliott. *The Advance of Baptist Associations Across America*. Nashville, TN: Broadman, 1979.

Smith, Steve, and Ying Kai. *T4T: A Discipleship ReRevolution*. Monument, CO: WIGTake Resources, 2011.

Smyth, John. *Short Confession of Faith in XX Articles by John Smyth*. In *Baptist Confessions of Faith*, edited by William Lumpkin, 100–101. Rev. ed. Valley Forge, PA: Judson, 1969.

Soden, Dale E. *The Reverend Mark Matthews: An Activist in the Progressive Era*. Seattle, WA: University of Washington, 2001.

Sproul, R. C. *How Should I Think About Money?* Crucial Questions No. 23. Sanford, FL: Reformation Trust, 2016.

Spurgeon, Charles. "The Blessing of Public Worship." In *Classic Sermons on Worship*, edited by Warren W. Wiersbe, 31–43. Peabody, MA: Hendrickson, 1988.

_____. *Lectures to My Students: A Selection from Addresses Delivered to the Students of the Pastors' College, Metropolitan Tabernacle*. Lynchburg, VA: The Old-Time Gospel Hour, 1992.

_____. "The Lord with Two or Three." In *Classic Sermons on Worship*, edited by Warren W. Wiersbe, 45–59. Peabody, MA: Hendrickson, 1988.

Stetzer, Ed, and Warren Bird. *Viral Churches: Helping Church Planters Become Movement Makers*. San Francisco, CA: Jossey-Bass, 2010.

Stetzer, Ed, and Mike Dodson. *Comeback Churches: How 300 Churches Turned Around and Yours Can Too*. Nashville, TN: Broadman & Holman, 2007.

Stetzer, Ed, and Thom Rainer. *Transformational Church: Creating a New Scorecard for Congregations*. Nashville, TN: Broadman & Holman, 2010.

Still, Todd D. *Philippians and Philemon*. Smith & Helwys Bible Commentary. Macon, GA: Smith & Helwys, 2011.

Strauch, Alexander. *The New Testament Deacon: Minister of Mercy*. Colorado Springs, CO: Lewis & Roth, 1992.

Strong, Augustus Hopkins. *Systematic Theology: A Compendium and Common-place-Book Designed for the Use of Theological Students.* Vol. 3. Philadelphia, PA: Judson, 1909.

Strong, James. *The New Strong's Concise Dictionary of Bible Words.* Nashville, TN: Nelson, 2000.

Surratt, Geoff, Greg Ligon, and Warren Bird. *The Multi-Site Church Revolution: Being One Church in Many Locations.* Grand Rapids, MI: Zondervan, 2006.

————. *A Multi-Site Church Road Trip: Exploring the New Normal.* Grand Rapids, MI: Zondervan, 2009.

Taylor, L. Roy. "Presbyterianism." In *Who Runs the Church?: 4 Views on Church Government,* edited by Steven B. Cowan, 71–98. Grand Rapids: Zondervan, 2004.

Terry, John Mark. *Evangelism: A Concise History.* Nashville, TN: Broadman & Holman, 1992.

Thielman, Frank. *Ephesians.* Baker Exegetical Commentary on the New Testament. Grand Rapids, MI: Baker, 2010.

Thomas, J. V. *Investing in Eternity.* Dallas, TX: J. V. Thomas, 1991.

Thomas, John Christopher, and Frank D. Macchia. *Revelation.* Grand Rapids, MI: Eerdmans, 2016.

Tomberlin, Jim, and Warren Bird. *Better Together: Making Church Mergers Work.* San Francisco, CA: Jossey-Bass, 2012.

Toon, Peter. "Episcopalianism." In *Who Runs the Church?: 4 Views on Church Government,* edited by Steven B. Cowan, 19–41. Grand Rapids: Zondervan, 2004.

Towns, Elmer. *An Inside Look at 10 of Today's Most Innovative Churches: What They're Doing, How They're Doing It, and How You Can Apply Their Ideas in Your Church.* Ventura, CA: Regal, 1990.

————. *Getting a Church Started: A Student Manual for the Theological Foundation and Practical Techniques of Planting a Church.* 3rd ed. Lynchburg, VA: Liberty University, 1993.

Towns, Elmer, Ed Stetzer, and Warren Bird. *11 Innovations in the Local Church: How Today's Leaders Can Learn, Discern, and Move into the Future.* Ventura, CA: Regal, 2007.

Truett, George. *A Quest for Souls: Comprising All the Sermons Preached and Prayers Offered in a Series of Gospel Meetings, Held in Fort Worth, Texas, June 11–24, 1917,* edited by J. B. Cranfill. Dallas, TX: Baptist Standard, 1920.

Trumbull, Clay H. *The Sunday-School: Its Origins, Mission, Method, and Auxiliaries. The Lyman Beecher Lectures Before Yale Divinity School for 1888.* Philadelphia, PA: J. D. Wattles, 1893.

Turner, David L. *Matthew.* Baker Exegetical Commentary on the New Testament. Grand Rapids, MI: Baker, 2008.

VanGemeren, Willem A. *Psalms*. The Expositor's Bible Commentary. Vol. 5. Rev. ed. Grand Rapids, MI: Zondervan, 2008.

Van Rheenen, Gailyn. "Reformist View." In *Evaluating the Church Growth Movement: 5 Views*, edited by Gary L. McIntosh, 165–89. Grand Rapids, MI: Zondervan, 2004.

Vaughn, Curtis, and Thomas D. Lea. *1 Corinthians*. Bible Study Commentary. Grand Rapids, MI: Lamplighter, 1983.

Vaughan, John N. *The Large Church: A Twentieth Century Expression of the First-Century Church*. Grand Rapids, MI: Baker, 1985.

_____. *Megachurches and American Cities*. Grand Rapids, MI: Baker, 1993.

Verbrugge, Verlyn D. "1 Corinthians." In *Romans–Galatians*, edited by Tremper Longman III and David E. Garland. The Expositor's Bible Commentary. Vol. 11. Rev. ed. Grand Rapids, MI: Zondervan, 2008.

_____, ed. *The NIV Theological Dictionary of New Testament Words*. Grand Rapids, MI: Zondervan, 2000.

Vincent, Rick. *The Micro-Church Revolution!: The Complete Guide to Starting and Growing a Micro-Church*. Palm Coast, FL: Just the Word, 2019.

Vines, Jerry, and Jim Shaddix. *Power in the Pulpit: How to Prepare and Deliver Expository Sermons*. Rev. ed. Chicago, IL: Moody, 2017.

Warren, Rick. *The Purpose Driven Church: Growth Without Compromising Your Message and Mission*. Grand Rapids, MI: Zondervan, 1995.

Wayland, Francis. *The Principles and Practices of Baptist Churches*. London: J. Heaton & Son, 1861.

Welsh, Robert L. *The Presbytery of Seattle, 1858–2005: The "Dream" of a Presbyterian Colony in the West*. Bloomington, IN: Xlibris, 2006.

Wenham, Gordan J. *The Book of Leviticus*. The New International Commentary on the Old Testament. Grand Rapids, MI: Eerdmans, 1979.

White, James R. "The Single-Elder Led Church: Response by James R. White." In *Perspectives on Church Government: 5 Views*, edited by Chad Owen Brand and R. Stanton Norman, 85–86. Nashville, TN: Broadman & Holman, 2004.

White, Thomas. "A Baptist's Theology of the Lord's Supper." In *Restoring Integrity in Baptist Churches*, edited by edited by Thomas White, Jason G. Duesing, and Malcolm B. Yarnell III, 137–61. Grand Rapids, MI: Kregel, 2008.

_____. "What Makes Baptism Valid?" In *Restoring Integrity in Baptist Churches*, edited by Thomas White, Jason G. Duesing, and Malcolm B. Yarnell III, 107–18. Grand Rapids, MI: Kregel, 2008.

White, Thomas, Jason G. Duesing, and Malcolm B. Yarnell III, eds. *Restoring Integrity in Baptist Churches*. Grand Rapids, MI: Kregel, 2008.

White, Thomas, and John M. Yeats. *Franchising McChurch: Feeding Our Obsession with Easy Christianity*. Colorado Springs, CO: David C. Cook, 2009.

Whitney, Donald S. *Spiritual Disciplines for the Christian Life*. Colorado Springs, CO: NavPress, 1991.

_____. *Spiritual Disciplines Within the Church: Participating Fully in the Body of Christ*. Chicago, IL: Moody, 1996.

Williams, William. *Apostolic Church Polity*. Waterton, WI: Classic Baptist Books, 2012.

Wills, Gregory A. *Democratic Religion: Freedom, Authority, and Church Discipline in the Baptist South 1785–1900*. New York, NY: Oxford University, 1997.

_____. "Southern Baptists and Church Discipline: Development and Decline." In *Restoring Integrity in Baptist Churches*, edited by Thomas White, Jason G. Duesing, and Malcolm B. Yarnell III, 179–97. Grand Rapids, MI: Kregel, 2008.

Wright, Shawn D. "Baptism in History, Theology, and the Church." In *Baptist Foundations: Church Government in an Anti-Institutional Age*, edited by Mark Dever and Jonathan Leeman, 107–30. Nashville, TN: Broadman & Holman, 2015.

Yarnell, Malcolm B., III. "'Upon This Rock I Will Build My Church': A Theological Exposition of Matthew 16:13–20." In *Upon This Rock: The Baptist Understanding of the Church*, edited by Jason Duesing, Thomas White, and Malcolm B. Yarnell III, 24–56. Nashville, TN: Broadman & Holman, 2010.

JOURNAL AND NEWS ARTICLES

Allison, Gregg. "Theological Defense of Multi-Site." *9Marks Journal* 6, no. 3 (June 2010): 7–18. https://www.9marks.org/article/theological-defense-multi-site/.

Boot, H. M. "Real Incomes of the British Middle Class, 1760–1850: The Experience of Clerks at the East India Company." *The Economic History Review* 52, no. 4 (Nov. 1999): 638–68.

Button, Mark, and Fika J. Van Rensburg. "The 'House Churches' in Corinth." *Neotestamentica* 37, no.1 (2003): 1–28.

Chandler, Diana. "Churches Worshiped Online, Onsite in COVID-19 Pandemic." *BaptistPress*, March 16, 2020. https://www.baptistpress.com/resource-library/news/churches-worshiped-online-onsite-in-covid-19-pandemic/.

Chandler, Matt. "Clouds on the Horizon." *9Marks Journal* 6, no. 3 (2010): 32. http://www.9marks.org/article/clouds-horizon/.

Cooper, Clint. "Chattanooga's Iconic Highland Park Baptist Church Will Move." *Chattanooga Times Free Press*. September 10, 2012.

Earls, Aaron. "Southern Baptists Grow in Attendance and Baptisms, Decline in Membership." Baptist Press, May 9, 2023. https://www.baptistpress.com/resource-library/news/southern-baptists-grow-in-attendance-and-baptisms-decline-in-membership/.

Earls, Aaron, and Carol Pipes. "Multisite Church ID Shift to Help SBC Ties." *Baptist Press*. August 27, 2019. http://www.bpnews.net/53506/multisite-church-id-shift-to-help-sbc-ties.

Ferguson, Dave. "The Multi-Site Church." *CT Pastors*. April 1, 2003. https://www.christianitytoday.com/pastors/2003/spring/21.81.html.

Ferguson, Everett. "Lord's Supper and Love Feast." *Christian Studies Journal* 21 (Jan. 2005): 27–38.

_____. "'When You Come Together': *Epi to Auto* in Early Christian Literature." *Restoration Quarterly* 16, no. 3/4 (1973): 202–8.

Gaines, Grant. "Exegetical Critique of Multi-Site: Disassembling the Church?" *9Marks Journal* 6, no. 3 (2010): 33–37. https://www.9marks.org/article/exegetical-critique-multi-site-disassembling-church/.

Gardner, Andrew. "Mark Dever Says In-Person Worship Is Essential to Biblical Christianity." *Baptist News Global*. October 8, 2020. https://baptistnews.com/article/mark-dever-says-in-person-worship-is-essential-to-biblical-christianity/#.X_Jk4NhKiM8.

Gilbert, Greg. "What Is This Thing, Anyway? A Multi-Site Taxonomy." *9Marks Journal* 6, no. 3 (2010): 25–27. https://www.9marks.org/article/what-thing-anyway-multi-site-taxonomy/.

Grace, W. Madison, II. "Early English Baptists' View of the Lord's Supper." *Southwestern Journal of Theology* 57, no. 2 (Spring 2015): 159–79.

Greear, J. D. "A Pastor Defends His Multi-Site Church." *9Marks Journal* 6, no. 3 (2010): 19–24. https://www.9marks.org/article/pastor-defends-his-multi-site-church/.

Guder, Darrell L. "Evangelism and the Debate over Church Growth." *Interpretation* 47 (April 1994): 147–55.

Hammett, John S. "Book Review: *The Multi-Site Church Revolution*, by Geoff Surratt . . . Greg Ligon, and Warren Bird." *9Marks Journal* 6, no. 3 (2010): 63–65. https://www.9marks.org/review/multi-site-church-revolution-geoff-surratt-greg-ligon-and-warren-bird/.

_____. "Have We Ever Seen This Before?" *9Marks Journal* 6, no. 3 (2010): 28–31. https://www.9marks.org/article/have-we-ever-seen-multi-site-precedents/.

_____. "What Makes a Multi-Site Church One Church?" *Great Commission Research Journal* 4, no. 1 (2012): 95–107.

Howe, Jonathan, and Amy Whitfield. "Floyd Issues Vision 2025 Call to Reach Every Person With the Gospel." *Baptist Press*. February 17, 2020. http://www.bpnews.net/54341/floyd-issues-vision-2025-call-to-reach-every-person-with-the-gospel.

Jamieson, Bobby. "Book Review: *Multi-Site Churches*, by Scott McConnell." *9Marks Journal* 6, no. 3 (2010): 55–57. https://www.9marks.org/review/multi-site-churches/.

_____. "Book Review: *One Church, Many Congregations*, by J. Timothy Ahlen and J. V. Thomas." *9Marks Journal* 6, no. 3 (2010): 61–62. https://www.9marks.org/review/one-church-many-congregations/.

_____. "Giving Time, Talents, and Treasures." *TableTalk*. February 2019. https://tabletalkmagazine.com/article/2019/02/giving-time-talents-treasures/.

_____. "Historical Critique of Multi-Site: Not Over My Dead Body." *9Marks Journal* 6, no. 3 (2010): 46–48. https://www.9marks.org/ article/historical-critique-multi-site-not-over-my-dead-body/.

Laura, Robert. "Pastor Rick Warren Is Well Prepared for a Purpose Driven Retirement." *Forbes*. March 21, 2013. https://www.forbes.com/sites/robert-laura/2013/03/21/pastor-rick-warren-is-practicing-what-he-preaches-and-getting-ready-for-retirement/ ?sh=31a6cab74dbf.

Leeman, Jonathan. "The Alternative Case: Why Don't We Plant?" *9Marks Journal* 6, no. 3 (2010): 52–54. https://www.9marks.org/article/alternative-why-dont-we-plant/.

_____. "Book Review: *Franchising McChurch*, by Thomas White and John Yeats." *9Marks Journal* 6, no. 3 (2010): 58–60. https://www.9marks.org/review/franchising-mcchurch/.

_____. "Regulative Like Jazz." *9Marks Journal* (July/August 2013): 38–42. http://www.9marks.org/ wp-content/uploads/2013/07/9Marks_Journal_2013_jul-aug_scripture.pdf.

_____. "Theological Critique of Multi-Site: What Exactly Is a 'Church'?" *9Marks Journal* 6, no. 3 (2010): 38–45. https://www.9marks.org/article/theological-critique-multi-site-what-exactly-church/.

Leeman, Jonathan, ed. "Is Scripture Enough?" *9Marks Journal*. July–August 2013. http://www.9marks.org/wp-content/uploads/2013/07/9Marks_Journal_2013_jul-aug_scripture.pdf.

Mappes, David. "The 'Elder' in the Old and New Testaments." *Biblotheca Sacra* 154, no. 613 (January 1997): 80–92.

Murashko, Alex. "Mars Hill Church: Don't Call Us 'Campuses' Anymore." *The Christian Post*. August 11, 2011. https://www.christianpost.com/news/mars-hill-church-dont-call-us-campuses-anymore.html.

Roach, David. "COVID-19's Lasting Changes." *CT Pastor's Special Issue: The State of Preaching* (Fall 2020): 28–33.

Scroggins, Jimmy, and BSCNC Communications. "Q&A: Jimmy Scroggins on Leadership, Vision, Evangelism, Church Culture, and More." *North Carolina Baptists*. January 14, 2020. https://ncbaptist.org/qa-jimmy-scroggins-on-leadership-vision-evangelism-church-culture-and-more/.

Shellnut, Kate. "J. D. Greear Transformed His Church Through Missions. Can He Do the Same for the Southern Baptist Convention?" *Christianity Today.* May 18, 2018. https://www.christianitytoday.com/ct/2018/june/jd-greear-southern-baptist-president-candidate-summit-nc.html.

Welch, Craig. "The Rise and Fall of Mars Hill Church." *Seattle Times.* February 4, 2016. https://www.seattletimes.com/seattle-news/the-rise-and-fall-of-mars-hill-church/.

White, Thomas. "Nine Reasons I Don't Like Multi-Site Churches." *9Marks Journal* 6, no. 3 (2010): 49–51. https://www.9marks.org/article/nine-reasons-i-dont-multi-site-churches/.

Wishall, Garret E. "Matt Chandler." *Towers* 8, no. 10 (2010): 3, 6.

Zadrozny, Brandy. "Controversial Megachurch Pastor Mark Driscoll Finds a New Flock." *Daily Beast.* April 13, 2017. https://www.thedailybeast.com/controversial-megachurch-pastor-mark-driscoll-finds-a-new-flock.

DISSERTATIONS, THESES, PROJECTS, AND PAPERS

Aum, Chongoh. "The Cell Church Model as a Viable Approach for Urban Church Planting." PhD diss., Mid-America Baptist Theological Seminary, 1997.

Edwards, Jamus Howell, II. "Leadership Structures and Dynamics in Multisite Churches: A Quantitative Study." PhD diss., The Southern Baptist Theological Seminary, 2016.

Ferguson, Earl. "The Multi-Site Church and Disciplemaking." DMin project, McCormick Theological Seminary, 1997.

Floyd, Nick. "A Multi-Plantation Ministry: Blending a Multi-Site and Church Planting Strategy in the Local Church." DMin diss., Liberty Baptist Theological Seminary, 2009.

Frye, Brian Nathaniel. "The Multi-Site Church Phenomenon in North America: 1950–2010." PhD diss., The Southern Baptist Theological Seminary, 2011.

Gaines, Grant. "One Church in One Location: Questioning the Biblical, Theological, and Historical Claims of the Multi-Site Church Movement." PhD diss., The Southern Baptist Theological Seminary, 2012.

Hawkins, O. S. "Two Kinds of Baptists: Re-Examining the Legacies of John Franklyn Norris and George Washington Truett." PhD diss., Southwestern Baptist Theological Seminary, 2020.

Herrington, Robert. "A Theological and Philosophical Evaluation of Simulcast Preaching within the Multi-Site Church Movement." PhD diss., Southeastern Baptist Theological Seminary, 2017.

Hughes, William Beau. "Preparing and Transitioning a Multi-Site Campus to a Local Church at The Village Church in Denton, Texas." DMin project, The Southern Baptist Theological Seminary, 2016.

Kahlbau, Heath. "Is Anything New Under the Sun? A Comparative Evaluation of the Ante-Nicene Patristic Episcopacy and Common Polity Models Within the Contemporary Multi-Site Church Movement." PhD diss., Southeastern Baptist Theological Seminary, 2014.

Kouba, Christoper Barton. "Role of the Campus Pastor: Responsibilities and Practices in Multisite Churches." DMin diss., The Southern Baptist Theological Seminary, 2014.

McKinley, Angus Richards. "The Cell Church Strategy of Ralph W. Neighbour in Evangelism and Discipleship." PhD diss., Southwestern Baptist Theological Seminary, 1999.

Mullins, J. Todd. "Online Church: A Biblical Community." DMin project, Liberty Theological Seminary, 2011.

Patterson, Joshua Rice. "Leveraging the Multi-Site Church Approach as a Long-Term Church Planting Strategy at the Village Church in Dallas-Fort Worth." DMin project, The Southern Baptist Theological Seminary, 2014.

Pigott, Kelly David. "A Comparison of the Leadership of George W. Truett and J. Frank Norris in Church, Denominational, Interdenominational, and Political Affairs." PhD diss., Southwestern Baptist Theological Seminary, 1993.

Reavely, R. Scott. "An Ecclesiology for Multi-Site Churches: Thinking Biblically About the Local Church in Multiple Locations." DMin project, Western Seminary, 2007.

Reed, Nathan A. "A Comparative Analysis of Church Membership Practices in Large, Multi-Site Churches." EdD diss., Southeastern Baptist Theological Seminary, 2019.

Shelby, Robert L. "One Church with Multiple Locations: Exploring Community at a Multisite Religious Organization." MA thesis, Western Illinois University, 2011.

Slaton, Dustin. "The Citywide Church: Biblical Evidence and Practical Application." Southwestern Baptist Theological Seminary, 2019. Church Growth and Vitalization Seminar. https://www.academia.edu/104190305/The_Citywide_Church_Biblical_Evidence_and_Practical_Application.

———. "Congregational Polity in Multisite Baptist Churches." Southwestern Baptist Theological Seminary, 2017. Church and Ministry Seminar. https://www.academia.edu/104190587/Congregational_Polity_in_Multisite_Baptist_Churches.

———. "Discovering Evidence of Multisite Ekklesia: An Investigation of the New Testament Church in Acts." Southwestern Baptist Theological Seminary, 2017. Current Issues in Church Revitalization Seminar. https://www.academia.edu/104190166/Discovering_Evidence_of_a_Multisite_Ekklesia.

Sullivan, Dennis Kyle. "Examining the Ecclesiological Soundness of the Southern Baptist Multisite Church Movement." PhD diss., The Southern Baptist Theological Seminary, 2019.

Taylor, Benjamin T. "A Study of Sermon Preparation Methods Regarding Three Memphis, Tennessee Pastors with Simulcast-Satellite Campuses." PhD Diss., Mid-America Baptist Theological Seminary, 2018.

Wamble, G. Hugh. "The Concept and Practice of Christian Fellowship: The Connectional and Inter-Denominational Aspects Thereof, Among Seventeenth Century English Baptists." DTh diss., The Southern Baptist Theological Seminary, 1955.

Willis, Patrick Graham. "Multi-Site Churches and Their Undergirding Ecclesiology: Questioning Its Baptist Identity and Biblical Validity." PhD diss., Southwestern Baptist Theological Seminary, 2014.

BLOG ARTICLES

Alexander, Paul. "8 Reasons Your Excuses for Not Practicing Church Discipline Don't Work." *9Marks*. September 24, 2018. https://www.9marks.org/article/8-reasons-your-excuses-for-not-practicing-church-discipline-dont-work/.

Anyabwile, Thabiti. "Multi-Site Churches Are from the Devil." *The Gospel Coalition*. September 27, 2011. https://www.thegospelcoalition.org/blogs/thabiti-anyabwile/multi-site-churches-are-from-the-devil/.

Austin, Chad. "The Origin of the '3 Circles' and Why It's Relevant to Your Ministry." *North Carolina Baptists*. March 3, 2020. https://ncbaptist.org/the-origin-of-the-3-circles-and-why-its-relevant-to-your-ministry/.

Barcley, William. "The Bible Commands Christians to Tithe." *The Gospel Coalition*. March 28, 2017. https://www.thegospelcoalition.org/article/7-reasons-christians-not-required-to-tithe/.

Bird, Warren. "Big News-Multisite Churches Now Number More Than 5,000." *Leadership Network*. January 9, 2019. https://leadnet.org/big-news-multisite-churches-more-than-5000/.

———. "Lyle E. Schaller (1925–2015): Intellectual Pillar of Leadership Network." *Leadership Network*. March 27, 2015. https://leadnet.org/lyle-e-schaller-1923–2015-intellectual-pillar-of-leadership-network/.

Chandler, Matt. "Instagram Post from October 23, 2022." *Instagram*. https://www.instagram.com/p/CkEBezBuo8v/.

———. "Is Church Membership Biblical?" *Church Leaders*. February 7, 2019. https:// churchleaders.com/pastors/pastor-articles/151320-is-church-membership-biblical.html.

Christopherson, Jeff. "Can Multisite Be Missional?" *The Exchange with Ed Stetzer*. Blog. April, 2, 2019. *Christianity Today*. https://www.christianitytoday.com/edstetzer/2019/april/can-multisite-churches-be-missional.html.

Conrad, Andrew. "5 Biggest Online Churches." *Capterra*. May 10, 2019. https://blog.capterra.com/the-5-biggest-online-churches/.

Emadi, Sam. "7 Well-Meaning Objections to Church Discipline—and How Pastors Ought to Respond to Them." *9Marks*. July 5, 2019. https://www.9marks. org/article/7-well-meaning-objections-to-church-discipline-and-how-pastors-ought-to-respond-to-them/.

First Presbyterian Church of Seattle. "First Presbyterian Church of Seattle: A Brief History of the First Presbyterian Church of Seattle." *Secretary of State Kim Wyman*. Website. https://www.sos.wa.gov/legacy/cities_detail.aspx?i=27.

"Foundational Documents." *The Gospel Coalition*. April, 12, 2011. https://media. thegospelcoalition.org/wp-content/uploads/2020/05/20161257/TGC-Foundation-Documents-2020-Final-5–20.pdf.

Graves, Marlena. "Prodigal Children: If It Can Happen to John Piper, It Can Happen to You." *Christianity Today*. June 20, 2012. https://www.christianitytoday.com/ ct/2012/juneweb-only/prodigal-children-if-it-can-happen-to-john-piper-it-can.html.

Greear, J. D. "How to Judge the Success of a Church: Does It Make Disciples?" *IMB*. July 22, 2019. https://www.imb.org/2019/07/22/make-disciples/.

_____. "Is Multi-Site a Biblically Sound Model?" *J. D. Greear Ministries*. October 23, 2014. https://jdgreear.com/multi-site-a-biblically-sound-model/.

_____. "Multisite or 'One-Service-Only?' A Question of Evangelical Faithfulness." *J. D. Greear Ministries*. October 22, 2014. https://jdgreear.com/ multi-site-an-evangelistically-effective-model/.

Hamilton, Jim. "A Biblical Theology of Corporate Prayer." *9Marks*. February 25, 2010. https://www.9marks.org/article/biblical-theology-corporate-prayer/.

Helopoulos, Jason. "Pastor, Include More Prayer in Your Church Service." *The Gospel Coalition*. September 13, 2018. https://www.thegospelcoalition.org/ article/include-more-prayer-church-service/.

Hernandez, Salvador. "Pastor Rick Warren's Final Saddleback Church Sermon Is a Lot Like His First One in 1980." *Los Angeles Times*. August 29, 2022. https://www.latimes.com/ california/story/2022–08–29/pastor-rick-warren-retires-final-saddleback-church-sermon.

Hyatt, Bob. "Contribution to 'Multi-Site Churches Are Here, and Here, and Here to Stay,' by Ed Stetzer." *The Exchange*. Blog. *Christianity Today*. February 24, 2014. https://www. christianitytoday.com/edstetzer/2014/february/ multisite-churches-are-here-to-stay.html.

Im, Daniel. "10 Signs You Shouldn't Be a Campus Pastor." *Facts and Trends*. July 20, 2015. https://factsandtrends.net/2015/07/20/10-signs-you-shouldnt-be-a-campus-pastor/.

_____. "Multi-Site Churches and Discipleship: A Contradiction?" *Daniel Im*. April 4, 2013. https://www.danielim.com/2013/04/04/multi-site-churches-and-discipleship-a-contradiction/.

Jamieson, Bobby. "Biblical Theology and Corporate Worship." *9Marks*. September 20, 2014. https://www.9marks.org/article/biblical-theology-and-corporate-worship/.

Leeman, Jonathan. "Mailbag #10—Lord's Supper in Nursing Home; Christians Dating a Non-Christian; Role of Small Group Leaders; New Pastor in Need of Help." *9Marks*. July 31, 2015. https://www.9marks.org/mailbag/mailbag-10-lords-supper-in-nursing-homechristians-dating-a-non-christian-role-of-small-group-leaders-new-pastor-in-need-ofhelp/.

———. "MultiChurch a More Biblical Version of Multisite?" *The Gospel Coalition*. December 17, 2018. https://www.thegospelcoalition.org/reviews/multichurch-exploring-future-multisite/.

———. "Twenty-Two Problems with Multi-Site Churches." *9Marks*. October 1, 2014. https://www.9marks.org/article/twenty-two-problems-with-multi-site-churches/.

Ligon, Greg. "What Makes a Great Campus Pastor?" *Exponential*. December 22, 2016. https://exponential.org/great-campus-pastor/.

"Local Churches Update." *Mars Hill Church Archive*. November 12, 2014. http://marshill.se/marshill/2014/11/12/local-churches-update.

Malphurs Aubrey. "The Need for Church Planting and Revitalization." *The Malphurs Group*. Accessed July 23, 2020. http://malphursgroup.com/the-need-for-church-planting-and-revitalization/.

Merker, Matt. "How Contemporary Worship Music Is Shaping Us—For Better or Worse." *The Gospel Coalition*. February 6, 2019. https://www.thegospelcoalition.org/reviews/singing-congregation-contemporary-worship/.

Niehwhof, Carey. "The Pros and Cons of a Celebrity Pastor." *Carey Nieuwhof*. October 28, 2013. https://careynieuwhof.com/the-pros-and-cons-of-a-celebrity-pastor-culture/.

Piper, John. "Avoid the Unrepentant—But What if They're Family?" *Desiring God*. November 21, 2014. https://www.desiringgod.org/interviews/avoid-the-unrepentant-but-what-if-theyre-family.

———. "The Danger of Deserting Community." *Desiring God*. October 31, 2013. https://www.desiringgod.org/interviews/the-danger-of-deserting-community.

———. "Inspired by the Incredible Early Church." *Desiring God*. April 4, 1994. https://www.desiringgod.org/articles/inspired-by-the-incredible-early-church.

———. "The Leniency of Excommunication." *Desiring God*. March 27, 2008. https://www.desiringgod.org/articles/the-leniency-of-excommunication.

———. "No Prayer, No Power." *Desiring God*. March 27, 1989. https://www.desiringgod.org/articles/no-prayer-no-power.

_____. "Treasuring Christ Together Above All Things." *Desiring God*. June 26, 2005. https://www.desiringgod.org/messages/treasuring-christ-together-above-all-things.

_____. "Treasuring Christ Together as a Church on Multiple Campuses." *Desiring God*. November 4, 2007. https://www.desiringgod.org/messages/treasuring-christ-together-as-a-church-on-multiple-campuses.

_____. "Treasuring Christ Together, Part 1." *Desiring God*. September 7, 2003. https://www.desiringgod.org/messages/treasuring-christ-together-part-1.

_____. "What Are the Key Issues in Thinking Through the Multi-Campus Church Movement?" *Desiring God*. June 5, 2009. https://www.desiringgod.org/interviews/what-are-the-key-issues-in-thinking-through-the-multi-campus-church-movement.

_____. "What Is Discipleship and How Is It Done?" *Desiring God*. January 25, 2016. https://www.desiringgod.org/interviews/what-is-discipleship-and-how-is-it-done.

_____. "Where I Am There Will My Servant Be: A Call to Treasure Christ Together." *Desiring God*. September 3, 2006. https://www.desiringgod.org/messages/where-i-am-there-will-my-servant-be-a-call-to-treasure-christ-together.

_____. "Who Are the Elders?: Then and Now." *Desiring God*. June 2, 1991. https://www.desiringgod.org/messages/who-are-the-elders.

_____. "Why Is Differentiating Between Evangelism and Missions Important?" *Desiring God*. August 17, 2008. https://www.desiringgod.org/interviews/why-is-differentiating-between-evangelism-and-missions-important.

Platt, David. "12 Characteristics of a Healthy Church." *IMB*. August, 31, 2016. https://www.imb.org/2016/08/31/2016083112-characteristics-healthy-church/.

_____. "The Four Steps of Restorative Church Discipline." *Radical*. October 9, 2020. https://radical.net/articles/the-four-steps-of-restorative-church-discipline/.

Pope, Randy. "3 Reasons We Stopped Doing Multisite Church." *Christianity Today Pastors*. Blog. July 6, 2015. https://www.christianitytoday.com/pastors/2015/summer-2015/3-reasons-we-stopped-doing-multisite-church.html.

Rainer, Thom. "Five Examples of Effective Prayer Ministries." *Thom S. Rainer*. July 4, 2018. https://archive.thomrainer.com/2018/07/five-examples-effective-prayer-ministries/.

———. "The Healthy Church in 2029: Ten Major Changes in Ten Years." *Church Answers*. June 10, 2019. https://churchanswers.com/blog/the-healthy-church-in-2029-ten-major-changes-in-ten-years/.

———. "Is the Multisite Church Movement Still Growing? Six Updates." *Church Answers*. June 24, 2019. https://churchanswers.com/blog/is-the-multisite-church-movement-still-growing-six-updates/.

———. "New Research and Insights on the Online Church." *Church Answers*. March 11, 2019. https://churchanswers.com/blog/new-research-and-insights-on-the-online-church/.

———. "Twelve Major Trends for Churches in 2021." *Church Answers*. December 21, 2020. https://churchanswers.com/blog/twelve-major-trends-for-churches-in-2021/.

Raymond, Erik. "Living on Mission Means Living on Purpose." *The Gospel Coalition*. November 27, 2018. https://www.thegospelcoalition.org/blogs/erik-raymond/living-mission-means-living-purpose/.

Reardon, JoHannah. "Stewardship Is More Than Giving Money." *Christianity Today*. June 14, 2011. https://www.christianitytoday.com/biblestudies/articles/churchhomeleadership/ accountablegod.html.

Roys, Julie. "Matt Chandler Signals Imminent Return to Ministry in Social Media Post." *The Roys Report*. October 25, 2022. https://julieroys.com/matt-chandler-signals-imminent-return-ministry-social-media-post/.

Scroggins, Jimmy. "10 Ways to Build an Evangelistic Culture." *Facts and Trends*. August 7, 2019. https://factsandtrends.net/2019/08/07/10-ways-to-build-an-evangelistic-church-culture/.

Silliman, Daniel. "Matt Chandler Steps Aside After Inappropriate Online Relationship." *Christianity Today*. August 28, 2022. https://www.christianitytoday.com/news /2022/august/matt-chandler-village-church-online-inappropriate-leave.html.

Smith, Steven. "The Essential Elements of Text-Driven Preaching." *Preaching Source*. September 1, 2016. https://preachingsource.com/blog/the-essential-elements-of-text-driven-preaching/.

Stetzer, Ed. "4 Reasons Small Groups Are Vital to Your Church's Health." *The Exchange with Ed Stetzer*. Blog. March 30, 2015. *Christianity Today*. https://www.christianitytoday. com/edstetzer/2015/march/4-reasons-small-groups-are-vital-to-your-churchs-health.html.

———. "Ending the Worship War without a Truce." *The Exchange with Ed Stetzer*. Blog. *Christianity Today*. October 15, 2009. https://www.christianitytoday.com/edstetzer/ 2009/october/ ending-worship-war-without-truce.html.

_____. "Membership Matters: 3 Reasons for Church Membership." *The Exchange with Ed Stetzer*. Blog. *Christianity Today*. April 7, 2015. https://www.christianitytoday.com/ edstetzer/2015/july/membership-matters-3-reasons-for-church-membership.html.

_____. "Multisite Churches Are Here, and Here, and Here to Stay." *The Exchange with Ed Stetzer*. Blog. *Christianity Today*. February 24, 2014. https://www.christianitytoday.com/edstetzer/2014/february/multisite-churches-are-here-to-stay.html.

_____. "Multisite Evolution." *The Exchange with Ed Stetzer*. Blog. *Christianity Today*. June 18, 2013. https://www.christianitytoday.com/edstetzer/2013/june/multisite-evolution.html.

_____. "Questions for McChurch." *The Exchange with Ed Stetzer*. Blog. *Christianity Today*. June 4, 2008. https://www.christianitytoday.com/ edstetzer/2008/june/questions-for-mcchurch.html.

Stetzer, Ed, and Geoff Surratt. "Questions for 'Questions for McChurch.'" *The Exchange with Ed Stetzer*. Blog. *Christianity Today*. June 5, 2008. https://www.christianitytoday.com/ edstetzer/2008/june/questions-for-questions-for-mcchurch.html.

Taylor, Justin. "Mark Dever's Original Letter to a Church Plant on 'The 9 Marks of a Healthy Church.'" *The Gospel Coalition*. February 15, 2019. https://www.thegospelcoalition.org/ blogs/evangelical-history/mark-devers-original-letter-church-plant-9-marks-healthy-church/.

Tomberlin, Jim. "How to Handle Governance in Multisite Churches." *Outreach Magazine*. June 6, 2019. https://outreachmagazine.com/features/mega-church/43398-how-to-handle-governance-in-multisite-churches.html.

_____. "What Makes a Great Campus Pastor?" *Leadership Network*. July 28, 2015. https://leadnet.org/what-makes-a-great-campus-pastor/.

Van Skaik, Michael, Larry Osborne, Jon Phelps, and Matt Rogers. "Pastor Mark Driscoll's Resignation." *Mars Hill Church Archive*. October 15, 2014. http://marshill.se/marshill/2014/10/15/pastor-mark-driscolls-resignation.

Vaters, Karl. "If We Can Worship Anywhere, Why Go to Church?" *Pivot*. Blog. *Christianity Today*. October 17, 2018. https://www.christianitytoday.com/karl-vaters/2018/october/worship-anywhere-why-church.html.

Warren, Rick. "News and Views." *Saddleback Church*. February 9, 2012. https://saddleback.com/archive/blog/pastor-ricks-news-views/2012/02/09/news-views-02-09-12.

Wasem, James. "Mixing Sound for the Multi-Site Church." *Church Tech Today*. October 5, 2016. https://churchtechtoday.com/2016/10/05/mixing-sound-multi-site-church/.

Wax, Trevin. "The Mars Hill Postmortem." *The Gospel Coalition*. Oct. 16, 2014. https://www.thegospelcoalition.org/blogs/trevin-wax/the-mars-hill-postmortem/.

_____. "New Research: Churches Going Digital While Offerings Drop." *The Gospel Coalition*. April 2, 2020. https://www.thegospelcoalition.org/blogs/trevin-wax/new-research-churches-going-digital-while-offerings-drop/.

Zylstra, Sarah Eekhoff. "Seattle Reboot: Life After Mars Hill." *The Gospel Coalition*. May 30, 2017. https://www.thegospelcoalition.org/article/seattle-reboot-life-after-mars-hill/.

_____. "The 'Unintended Consequence' Overtaking the Multisite Church Movement." *The Gospel Coalition*. February 24, 2017. https://www.thegospelcoalition.org/article/the-unintended-consequence-thats-overtaking-the-multisite-church-movement/.

Zylstra, Sarah Eekhoff, Morgan Lee, and Bob Smietana. "Former Member Accepts Acts 29 Megachurch Apology in Church Discipline Case." *Christianity Today*. June 10, 2015. https://www.christianitytoday.com/ct/2015/may-web-only/matt-chandler-apologizes-for-village-churchs-decision-to-di.html.

WEBSITES

"2018 Ministry Inquiries." North American Mission Board. 2018. http://www.sbc.net/cp/ministryreports/2018/pdf/namb/namb-ministry-inquiries.pdf.

"About." *9Marks*. Accessed April 2, 2021. https://www.9marks.org/about/.

"About David Platt." *Radical*. Accessed October 4, 2020. https://radical.net/about-david-platt/.

"About Hillsong." *Hillsong Church*. Accessed July 22, 2020. https://hillsong.com/about/.

"About J. D. Greear." *Southern Baptist Convention*. Accessed July 22, 2020. http://www.sbc.net/presidentspage/about.asp.

"About Larry." *Larry Osborne*. Accessed October 24, 2020. https://larryosborne.com/about/.

"About Us." *Summit Collaborative*. Accessed December 31, 2020. https://summitcollaborative.org/about/.

"About Vision 2025." *Vision 2025*. Accessed January 1, 2021. http://sbcvision2025.com.

"Acts 29: A Diverse, Global Family of Church-Planting Churches." *Acts 29*. Accessed December 31, 2020. https://www.acts29.com/about/.

"The Baptist Faith and Message: The 2000 Baptist Faith and Message." *Southern Baptist Convention*. Accessed July 2, 2023. https://bfm.sbc.net/bfm2000/.

"Bylaws." *The Village Church*. Accessed November 6, 2020. https://www.thevillagechurch.net/about/beliefs/bylaws/.

"Campuses, Service Times, Locations." *North Coast Church*. Accessed December 18, 2020. https://www.northcoastchurch.com/locations/.

"Campus Transitions." *TVC Resources.* Accessed December 19, 2020. https://www.tvcresources.net/resource-library/articles/campus-transitions/.

"Carillon." *Community Christian Church.* Accessed July 22, 2020. https://communitychristian.org/carillon/.

Carrie, Jim. "Jim Carrie." *LinkedIn.* Accessed November 20, 2020. https://www.linkedin.com/in/jim-carrie-7183954/.

"Church for the Rest of Us." *Family Church Network.* Accessed December 31, 2020. https://www.familychurchnetwork.com/.

"Church Planting." *The Village Church.* Accessed November 14, 2022. https://thevillagechurch.net/ministries/church-planting.

"Church Planting Residency." *Family Church Network.* Accessed September 18, 2020. https://www.familychurchnetwork.com/church-planting-residency/.

"Church Search." *9Marks.* Accessed April 2, 2021. https://www.9marks.org/church-search/.

"Community Locations." *Community Christian Church.* Accessed July 22, 2020. https://communitychristian.org/locations/.

"Comparison Chart." *SBC.* Accessed July 8, 2023. https://bfm.sbc.net/comparison-chart/.

Dever, Mark, and Capitol Hill Baptist Church (@chbcdc). "Letter to Capitol Hill Baptist Church Regarding Public Services." Twitter, March 13, 2020, 5:51 a.m. https://twitter.com/chbcdc/status/1238417328498446336.

"Don Overstreet." *Touch Publications.* Accessed August 18, 2020. http://www.touchpublishingservices.com/don-overstreet/.

"Dr. Tom Cheyney, Executive Director of Missions." *Greater Orlando Baptist Association.* Accessed August 18, 2020. https://www.goba.org/staff-tom-cheyney.

"Ebenezer's Coffee House." *National Community Church.* Accessed September 4, 2020. https://national.cc/expressions/ebenezers-coffeehouse.

"Family Church Network." *Family Church.* Accessed July 22, 2020. https://gofamilychurch.org/ family-church-network/.

"Fast Facts." *Southern Baptist Convention.* February 15, 2022. https://www.sbc.net/about/what-we-do/fast-facts/.

"FBC Winderemere—Teaching Pastor—Specs Updated." *Vanderbloemen.* Accessed December 19, 2020. https://drive.google.com/file/d/1k6EO2WccIrgNmcdRN0UZxd62vF3lvEX_/view.

Ferguson, Earl. "Earl Ferguson." *Facebook.* Accessed July, 22, 2020. https://www.facebook.com/earl.ferguson.378/.

———. "Earl Ferguson." *LinkedIn.* Accessed July 22, 2020. https://www.linkedin.com/in/earl-ferguson-86146a5/.

"Flint Campus." *Green Acres Baptist Church.* Accessed November 12, 2022. https://www.gabc.org/flint/.

"Gregg R. Allison." *The Southern Baptist Theological Seminary*. Accessed July 19, 2020. https://www.sbts.edu/academics/faculty/gregg-r-allison/.

"Home." *Chartwell Church*. Accessed November 20, 2020. https://www.chart wellchurch.com/.

"I'm New." *Sojourn Church*. Accessed July 19, 2020. https://sojournchurch.com/new.

"John Piper, D.Theol." *Bethlehem College and Seminary*. Accessed July 22, 2020. https://bcsmn.edu/profile/john-piper-faculty-2/.

"Leadership Team." *Community Christian Church*. Accessed July 22, 2020. https://communitychristian.org/ourteam/.

"Life Church Branding Guidelines." *Life Church Open Network*. September 2015. https://open.life.church/items/122018-lifechurch-branding-guidelines-pdf.

"Locations." *Life Church*. Accessed July 3, 2023. https://tinyurl.com/LCLocations.

"Locations." *Saddleback Church*. Accessed December 19, 2020. https://saddleback.com/visit/locations.

"Mission, Values, and Beliefs." Accessed July 19, 2020. *Sojourn Church*. https://sojournchurch.com/about-us.

"Multiply." *The Village Church*. Accessed December 19, 2020. https://multiply.thevillagechurch.net/.

"Multisite: Keeping Experiences Consistent Across Multiple Campuses." *Life Church Open Network*. Accessed December 19, 2020. https://open.life.church/training/20-keeping-experiences-consistent-across-multiple-campuses.

"Multisite Unstuck Process." *The Unstuck Group*. Accessed July 27, 2020. https://theunstuckgroup.com/multisite/.

"New Here?" *Green Acres Baptist Church*. Accessed November 12, 2022. https://www.gabc.org/new-here/.

"One Church in Multiple Locations," *Life Church*. Accessed December 19, 2020. https://bit.ly/3nB1noy.

"One Church. Two Locations." *Green Acres South*. Accessed July 22, 2020. https://gabcsouth.org/about/1-church-2-locations.

"Our History." *Living Creek Christian Church*. Accessed July 22, 2020. https://www.livingcreek.org/our-history/.

"Our Mission." *Harbor Network*. Accessed December 31, 2020. https://www.harbornetwork.com/about.

"Our Story." *Family Church*. Accessed September 18, 2020. https://gofamilychurch.org/story/.

"The Philadelphia Confession of Faith, 1742." *Baptist Studies Online*. Accessed October 3, 2020. http://baptiststudiesonline.com/wp-content/uploads/2007/02/philadelphia-confession.pdf.

"Plant: We Equip Leaders to Plant Churches." *Summit Collaborative*. Accessed December 31, 2020. https://summitcollaborative.org/plant/.

"Rodney A. Harrison." *Midwestern Baptist Theological Seminary.* Accessed August 18, 2020. https://www.mbts.edu/about/faculty/rodney-a-harrison/. "Sojourn Midtown." Sojourn Church. Accessed July 2, 2023. https://sojournchurch.com/.

"Staff." *Sojourn Church.* Accessed July 19, 2020. https://sojournchurch.com/leaders.

"Start New Churches. We'll Help." *NewChurches.* Accessed May 19, 2023. https://www.newchurches.com.

"Teaching Pastors." *North Coast Church.* Accessed December 18, 2020. https://www.northcoastchurch.com/about/teaching-pastors/.

"Ten Leading Indicators of a Healthy Church." *Evangelical Free Church of America.* Accessed October 4, 2020. https://www.efca.org/resources/document/ten-leading-indicators-healthy-church.

"Where Should We Explore?" *Life Church.* Accessed December 19, 2020. https://www.life.church/cities/.

AUDIO AND VIDEO

Chandler, Matt. "He Hears: How to Pray." *TVC Resources.* May 15, 2016. https://www.tvcresources.net/resource-library/sermons/how-to-pray/.

———. "Wanderer / Restorer." *TVC Resources.* May 31, 2015. https://www.tvcresources.net/resource-library/sermons/wanderer-restorer/.

Cosper, Mike. "The Brand." *The Rise and Fall of Mars Hill.* Podcast. *Christianity Today.* August 2, 2021. https://www.christianitytoday.com/ct/podcasts/rise-and-fall-of-mars-hill/rise-fall-mars-hill-podcast-mark-driscoll-brand.html.

———. *The Rise and Fall of Mars Hill.* Podcast. *Christianity Today.* Accessed November 13, 2022. https://www.christianitytoday.com/ct/podcasts/rise-and-fall-of-mars-hill/.

———. "Who Killed Mars Hill?" *The Rise and Fall of Mars Hill.* Episode 1. Podcast. *Christianity Today.* June 21, 2021. https://www.christianitytoday.com/ct/podcasts/rise-and-fall-of-mars-hill/who-killed-mars-hill-church-mark-driscoll-rise-fall.html.

Dever, Mark, Jonathan Leeman, and Matt Chandler. "On Multi-Site Churches (with Matt Chandler)." *Pastors' Talk.* Podcast. Ep. 26. *9Marks.* November 7, 2017. https://www.9marks.org/pastors-talk/episode-26-on-multi-site-churches-with-matt-chandler/.

Floyd, Ronnie. "Vision 2025 Presentation by Ronnie Floyd." Replayed on *SBC This Week.* Podcast. February 25, 2020. https://sbcthisweek.com/vision-2025-presentation-by-ronnie-floyd/.

Greear, J. D. "Gospel: The Revolutionary Power of the Christian Life (John 15:12; 13:34–35)." *The Summit Church.* October 10, 2019. https://bit.ly/3a6vcaL.

_____. "How Do You Prepare for Sermons?" *Ask Me Anything*. Podcast. *J. D. Greear Ministries*. December 3, 2018. https://jdgreear.com/podcasts/how-do-you-prepare-for-sermons/.

_____. "Why Is the Summit Multi-Site? Is Multi-Site Biblical?" *Ask Me Anything*. Podcast. *J. D. Greear Ministries*. December 7, 2020. https://jdgreear.com/podcasts/why-is-summit-multi-site-is-multi-site-biblical/.

Groves, J. C., Brian Edwards, and Nathan Cravatt. "The Power of a Story: JC's Story." *The Recovering Fundamentalist Podcast*. Episode 003. February 2, 2020.

Hardin, Steve. "A History of Faithfulness." *TVC Resources*. September 20, 2012. https://www.tvcresources.net/resource-library/sermons/a-history-of-faithfulness/.

Luden, Jennifer. "Big Churches Use Technology to Branch Out." *All Things Considered* on *NPR*. Audio. August 7, 2005. https://www.npr.org/templates/story/story.php?storyId=4788676.

Morgan, Tony. "Hiring Campus Pastors." *The Unstuck Group Podcast*. Podcast. *Tony Morgan Live*. May 30, 2018. https://tonymorganlive.com/2018/05/30/hiring-multisite-campus-pastors/.

Morgan, Tony, and Christ Surratt. "Centralized vs. De-centralized Multisite Models: Which Is Best?" *Tony Morgan Live*. December 15, 2017. https://youtu.be/PTempuK0m6A.

Rainer, Thom, and Kevin Ezell. "Why the Intersection of the Multi-site Movement and the Replanting Movement Is So Powerful." *Revitalize and Replant*. Podcast. Episode 125. December 26, 2019. *Church Answers*. https://churchanswers.com/podcasts/revitalize-and-replant/why-the-intersection-of-the-multi-site-movement-and-the-replanting-movement-is-so-powerful-revitalize-and-replant-episode-125/.

Rainer, Thom, and Jonathan Howe. "Pastoral Leadership, Prayer, and Church Health." *Rainer on Leadership*. Podcast. Ep. 316. April 4, 2017. *Thom S. Rainer*. https://archive.thomrainer.com/2017/04/pastoral-leadership-prayer-and-church-health-rainer-on-leadership-316/.

_____. "Seven Ways Churches Make Prayer Central to Their Worship Services." *Rainer on Leadership*. Podcast. Ep. 518. March 12, 2019. *Church Answers*. https://churchanswers.com/podcasts/rainer-on-leadership/seven-ways-churches-make-prayer-central-to-their-worship-services-rainer-on-leadership-518/.

_____. "Why Small Churches Are Going Multisite." *Rainer on Leadership*. Podcast. Ep. 296. January 24, 2017. *Church Answers*. https://churchanswers.com/podcasts/rainer-on-leadership/smaller-churches-going-multisite-rainer-leadership-296/.

Rainer, Thom, and Sam Rainer. "Four Things Your Church Should Know about Fostering a Church." *Rainer on Leadership*. Podcast. Ep. 586. November 5, 2019. *Church Answers*. https://churchanswers.com/podcasts/rainer-on-leadership/four-things-your-church-should-know-about-fostering-a-church/.

————. "Understanding the Differences Between Church Adoption, Church Fostering, and Church Revitalization." *Rainer on Leadership*. Podcast. Ep. 598. December 17, 2019. *Thom S. Rainer*. https://archive.thomrainer.com/2019/12/understanding-the-differences-between-church-adoption-church-fostering-and-church-revitalization/.

Scroggins, Jimmy. "Vintage Church: Church Discipline." *Family Church*. March 7, 2010. https://gofamilychurch.org/messages/church-discipline/.

Scroggins, Jimmy, and Steve Wright. "Autonomous Launch." *Church for the Rest of Us*. Podcast. Episode 0017. December 11, 2017. *Family Church Network*. https://www.familychurchnetwork.com/cftrou-0017-autonomous-launch/.

————. "Building A New Church Culture, Not New Church Programs: Membership." *Church for the Rest of Us*. Podcast. Episode 0021. January 8, 2018. *Family Church Network*. https://www.familychurchnetwork.com/cftrou-0021-building-new-church-culture-not-new-church-programs-membership/.

————. "Five Free Strategies for Church Growth that will Cost You Your Life." *Church for the Rest of Us*. Podcast. Episode 0008. October 9, 2017. *Family Church Network*. https://www.familychurchnetwork. com/cftrou-0008-five-free-strategies-church-growth-will-cost-life/.

————. "How Family Church Does Multisite." *Church for the Rest of Us*. Podcast. Episode 0013. November 13, 2017. *Family Church Network*. https://www.familychurchnetwork.com/cftrou-0013-family-church-multisite/.

REPORTS

Atchison, David W., ed. *Annual of the Southern Baptist Convention: Nineteen Hundred and Ninety-Five*. Atlanta, GA: Southern Baptist Convention, June 20–22, 1995. http://media2.sbhla.org.s3.amazonaws.com/annuals/SBC_Annual_1995.pdf.

————, ed. *Annual of the Southern Baptist Convention: Nineteen Hundred and Ninety-Six*. New Orleans, LA: Southern Baptist Convention, June 11–13, 1996. http://media2.sbhla.org.s3.amazonaws.com/annuals/SBC_Annual_1996.pdf.

Bird, Warren. "Campus Pastor as Key to Multisite Success: New Research, Sample Job Descriptions." *Leadership Network*, 2015. http://multisitesolutions.com/wp-content/uploads/2015/10/Campus_Pastor_as_Key_to_Multisite_Success.pdf.

_____. "Latest Multisite Trends: How a New Generation of Pastors is Shifting to Strategies that Reproduce and Multiply." *Leadership Network*, 2018. https://www.portablechurch.com/resources/latest-multisite-trends-report/.

Bird, Warren, and Kristin Walters. "Multisite Is Multiplying." *Leadership Network*, 2010. http://pastoralized.com/wp-content/uploads/2013/01/LN_multisite_report-1.pdf.

_____. "Leadership Network/Generis Multisite Church Scorecard." *Leadership Network*, 2014. https://www.beboldacademy.org/images/uploads/Multisite_Church_Scorecard_Report_v2.pdf.

Finn, Nathan, ed. *Book of Reports of the 2023 Southern Baptist Convention*. New Orleans, LA, June 13–14, 2023. https://www.baptistpress.com/wp-content/uploads/2023/05/2023-Book-of-Reports-Final-Online.pdf.

"National Congregations Study, Cumulative Dataset (1998, 2006–2007, and 2012), Version 2." *Association of Religious Data Archives*. Report. 2012. http://www.thearda.com/Archive/Files/Descriptions/NCSIII.asp.

Travis, Dave. "Multi-Site/Multiple-Campus Churches: Report from a Leadership Network Forum." Report. Leadership Network. September 11–12, 2001. http://bgav.org/wp-content/uploads/2013/08/Multi-Site-Report.pdf.

Yeats, John L., ed. *Annual of the 2007 Southern Baptist Convention*. San Antonio, TX: Southern Baptist Convention, June 12–13, 2007. http://media2.sbhla.org.s3.amazonaws.com/annuals/SBC_Annual_2007.pdf.

_____, ed. *Annual of the 2009 Southern Baptist Convention*. Louisville, KY: Southern Baptist Convention. June 23–24, 2009. http://media2.sbhla.org.s3.amazonaws.com/annuals/SBC_Annual_2009.pdf.

_____, ed. *Annual of the 2010 Southern Baptist Convention*. Orlando, FL: Southern Baptist Convention, June 15–16, 2010. http://media2.sbhla.org.s3.amazonaws.com/annuals/SBC_Annual_2010.pdf.

_____, ed. *Annual of the 2011 Southern Baptist Convention*. Phoenix, AZ: Southern Baptist Convention, June 14–15, 2011. http://media2.sbhla.org.s3.amazonaws.com/annuals/SBC_Annual_2011.pdf.

_____, ed. *Annual of the 2013 Southern Baptist Convention*. Houston, TX: Southern Baptist Convention, June 11–12, 2013. http://media2.sbhla.org.s3.amazonaws.com/annuals/SBC_Annual_2013.pdf.

_____, ed. *Annual of the 2016 Southern Baptist Convention*. St. Louis, MO: Southern Baptist Convention, June 14–15, 2016. http://media2.sbhla.org.s3.amazonaws.com/annuals/SBC_Annual_2016.pdf.

_____, ed. *Book of Reports Prepared for 2020 SBC Advance*. Nashville, TN: Southern Baptist Convention, 2020. http://www.sbc.net/advance/pdf/2020%20SBC%20Book%20of%20Reports.pdf.

_____, ed. *Book of Reports of the 2021 Southern Baptist Convention*. Nashville, TN: Southern Baptist Convention, June 15–16, 2021. https://sbcannualmeeting. net/wp-content/uploads/2021/05/2021-Book-of-Reports-with-links.pdf.

_____, ed. *Book of Reports of the 2022 Southern Baptist Convention*. Anaheim, CA: Southern Baptist Convention, June 14-15, 2022. https://www.baptistpress. com/wp-content/uploads/2022/05/2022-SBC-Book-of-Reports.pdf.

Yeats, John L., and Allison Young, eds., *Annual of the Southern Baptist Convention Prepared for the Year 2020*. Nashville, TN: SBC Executive Committee, 2020. https://www.sbc.net/wp-content/uploads/2020/09/2020-SBC-Annual.pdf.

ABOUT THE AUTHOR

DUSTIN SLATON (PhD, Southwestern Baptist Theological Seminary) is the lead pastor at First Baptist Church in Round Rock, TX. He served for more than ten years in youth ministries in Arkansas, Colorado, and Texas before serving six years as the campus pastor at Green Acres Baptist Church in Tyler, TX. In addition to his PhD, he has a BA in Theology from Ouachita Baptist University and an MDiv from Southwestern Baptist Theological Seminary.